50

D0754494

DATE DUE

JAMES RUSSELL LOWELL

Portrait of a Many-Sided Man

From a photograph by F. Gutekunst

JAMES RUSSELL LOWELL

Portrait of a Many-Sided Man

EDWARD WAGENKNECHT

> Illusion, Temperament, Succession, Surface, Surprise, Reality, Subjectiveness,—these are the threads on the loom of time, these are the lords of life. . . . Temperament is the iron wire on which the beads are strung.
>
> R. W. Emerson: "Experience"

NEW YORK   OXFORD UNIVERSITY PRESS   1971

PREFACE

For many years I have wished to do a psychograph or character portrait of Lowell. Various circumstances conspired to delay me, and when I heard that Martin Duberman was at work upon what I was sure would be the definitive modern biography, I deliberately postponed my book until after his should have appeared, both because it seemed to me that his work ought logically to precede mine and because I hoped to profit by his researches. As it turns out, I am even more indebted to him than I expected to be, for he has been kind enough to read my manuscript, and this at a very inconvenient time for himself. I am very grateful.

I am also, as usual, indebted to the Houghton Library at Harvard University, and I wish to thank Dr. William H. Bond, its director, and the always more than kind and helpful Miss Carolyn Jakeman and the assistants in the reading room to whom she always somehow manages to impart the courtesy which comes natural to herself. To a lesser extent I have also drawn upon materials in the Massachusetts Historical Society, the Boston Public Library, the Boston Athenaeum, and the Mugar Memorial Library at Boston University.

For the sake of uniformity, I italicize all book titles, even in quotations from writers who may have followed a different system. I use the conventional three periods to indicate omissions within a passage quoted, but since I do not pretend to be quoting complete documents generally not at the beginning or the end.

E. W.

CONTENTS

JAMES RUSSELL LOWELL

Portrait of a Many-Sided Man

CHAPTER ONE

THE LOWELL PROBLEM

Here lies that part of J.R.L.
Which hampered him from doing well;
Here lies that film of muddy clay
Which kept the sight of Heaven away:
If now his faults thou canst not brook,
Into his heart a moment look;
If still to judge him thou incline,
O, Unforgiving, look in thine!

JRL, 1845

I

In a toast offered at a dinner of the Holy Cross alumni in 1910,
John Collins Bossidy created what is probably the best-known
"poem" ever achieved about Boston:

And this is good old Boston,
The home of the bean and the cod,
Where the Lowells talk only to Cabots
And the Cabots talk only to God.

But more than forty years have now passed since a Bostonian of
non-Anglo-Saxon derivation got tired of being called Kabotznick
and shortened his name to Cabot. Though he had hardly effected
a greater change than thousands of other immigrants have made,
the Cabot family did not welcome the new member with open
arms, and litigation ensued. When the judge decided in the immi-
grant's favor, a newspaper poet quipped:

> And this is good old Boston,
> The home of the bean and the cod,
> Where the Lowells have no one to talk to,
> 'Cause the Cabots talk Yiddish, by God!

Despite this adverse verdict, both the Lowells and the Cabots might be said to have held their place in twentieth-century Boston, but it may not seem that the same thing could be said for James Russell Lowell's literary reputation. During his later years he was generally regarded as the leading American man of letters, and when he died in 1891 he was treated like a great man.[1] Such judgments have sometimes been reaffirmed during more recent years—by Joseph J. Reilly, amazingly, who in 1915 published a snakes-in-Ireland kind of book on *James Russell Lowell as a Critic*, which concluded with the observation that Lowell was not a critic at all, thus leaving the reader wondering helplessly what he had been writing about, and by both Robert Underwood Johnson and Joseph Edgar Chamberlain[2] at the time of the centenary celebration of Lowell's birth in 1919. By this time, such judgments seemed somewhat idiosyncratic however, and Chamberlain for one had considerable difficulty agreeing with himself, for though he spoke of "the wellnigh Shakespearean magic of this man with words," the "want of music, of song" in Lowell's lines caused him to suspect that he must have been tone deaf, and he thought *A Fable for Critics* quite unreadable! On the other hand, none other than Harold Laski has been ready to go on record that "criticism of literature as criticism of life begins, as a serious matter, with James Russell Lowell."[3]

Between 1901, when Horace E. Scudder's authorized biography of Lowell appeared, and 1966, when Martin Duberman published his excellent book, Lowell was unfortunate in his biographers. Ferris Greenslet would have to be exempted, but his book in the "American Men of Letters series" is only a sketch, and in *The Lowells and their Seven Worlds* the poet is necessarily one of many. Richmond C. Beatty's *James Russell Lowell* (1942) consists largely of a paraphrase of what Lowell himself wrote, accompanied by a running fire of snide comment by one who unfortunately had not yet been able to realize that the Civil War was over. And though Leon Howard's *Victorian Knight-Errant* (1952), which deals only with Lowell's early career, is a vastly more intelligent book, it is hardly more sympathetic. I might add that if my own experience in this area affords any criterion, this is one subject on which the "reactions" of the American undergraduate run parallel to those of his guides and mentors. In my own classes in American literature, Longfellow often runs neck-and-neck with Whitman (even those who greatly prefer Whitman often finding Longfellow a much better writer), but very seldom have I found anyone expressing a special interest in Lowell.

I do not believe that any of this can be explained in terms of the now simple and popular formula of the "conflict between generations." Nothing about Lowell is simple. Nor has it been left for contemporary critics to discover his weaknesses and limitations as poet and critic. Not even Reilly did a more thoroughgoing job than William Cleaver Wilkinson had done in *Scribner's Monthly* in 1872 and two years later in his book, *A Free Lance in the Field of Life and Letters.*[4] When Bliss Perry spoke at Harvard's centenary celebration in 1919, he certainly did not mean to be disparaging, but he did admit that both Hawthorne and Poe outranked Lowell "in purely literary fame" and that Emerson outranked him "in range of vision, Longfellow in craftsmanship, and Walt Whitman in sheer power of emotion and phrase." Fourteen years before that, Curtis Hidden Page had already declared that

there is something lacking in most of his work, something of charm, especially of rhythmic charm, something of poetic suggestiveness, something which he seems always striving after . . . and which now and then he does almost attain. . . . He lacks, usually, just that last touch of genius, that "St. Elmo's Fire" playing over all, which he so well describes in his essay on Keats.[5]

And if we wish to go back to 1893, we can even find Lowell's great friend, Sir Leslie Stephen, saying of his poems, "I like them, but they do not take hold of me as first-rate. It sounds almost disloyal to be saying this; and I do not love him one jot the less."

We do not have here, then, the familiar phenomenon of the writer who is overrated by his contemporaries and cut down to size by posterity; instead we have a writer who wins a leading place in spite of the fact that his contemporaries are almost as conscious as posterity itself of what Hyatt H. Waggoner was to call his "unrealized potential." [6] The explanation of this "unrealized potential" most favored by those who insist upon summing up problems in a phrase is that Lowell tried to do too much, or, as Gustav Pollak put it, he was "a poet whose Commemoration Ode stirred the heart of the nation to its depths, a brilliant satirist in prose and verse, a political writer of singular power, an admirable teacher and lecturer, a fascinating orator, a conversationalist, and lecture-writer, a skilful and dignified diplomat, and, above all, a pure and sagacious patriot." Even the subtle John Livingston Lowes inclined toward some such explanation in 1919 ("when one is at the same time a scholar and a poet and a man, life is apt to be somewhat complex" [7]), and William Dean Howells, who knew and loved Lowell so well, says that he made not one impression but a thousand.

Yet I think one must say also that if Lowell had been able to satisfy all his needs simply by writing poetry, then he would have done just that; only, had this been the case, he would obviously not have been the Lowell we know. Moreover, we cannot be sure that, under these altered conditions, he must have produced better poetry than he actually wrote. When they assume that he would, his detractors pay him a greater compliment than his warmest admirers. It may well be that he wrote the very best poetry he could have been capable of writing under any circumstances. Possibly some of his contemporaries overestimated him because of the charm of his personality, but his contemporaries were not all personally acquainted with him. He attempted less ambitious enterprises than Longfellow, and often brought off what he tackled with less complete success, and he seldom achieved the autochthonism which will always keep Whittier alive as an American poet until the character of America shall have fundamentally changed. But he was a more "stylish" poet than either of these others, and in a way he carries an air of greater distinction. In every age, and in every line of human endeavor, there are human beings who impress us as in some way more important than the sum of what they do, and it is clear that Lowell was one of them. As I have already said, nothing about him was simple, and he was a many-sided man personally as well as professionally. "I believe neither in heroes nor in saints," wrote Howells; "but I believe in great and good men, for I have known them; and among such men Lowell was of the richest nature I have known." We cannot hope to understand him without exploring all these aspects and, having done so, discovering their interrelationships and the principles of integration that formed them into a character and not a chaos. But before we attempt this, it will be well to remind ourselves briefly of the basic facts of his life experience.

II

When James Russell Lowell was born at Elmwood on the birthday of the Father of his Country in the year 1819, Cambridge, Massachusetts, was still a country town whose old-time Puritan earnestness had been leavened by the new intellectualism and savoir faire of Harvard College. During his early years the little boy loved to go to the blacksmith shop, where a friendly smith allowed him to blow the bellows. The house in which he was born, and where he died, still stands where it stood then (now the property of Harvard and the residence of one of its deans), but the grounds now embrace much less than the thirty acres which the Lowells knew. Originally they stretched clear to the entrance of what is now Mount Auburn. In those days this was Stone's Woods or "Sweet Auburn" and the property of the Massachusetts Horticultural Society; it was not sold for cemetery purposes until 1831. During part of Lowell's own life at Elmwood, farming was practised there on a small scale, and he took on the life of a country squire in addition to all his other functions, but he himself sold off a good deal of the land to avoid ruinous taxation, and when the Leslie Stephens visited Elmwood in the 'sixties they were scandalized by the "roughness" of the place and the absence of flowers. Lack of adequate help had left the grounds in a "slovenly" state, and cows were tethered on the lawn, just under the dining room windows.

In Lowell's boyhood, Elmwood stood at the end of "Tory Row." It was, and is, as Horace E. Scudder remarked, a Georgian brick manor house re-created in terms of New England wood, less impressive than the Craigie House, which became the Long-fellow House, but reflecting the same general taste. It had been built in 1767 for Thomas Oliver, the son of a West Indies merchant, and lieutenant governor of the Province, who married a daughter of Colonel John Vassall and was made President of the Council by King George III. On the morning of September 2, 1774, his residence was surrounded by some 4000 freemen, in obedience to whose commands he was obliged to resign his offices, after which he left Cambridge, and his house was seized for public uses. During the war it was used as a hospital. Later it was sold to Arthur Cabot, of Salem, then to Elbridge Gerry, one of the signers of the Declaration of Independence. Lowell's father, the Reverend Charles Lowell, purchased it in 1818.

The American establishment of the Lowells had been achieved by "old" Percival Lowle, at Newbury, Massachusetts, in 1639. Back of the poet lay three generations of Harvard-trained lawyers and clergymen. One uncle, Francis Cabot Lowell, who became one of the founders of the New England textile industry, and consequently one of the great architects of the family fortune, lent his name to the city of Lowell, and another, John Lowell "the Rebel," founded the Lowell Institute. The "Russell," which the poet afterwards thought, or pretended to think, indicated Jewish extraction, came from his grandfather, Judge James Russell of Charlestown.[8]

Charles Lowell purchased Elmwood because he had worn himself out as pastor of Boston's West Church, and a country residence had been prescribed for him. Even in those days, the building stood on the edge of a dangerous black-and-white slum area, but the fearless pastor moved freely among its denizens, carrying not only good counsel but food and medicines when they were needed. He has often been called a Unitarian, but this is not correct. He was pastor of a Congregational church, and when the split between Trinitarian and Unitarian came, he refused to be drawn into the controversy. "I have adopted," he wrote, "no other religious creed than the Bible, and no other name than Christian as denoting my religious faith," and Francis H. Underwood recorded, on James Russell Lowell's own authority, that the pastor once marshalled all the arguments he could find "for Congregationalism" in his "antique theological armory" for the benefit of one of his sons.[9] Charles Lowell preached his first sermon in West Church (Thomas Wentworth Higginson says his sermons were only fifteen minutes long[10]) on the text

"Rejoice in the Lord always; and again I say, Rejoice." It was his aim to present religion "in the garb of cheerfulness, and not of melancholy; as the inspirer of peace and hope, and not of wretchedness and despair," directing his hearers to God "as your Father and your best friend, and—as our religion presents him to us—as God in Christ, reconciling the world to himself."

I am not, and never have been a believer in that system which would dress up the gladsome spirit of youth in the weeds of sadness, and convert the accents, even of early childhood, into mournful regrets and lamentations—if, indeed, these could be felt and indulged—for the deformed scene on which they have entered, and the deformed nature they have brought with them.[11]

Charles Lowell had studied at Edinburgh under Dugald Stewart, and though Pope is said to have been his favorite poet, he had contacts with Wordsworth, Southey, and Scott. Though he was unable to sympathize with his son's "activist" abolitionist stand, he himself denounced the Fugitive Slave Law and prayed in Faneuil Hall that escaped slaves might not be recaptured, and it is said that his only outburst of rage that the family could remember came when he learned of the adoption of the Missouri Compromise. His health declined through many years, and after his stroke in 1852, both his mental and his bodily health were greatly impaired. In spite of all the differences between them, his youngest son never ceased to think of him as "the very simplest and charmingest of men." As late as the time of his appointment as Minister to Spain, he thought that "if my father were only alive to see this, I should be pleased by it."

Lowell's mother, Harriet Spence, came of a Tory, Episcopal family, ultimately of Orkney Islands and Scottish Highlands extraction, and it pleased her to count the ballad hero, Sir Patrick Spens, among her forebears.[12] The Lowells credited her with having brought "the Spence negligence" into the family, though

James Russell himself speaks of "the indolence (I know not whether to call it intellectual or physical) that I inherited from my father." If his mother brought him indolence, she brought him something more important also. She was a hypersensitive, rather exquisite person, a see-er of visions, a teller of tales and singer of ballads, and she influenced the imaginative side of his character importantly. As a child he was read to sleep from Shakespeare and *The Faerie Queene*, and Spenser took such a hold upon him that he used to fancy himself accompanied by Spenser's characters when he went to school. On March 19, 1845, when the poet-to-be was twenty-six, she was admitted to McLean Hospital, but the extract from the hospital records preserved in the Houghton Library[13] reports her as having already been insane "for very many years," and though she was taken back home on November 10, she was never to be well again. Lowell, whose poem "The Darkened Mind" refers to his mother's tragedy, apparently believed that her illness was triggered by the circumstances attending the "disgrace" which engulfed her eldest son, Charles Russell Lowell, in 1837, when, through mismanagement, and perhaps through what Longfellow called "moral delinquencies," he lost a large part of his father's fortune, which he had been managing for him. Though all these circumstances may cause the modern reader to shudder, he may perhaps shudder almost as much when he finds Mrs. Lowell addressing her eighteen-year-old son as "Babie Jamie."

Lowell was the youngest of six children. When he was born, "Charles was between eleven and twelve, Rebecca ten, Mary a little over eight, William between five and six, and Robert between two and three." [14] William died when James was four, and Rebecca inherited her mother's aberration. Since Rebecca kept house for her father in later years, Mrs. Longfellow's reference to her as Lowell's "mad sister" may seem a trifle exaggerated, but she was far from normal, and in 1875 Lowell wrote Charles Eliot

Norton that "our poor sister is grown violent." Lowell's child-hood relationship with his brother Charles was very close, but in 1839 they quarrelled so violently that James took a room outside of Elmwood; later he seems to have blamed himself for this. Whether this quarrel had any connection with Charles's financial difficulties I have no idea, but in later years Lowell admired his brother for the way he had rebuilt his life. When Charles died in 1870, Lowell wrote Norton:

Tell Jane I . . . was very grateful for her letter about Charles's death. I will not write about him yet—for there is too much to say about a life that shipwrecked as his did and one who stood by the wreck so long and gallantly as he.

The other two children both had literary talent, and both may be said to have lived distinguished lives. The Reverend Robert Traill Spence Lowell, an Episcopal clergyman, was first a missionary in Newfoundland, then a pastor in New Jersey, next headmaster of St. Mark's School in Southborough, Massachusetts, and finally Professor of Latin at Union College. He published a number of books in prose and verse, among which his novel *The New Priest in Conception Bay* (1858) was warmly admired though not widely read. Mary, later Mrs. Samuel R. Putnam, seems to have had at least as much to do with bringing up "Jamie" as his mother; very likely she did more. A learned, largely self-educated New England lady, of the type which Sarah Alden Ripley outstandingly exemplifies, and a phenomenal lin-guist, she lived nearly ninety years, and her *Records of an Obscure Man* is rated by Duberman as "far ahead of its own day" in "its learned, sophisticated defense of the Negro" and in "its awareness of past African achievements" ahead of ours.

The most important of Lowell's early masters was William Wells, an Englishman and a publisher, who kept a private school in Cambridge, where he combined stern discipline with thorough

training in Latin. In his autobiography in the Harvard Class
Book of 1838, Lowell boasted that

During the Freshman year, I did nothing, during the Sophomore
year I did nothing, during the Junior year I did nothing, and during
the Senior year I have thus far done nothing in the way of college
studies. I have undergone with the patience of a martyr "privates"
and "publics" without number, and three threats of dismissal.

This is more the smart-alecky boast of a bright young undergraduate than an accurate record. Lowell was certainly less interested in his classes than he was in his writings as a college
journalist, though he later spoke of these productions as having
been produced by "as great an ass as ever brayed, and thought it
singing." With a curriculum based mainly on Latin, Greek, and
mathematics, and a student body of about 250, engaged in grind-
ing out recitations, he could hardly have been expected to be
anything else. He was also an underground member of Alpha
Delta Phi, secret societies being forbidden by Harvard at this
time. But he would not have been himself had he not embarked
upon a wide range of reading in the Harvard Library, under his
own direction, and his college record, though far from brilliant,
is not disgraceful. When he graduated, his class chose him Class
Poet, but he was not allowed to appear and read his poem, since
he was undergoing punishment at the time for "continued
negligence in college duties," being "rusticated" at Concord in
care of the Reverend Barzillai Frost. The poem was printed,
however, and 170 copies were subscribed for.[15]

He must earn a living—but how? He pondered medicine, the
church, the law. For a time the law seemed the best of a bad
range of choices. He entered Harvard's Dane Law School and
received his Bachelor of Laws degree in 1840. But his hesitations
and uncertainties were pitiful, and the record would be amusing
if one could forget how many gifted youngsters have gone

through similar agonies in trying to find their places in the world. On February 26, 1837, which was before his graduation from Harvard, Lowell declares magniloquently that he expects to become Chief Justice, but by October 11, 1838, he is "reading Blackstone with as good a grace and as few wry faces as I may." That same month he decides to give up the law for business, but in November hearing a court case in which Daniel Webster participates gives him a new vision of what legal practice might be. By the following March this has worn off, and he is restrained from changing again only by the fear that people may think him a fool, "and yet I can hardly hope to be satisfied where I am." In May 1839 he is sure that he was "never made for a merchant" but begins to doubt "whether I was made for anything in particular but to loiter through life"; in June he thought he was beginning to like the law; in July he believed that though he might take his degree he would never practice. By June 1940 he would "as lief dig potatoes" as practice law—"*Something* I *must* do to get my bread. D—n!!!!"—and in August he rejects the argument of those who tell him that all young men have felt as he does: "Fools! that do not see that this is the strongest argument in my favor." In March 1841 he is in Charles G. Loring's office and "getting quite in love with the law," and in January 1842 he has been admitted to the bar and taken an office. Surely, then, he is at last settled? Far from it. By May he is speaking of "a calling which I hate, and for which I am not *well* fitted, to say the least." He reached the end of the road in 1843. On April 17, he wrote to Poe that he was

just on the eve of quitting the office which I occupy as "attorney and counsellor at law." I have given up that interesting profession, and mean to devote myself wholly to letters. I shall live with my father in Cambridge, in the house where I was born.

The first fruits of Lowell's literary ambitions had appeared between covers even before he made this decision. *A Year's Life and Other Poems* was published in 1841, with an epigraph which was not intended to be taken humorously—"Ich habe gelebt und geliebt." In 1843 Lowell and his friend Robert Carter attempted to establish a new literary magazine, *The Pioneer*, which, due largely to unwise financial arrangements with its publishers, expired after three numbers and left him saddled with debt, but not until after it had brought out Poe's "Lenore" and "The Tell-Tale Heart"; "The Hall of Fantasy" and "The Birthmark" by Hawthorne; and "The Maiden's Death" by Mrs. Browning. Many journals which have survived much longer cannot match this record.

By this time, Lowell's financial situation had been made more difficult by his desire to marry. His sweetheart was the high-minded, exquisite, and gifted Maria White, who wrote poetry which the granddaughter of her husband's cousin, Amy Lowell, was to consider better than her lover's, and who was a Transcendentalist, passionately interested in abolition and all good "causes." Her father was a Watertown citizen of substance, who, for the most part, preferred to allow his daughter and her husband to sink or swim on their own resources; Higginson speaks of him as a "recusant father-in-law." Lowell met Maria White late in 1839, and they became engaged in 1840, but marriage was not judged possible until December 26, 1844. Both had been members of "The Brother and Sister Club" or "The Band," an informal group of gay and earnest young people which included William Wetmore Story, Nathan Hale, Jr., and others. Before her always frail health was permanently shattered, and tuberculosis claimed her in 1853, Maria was to bear her husband four children—three daughters and a son—but all except one, Mabel, later Mrs. Edward Burnett, died almost in infancy, and even she did not long outlive her father.

The years of his marriage to Maria White marked the height

of Lowell's activity as a reformer. Thinking that Philadelphia might be kinder to her lungs than Boston, they went there shortly after their marriage. Lowell wrote for the *Philadelphia Freeman*, but his earnings were not large enough to support him and his wife, and in the spring of 1845 they came to live at Elmwood. Lowell's anti-slavery writing continued into 1850, however, and at one time he was "corresponding editor" of the *National Anti-Slavery Standard*, though, as he rightly insisted, his title was a contradiction in terms. In 1845 *Conversations on Some of the Old Poets* first showed what Lowell was worth critically.

The year 1848 was, as Greenslet called it, Lowell's annus mirabilis. Besides a two-volume *Poems*, in which he collected much of what he had been contributing to the magazines, he published separately *A Fable for Critics*, the First Series of *The Biglow Papers*, and *The Vision of Sir Launfal*. Both the *Fable* and *Biglow* demonstrated the humorous, satirical side of his poetic gift. In the first, this manifested itself in combination with his ability to achieve pungent criticism in verse, for the scheme of the work involved a cross section of contemporary American literature. In *The Biglow Papers*, the humorist wore prophetic robes, for this work was a bitter denunciation of the Mexican War and of war itself. *Launfal*, which has a highly romantic, chivalric, medieval setting, illustrated a more "refined," idealistic side of Lowell's endowment, and appealed profoundly to a generation which loved Tennyson's *Idylls of the King* and some of the more ambitious poems of Longfellow. For many, many years, it was the title which came first to mind when Lowell's name was spoken. Lowell was never to match the year 1848 again; if he could have kept up such a record, he would have outdistanced not only himself but all other American poets.

He went to Europe first in 1851–52 and again in 1855–56, the second trip being occasioned by his desire to qualify himself better for his duties as Smith Professor of French and Spanish and Professor of Belles-Lettres following Longfellow's resignation of the post. The appointment had been prompted, at least in part, by the strong impression he had made by his Lowell lectures on poetry. He became the first editor of *The Atlantic Monthly* when it was established in 1857 and continued to edit it until 1861, and from 1863 to 1868 he and Charles Eliot Norton jointly edited *The North American Review*. In 1857 he married Frances Dunlap, who had been looking after Mabel since her mother's death.

In 1864 Lowell published (in prose) his *Fireside Travels*; next year came the famous *Ode Recited at the Harvard Commemoration*. The Second Series of *The Biglow Papers*, which had been serialized in the *Atlantic* during the war, appeared in book form in 1867. Next year came the first collection of short poems in many years, *Under the Willows*, and in 1870 Lowell brought out one of his most ambitious poems, *The Cathedral*. It would probably not be just to call this a more "important" religious poem than Whittier's "Our Master" and "The Eternal Goodness," but it is certainly much more ambitious and intellectual. It is interesting that it should have been inspired by the same cathedral, Chartres, which was so greatly to enthrall Henry Adams.

Lowell's first mature collection of critical papers, *Among My Books*, appeared in 1870, and was sufficiently successful to be followed in kind by *My Study Windows* in 1871 and the second collection of *Among My Books* in 1876. His satisfaction in the publication of these volumes was modified by his dislike of their titles, which had been chosen by his publishers, and which he considered too egotistical.

He spent the years 1872–74 largely in Europe. He received honorary doctorates from both Oxford and Cambridge (as later from Edinburgh and Harvard). Upon his return to America, he took a more active part in politics than he had taken before. On the instigation of his kinsman by marriage, William Dean Howells, President Hayes made him American ambassador to Spain, where he served from 1877 to 1880, making an excellent record and showing how a man of letters writes state despatches! In 1880 he was awarded the leading post in the diplomatic service, the ambassadorship to England, from which he was removed in 1885 when the Democrat Cleveland came into office. The second Mrs. Lowell died in England in February 1885, and her death left her husband desolate, though it came at the end of a long and distressing illness, probably a brain lesion which, at intervals, had horribly affected her mind.

After his return to America, Lowell lived with his daughter and her family at Southborough, Massachusetts, with his sister Mrs. Putnam on Boston's Beacon Street, and, from November 1889, again at Elmwood. Besides a fresh series of Lowell lectures on the old English dramatists and a Presidential address for the Modern Language Association, he delivered an address at Harvard's 250th anniversary in 1886 and another in 1889, when the less venerable American nation celebrated the centenary of Washington's inauguration. Between 1885 and 1890 he made four more extended visits to England. He published *Democracy and Other Addresses* in 1886, both *Heartsease and Rue* and *Political Essays* in 1888, and *Latest Literary Essays and Addresses* in 1891, and saw the eleven-volume "Riverside Edition" of his writings through the press in 1890. He died at Elmwood on August 12, 1891, leaving *The Old English Dramatists* (1892) to be published posthumously.

III

In our time, every schoolchild knows that human character and behavior are importantly conditioned by heredity and environment. Many of the conditioning factors brought to bear upon James Russell Lowell will already have suggested themselves to the attentive reader of the foregoing sketch. He was the child of his time, of his family, of his social environment and the ideals cherished there. But there were simpler matters also. He was a man. He had a body. This body presented an outer aspect to the world; its inner climate expressed itself in terms of his own physical well-being and the reverse thereof. He developed behavior patterns. And all this, and much besides, affected and was affected by the far from simpler matter we may call his temperament. Before we turn to the examination of his particular and peculiar characteristics as one belonging to the genus artist, it might be well to glance at some of these more universal considerations.

CHAPTER TWO

BASIC EQUIPMENT

Without anecdote, what is biography, or even history, which is only biography on a larger scale?

JRL, 1867

I

Thomas Wentworth Higginson remembered Lowell at William Wells's school as "a rather homely boy, yet with bright eyes and the beginning of the Apollo look as to the brow, which lighted up a face otherwise rather heavy." [1] He adds that William Wetmore Story, the Steerforth of the school, took the lead of him there, and that this was also true later in Cambridge society. Descriptions of his appearance later vary with the describer, the two extremes probably being marked by Agnes Repplier, who immensely admired him,[2] and the wildly intemperate John Jay Chapman, who found him "a literary fop—f-o-p, fop." [3] The face which peers out at us from the almost sinister depths of William Page's canvas is that of a supersubtle Elizabethan, seemingly disinclined to lay all his cards on the table.

He was five feet, seven or eight inches tall; some say slender, others stocky. (His pictures rather support the latter view.) E. S. Nadal says: "He had that build which is said to be one of the best for strength and endurance, deep chest and broad shoulders, set on short, stout legs." In 1867 he told Norton that he now weighed 167 pounds, which was eight pounds less than last year, and in 1871 he told Mabel that he had tipped the scales at 171—"I had no notion I was carrying about so much luggage." In 1873 he wrote Aldrich that he was getting gray and fat, being about half the size of Howells, and in 1876 he warned Mrs. S. B. Herrick that he had lost his waist. He walked rapidly and shook hands vigorously enough to create a tingling. His manner was warm and friendly, at least when he wanted it to be, sometimes quizzical, but always suave, cultivated, and courtly. "Although small in stature," says William Roscoe Thayer, "he left upon you the impression of great dignity." His blue-gray eyes were often called beautiful (one woman called them "the coaxin'est eyes"); they had dark mottlings in them; ordinarily "bright and cheery," they were penetrating in concentration, lustrous in excitement, and lighted up as with a flash when he was amused. It is interesting that Justin McCarthy, who at first thought his appearance that of a typical sturdy Briton, much more robust than his writing, should have felt it necessary to add that "there is a certain indecision about the eyes and mouth . . . which helps us to recognize the author of the over-thoughtful poems and the exquisitely poetical essays," [4] and another adds that his lips were "perhaps irrepressible in their tendency to twitch or to quiver." But the voice that emerged through the lips was always beautiful, vibrantly tender, and marked by "crisp clearness," "perfect modulation, clear enunciation," and "exquisite accent." [5]

Some observers, like Charles Akers, call Lowell fastidious in person, always well and simply clothed. He once rebuked Akers for some unconventionality in his appearance, saying that it was modest and proper to dress like other people. He himself did not always do this, however. In 1850 he called on the Longfellows wearing "light nankeen trousers, a white Robespierre waistcoat, and collar turned over, with only a black ribbon for cravat." Much later, he liked to go without a winter overcoat, and within eight years of his death, he nearly froze E. S. Nadal, walking home from a function at Buckingham Palace, at two or three o'clock in the morning, in silk stockings and pumps. Howells says he astonished Cambridge by taking to a frock coat and high hat after his return from London, but Barrett Wendell had already encountered the hat, as part of a rather odd ensemble, in a Harvard classroom, at an earlier date.

My first impression was that he was surprisingly hirsute and a little eccentric in aspect. He wore a double-breasted sack-coat, by no means new. In his necktie, which was tied in a sailor-knot, was a pin—an article of adornment at that time recently condemned by an authority which some of us were then disposed to accept as gospel. On his desk lay a silk hat not lately brushed; and nobody, I then held, had any business to wear a silk hat unless he wore coat-tails too.

Hair seems always to have been a moral issue almost beyond any other aspect of human grooming or attire, and Saint Francis of Sales was quite exceptional when he replied to a penitent who wished to know whether she might follow the current fashion of powdering her hair: "Tell her to powder her hair, if she likes, so long as her heart is right; for the thing is not worth so much thinking about." When Lowell began wearing his auburn mop long, he was almost as unconventional as the "hippies" were to be in the 1960's before they themselves had established another convention and themselves fallen victim to it. In 1844 Mrs. Longfellow wrote in her journal:

Young Lowell, the poet, came at tea-time, to see us, looking very picturesque with his shapely beard. Talked à la jeune Amerique of the great reform this country is to display—the order of society to become more radical yet,—and men of all classes to know each other and love each other in communities &c. His pure and Christian notions are finely carried into everything with him—remarkable in a youth of imagination. He considers that beards should be worn or God would not have given them, and intends, when old, to sport one of patriarchal length.

Mrs. Longfellow did not care for beards (it is interesting to remember that she never saw her husband's), yet when she encountered Lowell again in 1852, for the first time since his had "succumbed to English prejudices," she admitted that "half the poetry" had gone out of his face. The hair was shorter during later years, but the beard grew again, and William Roscoe Thayer greatly disliked the "walrus tusks" of the mustache that were allowed to extend below it.

What twist of fancy could have led him to adopt this fashion cannot be guessed, for it was neither becoming nor beautiful, and I cannot believe that a man otherwise unaffected and reserved could have been tricked by vanity into choosing to make himself conspicuous in this way.

II

When his liver was out of order in 1875, Lowell called it the first illness he had ever had except for gout. On the contrary, he seems to me to have suffered from an extraordinary variety of maladies, and even to have been bedded with surprising frequency for a man who was not really an invalid. We hear of rheumatism, a swollen face, a "*fulness* in the head," and pain in the side which made him "half crazy." Once he complains that his back feels "as if it had been broken in two and awkwardly mended," and in 1877 he declared that a year ago he was "really pretty well crippled," though he did not look it. In 1881, in Dresden, he was fitted with "swaddling-bands of my second childhood" in the form of a truss by a technician who frightened him by telling him that he had been "on the eve of a great disaster" and might well have made himself "a disgusting cripple" for the rest of his life. The harness made him black and blue and left him fearful "of a jar or a long stride," and he planned to see a surgeon when he got to Rome. Perhaps he did so, and perhaps the Dresden man was merely a good salesman; at any rate, we hear nothing more about this particular menace.

He complains of his eyes as early as 1839, when he tells G. B. Loring that he cannot use them at night and only a little by day. He spent part of the winter of 1842–43 in New York, undergoing treatment by the great Dr. Samuel Elliot, who also treated Longfellow (his absence from Boston at this time was one of the things that wrecked *The Pioneer*), and he speaks of having "an application or an operation every day." In 1867 he had a tumor removed from an eyelid, and there are many complaints in the 'seventies. In March 1873 he writes Mabel from Paris that "the oculist recommends nippers"; does this mean that he has not worn glasses before? (As late as 1876 a letter to Howells contains the proud postscript: "Written without spectacles in his fifty-eighth year.") A month after his letter to Mabel, he tells her that "I have mounted an eyeglass but it wearies and pains me," and the very next month he tells his sister that he has had to consult an oculist about a disease which has somewhat damaged his left eye. Yet as late as 1878 he is writing his daughter that his eyes trouble him much and alarm him more, and that if they do not mend, he will be "driven" to consult an oculist, though he fears that he is too far gone now for medicine to help much. Toward the end of his life, he thought himself threatened with cataract, but I have found no evidence that this developed. While this is a somewhat motley array of references on eyes, I think it does add up to the conclusion that Lowell did not care for his eyes in anything like a consistent or systematic way.

The real plague of his life, healthwise, was gout. He regarded it as an hereditary complaint, "the unearned increment from my good grandfather's Madeira." It apparently appeared first in the late 'fifties, and thereafter was liable at any time to strike without warning, in either foot, or, worse still, in the stomach. Though the pain was dreadful, he learned to live with it.

I have had some exquisite variations of torture, almost unbearable at times, but have been well otherwise, and able to maintain, if not my serenity, at least the appearance of it, and an imperturbable good humor. I trust that the pain has been, as moralists tell us it is, for my good. What else it could be good for I can't make out.

He even tried to cultivate indifference to pain—"I think I can understand how men have borne the rack without flinching though I doubt if I could"—and when, at the very end of his life, he had occasion to complain of sciatica, he thought that "a sharp pain is better than the dull inexplicable ones I have been enduring so long."

Whether he suffered more or less from the cancer which killed him than he had suffered from gout, it would be hard to say. Its first effect, in January 1890, was a violent hemorrhage of the bladder, from which it spread to his liver and finally to his lungs. Apparently he never knew what ailed him. When he died the *Transcript* reported that the cause of his death was unknown, but an autopsy was performed, and the next day Child wrote: "Now we know the precise cause of his sufferings, it is a wonder that he didn't suffer much more." Yet he speaks of having been given opium as early as March 1890, and a few months before his death he wrote Sarah Orne Jewett that he had "few days, just now, in which I can control my wits enough to put words logically together." According to one report, he became delirious about two weeks before his death, now fancying himself entertaining royalty and again begging to be taken back to Elmwood, and his last words, on August 10, were "Oh, why don't you let me die?" But his illness went through many fluctuations, and though he told Henry James that when it first came upon him, he thought it was time for him to vanish like a ghost with "melodious twang," he was by no means consistently pessimistic. During the late summer of 1890 he actually seemed to be getting better. "I see no reason why I shouldn't get perfectly well again," he wrote Lady Lyttleton in December, and, even as late as February 1891, reporting to Dr. S. Weir Mitchell his inability to come to Philadelphia to lecture, he added, "But don't think me worse than I am. I do pretty well so long as I keep still and feel quite hopeful that I shall be as well as ever one of these days."

III

Except for his excessive smoking and intemperate study, Lowell seems to have led a hygienic life, though modern hygienists would not approve of all the things he did. We hear of 600 strokes with twenty-four-pound Indian clubs, so that his hands trembled afterwards, and of taking a cold bath by an open window, with the thermometer near zero. Once, in November, he writes Charles Briggs that they have so far had ice only once or twice, so that he has not yet been compelled to give up his swims in the Charles, "though they are shorter than in August." He seems to have been an excellent swimmer, but in spite of one ecstatic reference to a moonlight sail, I do not find that he cared much for sailing in general, and long sea voyages bored him as much as summer resorts. He skated in Germany (and presumably at home), and he was a mighty pedestrian; when Blanche was a baby, he looked forward to teaching her to walk twenty miles a day as he could. He developed a detailed knowledge of the streets of Paris, and in Rome, Maria reports him often walking out six or seven miles in spite of the bad condition of the roads after the heavy rains. Whether he rode horseback in his youth I do not know, but in 1877 he told Mabel he was thinking of buying a saddlehorse and taking to "vigorous equitation" for his health, and three years later he praised his grandson and namesake for showing "so much pluck in the saddle: I hope you will learn all manly exercises and accomplishments," he told him. "You will be a happier man for it all."

Shooting, fishing, nutting, and other country sports he came in contact with as a boy, but though he speaks of planning to get up at six o'clock in the morning to go fishing as late as 1866, Greenslet, who should certainly be a good judge in this area, does not believe he was a very persistent fisherman. Very likely he lacked the patience for it, as for the relish of sea voyages. Whatever hunting he did in later years seems to have been with the Adirondack Club, which embraced Emerson, Agassiz, E. R. Hoar, John Holmes, W. J. Stillman, and others. (Longfellow refused to go, not considering himself safe in the presence of firearms in the hands of such people!)[6] But though we hear of his having shot a bear and a deer, Lowell did not enjoy killing, and Stillman says he proposed to substitute archery for the actual hunting. What he did enjoy was the wilderness itself, "cutting paths through woods in which no paths had ever been made before" and scaling a reputedly unscalable pine tree, and he seems to have been capable of enjoying hardships for the stimulation they afforded, much as Theodore Roosevelt did. Later, when he was in Switzerland, however, he preferred to do his mountain-climbing with his eyes, through a telescope, and there is a late public address in which he raps "that very large class of men who have leisure without culture, and whose sole occupation is either the killing of game or the killing of time."

In college days, Lowell describes football in terms of Homeric burlesque,[7] but I find no later references to it or to other spectator sports. On shipboard in 1872 he played shuffleboard with

Francis Parkman against Henry Adams and T. W. Parsons, but the Lowell team lost. There are few references to dancing. What he did love, among indoor games, was whist, and for many years, he, John Holmes (the Autocrat's brother), John Bartlett, of *Familiar Quotations,* and Lowell's brother-in-law by marriage, Dr. Estes Howe, played it on Friday nights; Lowell kept the records, and they are still in the Houghton Library. But it is said that he was never too much absorbed in the game to stop to tell any story that might occur to him, and that when the laughter had subsided, he would blandly inquire, "What are trumps?" In 1877 he played whist with the captain on shipboard for "thrippeny" points and won five and six, which he gave to the sailors' poor box, adding a donation, as a penitential offering for his gambling. Of Thoreau he once wrote unsympathetically, "He wishes always to trump your suit and to *ruff* when you least expect it."

E. S. Nadal, who knew Lowell well, denied what he called the existence of essentially Yankee characteristics in him.

He had a power of enjoyment which was not Yankee, a power of enjoyment both mental and physical. He liked good food, drink and tobacco, and was altogether very fond of the earth. He sometimes spoke of this quality and said he had upon his ear a mark which is peculiar to the ear of the faun.

Whatever else Yankees may have been ascetic about, I have never observed in them any tendency toward asceticism in the areas mentioned, but this need not be debated here. Surprisingly little has been recorded about his tastes in food or his interest in it. Crossing the Atlantic with him in the summer of 1872, Mrs. Henry Adams found him revelling in "pig's cheek and cabbage followed by spiced tripe" when many others were unable to eat anything at all. Later, presumably after the sea had calmed, he joined her and her husband and Francis Parkman in

Welsh rarebit before retiring. Perhaps, after all, he was not exaggerating when, at the end of his life, Lowell wrote Lady Lyttleton that for seventy years he had hardly known he had a stomach.[8]

The references to drinking are nearly all to wine, though Nadal records that Lowell was very fond of Bass, which was bad for his gout. This notion may be incorrect, but if Lowell believed this and went on drinking Bass, the act is not without significance. When Thomas Hughes called on him at Cambridge early in the 'seventies, Lowell offered him sherry, but when it was poured out of the jar, it turned out to be whiskey, "and he hurried off to change the jar, explaining that the only alcohol in the house was in those jars, and he used it so seldom that he did not well know them apart." In 1868 Leslie Stephen drank whiskey toddy with Lowell at Elmwood, but the very next year, Lowell wrote Norton that he had had no whiskey in the house until he came down with a cold.[9]

There are many references to convivial drinking in the writings of Lowell's college years; in his Class Poem he argued that liquor is good because intolerance is bad, from which he went on to attack all who sought to apply intelligence to the whole problem of feeding. How much Lowell himself drank during his college years is problematical, though one letter of Loring's suggests that he was famous for it,[10] and Higginson apparently thought that if it had not been for Maria, he might easily have become a drunkard.[11] Though Edward Everett Hale indignantly denies such allegations,[12] Lowell's drinking, real or alleged, may well have influenced Abijah White's initial objection to him as a son-in-law.[13] We do know that he considered joining "the Anti-Wine" while still in college, and he was certainly a committed teetotaler in the early years of his marriage, though I am not able to say how long this lasted. When Maria appeared prominently at a temperance rally in Watertown, he was proudly in attendance. The only fault he could find with Dickens's *American Notes*, when he reviewed it in the first number of *The Pioneer*, was its

too frequent eulogy of brandy and water, and ill-concealed satire of the temperance reform,—a reform which has been and is doing incalculable good throughout the land; which is spreading peace and innocence where only degradation skulked before, and which is ensuring stability to our freedom, by teaching men to set free and respect *themselves*, without which they can have no true reverence for anything

(he had already refused to attend a dinner in Dickens's honor, when he was in Boston in 1842, because wine was to be served), and he was soon to rejoice in the news that temperance sentiment was making progress in Sweden under American inspiration.[14] In 1846 Longfellow recorded that Lowell was now so rabid on the subject of liquor that he wished to destroy all the wine in his cellar, and that same year the young poet criticized Oliver Wendell Holmes, who was ten years his senior, for what he considered his indifference to temperance, abolition, and other good causes.[15] There are many friendly references to temperance reform in the anti-slavery papers, and in *Conversations* John quotes from Mrs. Browning:

> Old Chaucer, with his infantine,
>   Familiar clasp of things divine,—
>   That stain upon his lips is wine.

Upon which he comments: "I had rather think it pure grape-juice." Philip, however, likes the third line as it stands, in spite of John's "cold-water prejudices."

Such references do not entirely disappear from Lowell's later writings. Birdofredum Sawin's opposition to the temperance reformers is certainly not intended to prejudice readers against them, and there is a late reference to the

> sand of bar-room floors
> Mid the stale reek of boosing boors.

Nevertheless, there was a change, and when, in later years, Lowell speaks of abstaining, it is clearly only a temporary measure, induced by health considerations. Once he calls the cellar the true foundation of the house, and upon arriving back at Elmwood in 1875 he rejoiced to find that John Holmes had laid in a store of "every possible tipple known to gods or men." He refused Higginson's invitation to address a temperance convention, and when Mrs. Stowe barred alcohol at an *Atlantic* dinner, he said she had "tied a witches-knot." In a review of *The Winthrop Papers* in 1867,[16] he quoted what he calls a cogent statement of the "anti-prohibition argument" from a letter of Thomas Shepard, minister at Cambridge, written in 1639:

This also I doe humbly intreat, that there may be no sin made of *drinking in any case one to another*, for I am confident he that stands here will fall and be beat from the grounds by his own arguments; as also that the consequences will be very sad, and the thing provoking to God and man to make more sins than (as yet is seene) God himself hath made.

Clarity is hardly the outstanding characteristic of this somewhat cryptic statement, but it can hardly be called an "argument" in any sense of the term. Lowell's interest, however, was not in the logic of the matter. That same year he wrote "Uncle Cobus's Story" for *Our Young Folks*, holding forth on the failure of the fairies to come to the new world with the Pilgrim Fathers, and even here he must say, apropos of Robin Goodfellow, "I hardly think gladsome Robin, even if he had come, would have cared to stay where even cider is sinful, unless it be turned to vinegar to keep some folks' faces well soured."

Lowell's recusancy to the temperance cause may have been simply a part of his turning away from extremism or comeoutism after his wife's death. As such it would be rather a strange phenomenon, however. He never ceased to mourn his wife and revere her memory; one might have thought that, once she had gone, he would have been all the more inclined to remain loyal to her principles as a memorial to her. There are indications, however, that even Maria became less of a reformer during her last years, and it may be that the change in Lowell was motivated less by her passing than by the passing of his youth, which, in its final aspect, she had so largely molded.

Tobacco, as I have already suggested, was much more important to him than alcohol—

> Nocotia, dearer to the Muse
> Than all the grape's bewildering juice.

It is referred to again and again both in his poetry and in his prose, and in an unpublished "ode of thanks" to Norton for "certain cigars" we learn that Bacchus himself planted it in the Western Hemisphere.

> He gave to us a leaf divine
> More grateful to the serious Nine
> Than fierce inspirings of the vine.
>
> And that he loved it more, this proved,—
> He gave his name to what he loved,
> Distorted now, but not removed.

Later we are told that

> The prayers of Christian, Turk and Jew
> Have one sound up there in the blue,
> And one smell all their incense too.
>
> Perhaps that smoke with incense ranks
> Which curls from 'mid life's jars and clanks,
> Graceful with happiness and thanks.

And finally,

> Hock-cups breed hiccups; let us feel
> The god along our senses steal
> More nobly and without his reel.

Chewing tobacco was a "vice" and a "vile habit" (in *The Biglow Papers* he attributes it to Southerners!), but smoking disgusted him only when the Spaniards and the Germans smoked in restaurants—"we never like the smell of our own vices in other people." When Nathan Hale, Jr., suggested that he give it up, he paraphrased Falstaff: "Banish plump Jack and banish all the world! My dear Nat it will never do—don't think of it." From time to time he did stop—or cut down—temporarily, but his reformation seems never to have lasted long, and if Maria objected to his drinking, she seems to have taken no stand on his smoking. Apparently there was something like a compulsive quality about it. In college he was already smoking eight to ten cigars a day when he could get them, and there is a letter to Loring in which he speaks of having smoked three cigars in an hour and another in which he reports having smoked until his hand trembled. In 1877 he reported to Mabel that he had smoked "enormously" on shipboard, adding that he planned to reform upon landing. Once he smoked in spite of a swollen face and lip, though it made the inside of his mouth "redhot," and once he speaks of smoking "my own tobacco which is very good— except that it takes the skin off the roof of my mouth. This however would only be an objection 'to the greener sort of boys,' for it gives a tearful pungency not without its charm." All of which may well remind the reader of Sam Weller's "Every one to his own taste, as the old lady said ven she kissed the cow." [17]

IV

One of the many myths about Lowell devoutly cherished by those who describe—and dismiss—him as a "Brahmin," without knowing quite what they mean by the word, is that he was born with a silver spoon in his mouth, and lived a comfortable life, sheltered from want and "reality." The truth of the matter is that during much of his life he was desperately poor, and that though he lived in a beautiful house, the residence was a white elephant and an unmanageable tax burden, horribly uncomfortable in winter because it was impossible to heat. In 1837 he wrote Loring that when he washed himself in the morning, the water froze in the basin.

As we have already seen, Dr. Lowell's personal fortune was lost through his oldest son's mismanagement, and after 1849, when he was compelled by ill health to reduce his ministerial activities, his income shrank to $1500 a year. Maria's father helped set up his daughter and her husband when they were married, but refused to do anything more for them. When he died the next year, leaving a fortune of about $300,000, Lowell worried about being forcibly deprived of the spiritual benefits of holy poverty, but, as it turned out, he received only about $500 a year. The *Atlantic* paid him first $2500, then $3000 a year, with extra for his own contributions, but he held his position there for only four years, after which the new owner, James T. Fields, desired to edit the magazine himself. The Harvard appointment was for $1200 a year, which was later modestly increased, but after he had been given tutorial assistance, it dropped down to $1200 again. He apparently had some railroad stock, though heaven only knows how he was ever able to buy it, and this entailed both gains and losses; in 1860, for example, Sam Ward sold some Michigan Central shares for him at a profit of $500. At the end, the ambassadorial salaries were high on paper ($12,500 in Spain and $17,500 in England), but after expenses were paid there was not much left, and the situation would have been worse if Mrs. Lowell's illness had not made it impossible for the ambassador to lead the active social life that would otherwise have been expected of him.

In the early days, of course, literature yielded little, and nearly all of this came from serial publication. In 1842 he wrote Poe that he thought he might

safely reckon on earning four hundred dollars by my pen the next year, which will support me. Between this and June, 1843, I think I shall have freed myself of debt and become an independent man. I am to have fifteen dollars a poem from the *Miscellany*, ten dollars from *Graham*, and I have made an arrangement with the editor of the *Democratic Review*, by which I shall probably get ten or fifteen dollars more. Prospects are brightening, you see.

But book publication at this time brought in little or nothing, and even when he was at his height, his reward seems pitifully meager for a writer of his eminence. In 1874 there was a contract with Osgood which guaranteed him a minimum of $1500 a year, and his book royalties during his last years have been placed between $1200 and $2000. In 1887 he wrote Thomas Hughes:

I get twenty-five cents, I think it is, on copies sold during the first eight months after publication, and then it goes into my general copyrights, for which I am paid £400 a year. Not much after nearly fifty years of authorship, but enough to keep me from the almshouse.

The worst of his poverty was shared with Maria, but hard times did not end with her death. In 1848 he says he has spent more than he earned every year since his marriage; that was the year when, after he had paid his taxes, he had $5.00 left. The Lowells sold land to go to Europe in 1851: "That is, we shall spend at the rate of about ten acres a year, selling our birthrights as we go along for messes of European pottage. Well, Raphael and the rest of them are worth it." After Maria's death, when he had about $1500 a year, he paid his brother-in-law, Estes Howe, $1100 to provide a home for Mabel and her governess, Frances Dunlap, who later became the second Mrs. Lowell. Ultimately he sold off about twenty-five of Elmwood's thirty acres, which was supposed to give him about $1500 a year and Mabel $1400 more, but these amounts later shrank somewhat. Financially considered, many of his letters make very painful reading. In November 1848 he writes Sydney Gay that his remittance for one of the slavery articles has arrived in the nick of time, for Lowell has not a cent to his name, and Mabel has no winter clothes yet. In May 1857 Norton is informed that he has had only three cents to his name for more than a week. And in August 1865 Fanny has had no new clothes since before the war, since she has been spending the little money available on Mabel. She has "only one decent gown and the invisible parts of her wardrobe are worn to gauze."

The question naturally arises was Lowell a good manager. It seems quite clear that he was not. He himself declares playfully that

Fate is capricious and sometimes thwarts the finest plans of Nature. Born with as rare a genius as ever man had for being a millionaire, with a skill for spending in an inverse ratio to my small talent for getting, I have never been in a condition to display my abilities.

When he was in Europe preparing for his Smith professorship, he left when he did because his London bankers mistakenly informed him that his balance had been exhausted, and when the mistake was discovered and £700 sent to him, he used it to refurbish his house and felt that a fortunate error had been made. He is said once to have ordered a case of champagne because he needed the bottles to put up some home-made cider. Nobody with any business sense could have signed the absurd *Pioneer* contract,[18] and Akers says that though Lowell sometimes prided himself on absurd little economies, he did not even manage the barnyard and farming operations at Elmwood well.

Lowell's greatest financial handicap was his incorrigible generosity. He began with the idea that he must never refuse money to anybody who asked it of him, and he never really got over this. Half the time when he wanted money, he wanted it not for his own necessities but for some luxury to give a friend. As a poor young lawyer, he would not take money from a Negro client, though he had hardly any other, and when one of his Elmwood tenants fell three years behind in his rent, he did nothing, "since it seems to me that the man who tills the land and makes it useful has a better right to it than he who has merely inherited it." He gave Stillman $600 when he was leaving for Europe ("I shall never want it. I know that I shall never have another child, and I can well spare it"), and he sent Akers away for a tuberculosis cure. He made Briggs a present of the serial rights to *A Fable for Critics*, though he expected this work to be more profitable than anything else he had done. In 1887 he wrote Mabel from London that he had lent £50 to "a poor devil of whom I knew nothing" and that to his astonishment he had been repaid. With one exception, he said, this was a unique experience.

This does not mean that Lowell could not bargain with editors upon occasion. It is true that Godkin thought him "so skittish and shy about money matters that it is difficult to negotiate with him by letter," but Graham clearly regarded him as pretty canny. He suggested $100 for "The Fountain of Youth" in *Putnam's* but accepted $50. Having received $100, he once wrote Fields inquiring why it had not been $150, which he now regarded as his rate. Yet when he was, as he conceived it, overpaid for inferior work, his conscience tortured him, and he would plan to make it up to the publisher by producing something better. In 1887 he conditionally withdrew "The Cuckoo" from the *Atlantic,* while Aldrich was editing it, on the ground that he could get $1000 for it elsewhere, but before the end of the letter, he set a minimum of $250 on it, saying that this is what the *Century* has paid him for a similar poem. He has had a good deal of cloudy weather, he says, but the sun now seems to be shining. "As I don't know how long this meteoric phenomenon is to last, I must be diligent with my windrows and cocks that my crop may be in the mow before a change of weather." It is amusing to see Lowell bargaining thus with a man sitting in a seat which he had once occupied, but what he says was certainly true. Gilder offered him $12,000 for twelve articles in the *Century,* and the rash *New York Ledger* sent $1000 in advance for anything he might choose to send. In a sense, he was more money-minded now than he had been in his youth, for though he liked his son-in-law, Edward Burnett, he apparently did not have a very high regard for his financial capacities, and he wished to leave his daughter and her children independent. "Grandfathers get miserly," he says. But Fields and his partners and successors were, when all was said and done, his principal market, and though he sometimes asked the *Atlantic* to pay upon acceptance, instead of on publication, as was their custom, he gladly acknowledged the generosity of this group.

V

Less tangible but more important than any of the factors we have been considering was what, for want of a better word, may be called Lowell's temperament. "*Can* one get away from his nature?" Lowell was nearly fifty when he asked Charles Eliot Norton this question. "That always puzzles me. Your close-grained, strong fellows tell you that you can—but they forget that they are only acting out their complexion, not escaping it."

He had plenty of room for variety of experience and expression without escaping from it, for few writers have commanded such widely varied interior demesnes, and few have offered greater difficulties to those bent on defining the figure in their carpets. Stanley T. Williams expressed it well when, commenting upon Lowell's Spanish experiences, he wrote that "his career was so complex, so fantastically multiple that what in another might be regarded as an imperious influence shrinks in Lowell to an episode." Extremists of course find here the key to what they are pleased to consider Lowell's "failure." Thus Reilly complains that he leaves words undefined and sometimes shifts his definitions in the course of his discussion. He is inconsecutive. He raises questions which he makes no attempt to resolve. His meaning is often vague. He was "a man of feeling rather than of thought." Others have pointed out that though Lowell achieved a collected edition, he never wrote a book, all his volumes being assemblies of short pieces, and even Bliss Perry, who sincerely admired him, admitted that his was

a nature never quite integrated with wholeness of structure into harmony with itself. His writing at its best, is noble and delightful, full of human charm, but it is difficult for him to master a certain waywardness and to sustain any note steadily.[19]

Lowell himself would not, I think, have found any of this slanderous. In "Uncle Cobus's Story," he tells of the boy whom the fairy Fan-ta-si-a reached ahead of El-bo-gres, and it is clear that he was not unmindful of the personal application of this. In 1847 he differentiated his aspects very carefully for Charles F. Briggs:

I do not know whether it is a common feeling or not, but I can never get to consider myself as anything more than a boy. My temperament is so youthful that whenever I am addressed (I mean by mere acquaintances) as if my opinion were worth anything, I can hardly help laughing. . . . This feeling is so strong that I have got into a way of looking on the Poet Lowell as an altogether different personage from myself, and feel a little offended when my friends confound the two. I find myself very curiously compounded of two utterly distinct characters. One half of me is clear mystic and enthusiast, and the other humorist. If I had lived as solitary as a hermit of the Thebais, I doubt not that I should have had as authentic interviews with the Evil One as they, and without any disrespect to the saint, it would have taken very little to have made a St. Francis of me. Indeed, during that part of my life in which I lived most alone, I was never a single night unvisited by visions, and once I thought I had a personal revelation from God himself. I can believe perfectly in the sincerity of those who are commonly called religious impostors, for, at one time, a meteor could not fall, nor lightning flash, that I did not in some way connect it with my own interior life and destiny. On the other hand, had I mixed more with the world than I have, I should probably have become a Pantagruelist.

This is early of course, and he probably would not have stated the case afterwards in quite the same terms, but the essentials did not greatly change, for in 1879 he told Norton that he did not yet know himself at sixty. Once he took ether for a swollen face. It did not touch the pain, but it did cause him to think himself twelve years old and ready to go out shooting, and all the rest of the night he thought life an illusion and himself "a poor puppet worked by some humorous higher power." In company he would sometimes watch himself "as if I were a third person, and hear the sound of my own voice," and he might come back from a walk fancying himself to be somebody else and expecting to find James Russell Lowell waiting for him in his room, after he had opened the door.

When he was in Spain, he discovered "something oriental" in his nature which sympathized with "this 'let her slide' temper of the hildalgos." Though this is an example of how easily a sensitive nature responds to its environment, it is more than that. As Lowell himself says, he sympathized more with butterflies than ants and liked Esau better than Jacob because he was a scatterbrain. It seems silly for a man who studied twelve hours a day to write, "You don't believe me when I tell you that my mind is sluggish, but it is." Actually, however, Lowell had a point. He enjoyed work more than thinking. "It is curious . . . how tyrannical the habit of reading is, and what shifts we make to escape thinking. There is no bore we dread being left alone with so much as our own minds." He had a tendency to neglect the systematic, mechanical side of both authorship and editorial work. All the virtues of his writing are those of sensitivity and quick, keen intuitive insight; none come from careful structure or patient logical development. Though he did not have much sympathy with the Transcendentalists, he resembled them in this.

He lived too early to speak of his "Peterpantheism," as H. G. Wells was later to do, but he had it and often described it in other terms. Almost beyond all others, the Peter Pan spirit seems to infuriate those who do not possess it; perhaps this is the secret of the almost savage antagonism that Lowell seems to awaken in some natures. It must be understood that in his case "Peterpantheism" never led to any attempt to escape adult responsibilities, which he was punctilious about discharging. It was rather a matter of the man's inner climate and the devices he employed to let off steam.

One expression of all this was Lowell's feeling of perpetual youth. The most extreme statement is in the famous story of his passing a "Home for Incurable Children," one day toward the close of his life, and remarking that he would probably have to go there sooner or later. He felt estranged from Yankees because they did not know how to play, and even in middle age, he was "grateful for anything that renews in me that capacity for mere delight which made my childhood the richest part of my life." Once he speaks to Mabel of "my unfortunate habit of thinking myself only twenty." Nadal compares his boyishness to Matthew Arnold's, and Henry James says that "the boy in him was never more clamorous than during the last summer that he spent in England two years before his death." Mrs. Henry Adams had noted the same tendency during his second wife's ultimately fatal illness: "Mr. Lowell reacts like a child, and is gay and happy at the least improvement." In one of the most charming of his many delightful letters to Lily Norton, Lowell told her that since he could not remember his first birthday, he could not reckon up the others and that consequently he had decided to be her age. "But as girls are always a little more mature than boys of the same age, I shall continue to treat you with the deference you deserve, and you must try to bear with me when I strike you as altogether *too* boyish." The feeling of youth returned to him temporarily and ironically even during his final illness—"but all of a sudden ten days ago I got up in the morning a new man"—and he told an interviewer that he did not feel his age even when he was near death.

But of course this is not the whole story. If it had been, Lowell must have been a freak or a case of arrested development. "The cunning years steal from us all but woe," and as time passes the milestones change to headstones. Growing old means losing your castles in Spain. Happiness is replaced by tranquility, and toasting one's toes before the fire takes the place of aspiration. Such and more is the testimony of the poems, and the letters reinforce it. It is not at all illogical that a man who especially cherishes his youth should be especially sensitive to its passing. "Oh, you'll begin to feel it pretty soon," he told Nadal, and certainly he himself worried about it long before it came. When he found the first gray hairs in his head, "it made me feel queerer than I should have expected for a few minutes." It was of course natural that after Maria's death he should have felt that though he might continue to live for fifty years, he had already begun to die. "The blood is no longer a pleasure to me running in my veins." Time brought healing as well as aging, but by 1860 he thought it would feel quite roomy in his black walnut box at Mount Auburn whenever the time came to move into it. Needless to say, he fought age every step of the way, and when, in later years, he tried to vault a wall in Howells's presence and did not succeed until the third try, he was obviously chagrined. I wonder what Whittier thought of Lowell's birthday letter of 1890: "the world will seem a worse world to me when you have left it, but it is not wholly so." One does not ordinarily remind birthday celebrants of their approaching end, nor yet observe that the world is going to be able to wag along without them!

All this goes back to Lowell's feeling that he was "a kind of twin . . . divided between grave and gay," as if he were the son of St. Theresa by Dick Steele. Hence he can say that "I know perfectly well that my nature is naturally joyous," and he can also speak of "an oasis in the arid desert of life," and ask "are the realities of life ever worth half so much as its cheats"? With most modern readers Lowell has probably worn best as a humorous poet, and it is not necessary to quote half *The Biglow Papers* and *A Fable for Critics* to show his power here, nor yet to discuss the relationship between humor and more solemn matters. There are passages in his Lowell lecture on "Humor, Wit, Fun, and Satire" [20] where he comes close to some of Mark Twain's ideas in *The Mysterious Stranger* and elsewhere ("man has a wholesome dread of laughter"); he knew that a sense of humor is a balance wheel on the machinery of life, but he also knew that humor is a "universal disenchanter." In some measure, a great man needs the fanaticism which humor undercuts. "The prophet knows his calling from childhood up," and "the disbelief of the whole world cannot shake that faith that he is God's messenger, which upbears him like a rock." On the other hand, he found Massinger's lack of humor indicating a limitation in him even as a tragic dramatist, doubting that either pathos or grandeur of imagination could exist without it.

In life, Lowell's humor overflowed into his letters and conversation and the high jinks in which he often indulged. He matured slowly, and it is not unfair to say that during his college years he often behaved like what Trollope called a "hobbledehoy" ("you used to frighten me with your wildness," wrote Loring, "and distress me with a strange ogre-like levity"), and he did not throw off these things with his graduation. When Fredrika Bremer visited Elmwood, she judged Maria's mind to have "more philosophical depth" than her husband's.

Singularly enough, I did not discern in him that deeply earnest spirit which charmed me in many of his poems. He seems to me occasionally brilliant, witty, gay, especially in the evening, when he has what he calls his "evening fever," and his talk is then like an incessant play of fireworks.

Lowell himself admits that when a clergyman offered a "Mrs. Grundyfied" view of the dear departed at a funeral, he would feel an impulse to rise and describe the true character of the deceased, and though he never did this, it seems to have been about the only impulse of the kind he ever resisted. He could improvise an imaginary opera, "Moses in the Bulrushes" upon an imaginary keyboard, supplying "lofty recitative, audacious rhyme, and fearful instrumental difficulties," and when his wife feared for his safety at night during a local crime wave, he marched to a Dante Club meeting at Longfellow's with an old-fashioned rifle over his shoulder. In the midst of a serious discussion during a walk with friends, he could jump up on one of the pillars at the edge of the Harvard Yard, crow like a cock, and then dismount and solemnly continue the discussion. At the whist club he would sometimes sustain an imaginary character throughout an evening, and once when a member's birthday fell on the day of the meeting, he walked backwards before the guest to the supper room, holding a pair of great silver candlesticks and bowing like a lord chamberlain. One closing example shows his kindness of heart alongside his cat-and-mouse whimsicality. One Sunday evening, E. H. House encountered him on the street in Cambridge and asked him if he knew where Professor Lowell lived. He said he did and offered to take House there, though he added that Professor Lowell was not presently at home. When House asked him if he knew Lowell, he replied that he himself was called Lowell, but even then his guest did not catch on. It was not until House asked him if he thought Professor Lowell would be willing to see an *Atlantic* contributor who had called so unceremoniously that he replied, "I shall be happy to see you as soon as we get to a light. Will you tell me who you are?"

If we ask whether Lowell was an optimist or a pessimist, the answer must be that, like all men who are neither cheerful idiots nor predestined suicides, he was both. The nineteenth-century faith in progress is very strong in his early poems, finding its most rhetorical and one of its most eloquent expressions in "The Present Crisis":

New occasions teach new duties; Time makes ancient good uncouth;
They must upward still and onward, who would keep abreast of
    Truth;
Lo, before us gleam her camp-fires! we ourselves must Pilgrims be,
Launch our Mayflower, and steer boldly through the desperate
    winter sea,
Nor attempt the Future's portal with the Past's blood-rusted key.[21]

He never believed that progress was automatic, but he did think that the good survives because it is in tune with the fundamental character of the universe.[22]

Inevitably the years brought doubts and questionings, and the realization that progress itself is sometimes Janus-faced. When Blanche came, he was foolish enough to believe that this would be a safe world for girls to walk abroad in by the time she grew up, a prophecy which takes on a grim suggestiveness from the fact that she never did grow up. But even toward the end of his life, though now finding much less improvement than his idealistic youth had looked for, he could tell the Civil Service Reform Association that they were living in what was

on the whole a better world, better especially in the wider distribution of the civilized and civilizing elements which compose it, better for the increased demands made upon it by those who were once dumb and helpless and for their increasing power to enforce their demands.

By this time he was well aware that new tastes, ideas, and standards (or lack of standards) were creating a world to which he found it increasingly hard to adjust himself, but he could still be sensible for others, as when he replied to a complaining letter from Mabel: "I can only say that life for the best and luckiest is very far from ideal. My own is certainly not at all what I would have it, but I try to go on as well as I can without complaint." And within months of his death, he writes Lady Lyttleton out of cancer, gout, dyspepsia, and racking cough, "In spite of this I am not turned pessimist and think a world which contains you and a few others well worth living in."

It is difficult to know how best to choose examples of Lowell's verbal pyrotechnics from his letters and informal writings which shall at once illustrate his quality and not unconscionably bore the reader. Sometimes he does this kind of thing very well, and sometimes he seems, to us at least, to do it very badly. We must remember that taste in humor changes very rapidly, and if we are bored by much of what the nineteenth century found amusing, we may be sure that the nineteenth century would gladly return the compliment if it were in a position to do so. Lowell's conversation seems at times to have taken the form of a veritable fusillade of puns and other forms of word-play, and here again it is much easier to be amused by something thrown off spontaneously in passing than by the same specimen of wit, solemnly quoted in a book. One of Lowell's best, though most ponderous puns was achieved when he was tempted to apply to a Shakespearean commentator "the quadrisyllabic name of the brother of Agis, King of Sparta," and it was really a little pedantic of C. C. Felton to look the matter up and report that actually it was the *father*, not the *brother*, of Agis IV who was called Eudamidas.[23] Puns of course are sadly out of fashion now, but this is merely a matter of taste. I doubt that anybody today would be amused by Lowell's remark concerning a feckless soul he was trying to help—"He seems to offer a pledge of a violin, but of course I should not dream of doing such violins to my own feelings as to accept it"—and only those temperamentally inclined to indulge Lowell will go for his remark concerning a translation of Homer by a Southerner named Worseley:

> For nobody'll ever translate him worseller.[24]

A larger number may be amused, however, by an invitation to Aldrich when he was editor of *Every Saturday*—"As you are busy only on every Saturday, surely you can play with us on Thursday"—or, later, after Aldrich had been promoted to the *Atlantic*, by the transformation of the letter T in his first name into a trident because he was "ruler of the Atlantic." But would any magazine editor today, writing to so distinguished a man as Ruskin, when Lowell himself was editor of the *Atlantic*, sign his letter "Hosea Biglow" in a feignedly unformed hand, and then

> by his next friend
> J. R. Lowell [25]

Unfortunately, the same intensity—and tension—which enabled Lowell to find delight in such trifles also increased his capacity for depression; as he himself observed,

> For me Fate gave, whate'er she else denied,
> A nature sloping to the southern side;
> I thank her for it, though when clouds arise
> Such natures double-darken gloomy skies.

"I fancy myself happy sometimes"—he writes Norton, "I am not sure—but then I never was for long," and to Henry James from Whitby, "I have been happy (after my hesitating fashion)." Once he wrote in a child's birthday book,

> Children's birthdays are all gold;
> They turn copper when we're old.[26]

As early as 1869 he calls Hawthorne's American notes "a very sad note-book . . . but who ever found the study of life a cheerful one?" [27] and as late as 1880 he wrote, "If one is good for anything, the world is not a place to be happy in—though, thank God, there are better things than being happy."

Sometimes his expression is more directly personal, and he sings his own hymn to death. In 1850 he wishes every day to die and be out of the world. "The only credit I claim is that I don't bother other people with it much." In 1882 he doesn't "*hanker arter* much more of this world." In 1885 he agrees to grow old only because he can't help it, and in 1886 he laments having been stupid enough to live nearly sixty-eight years. But he adds, "Not that I should be tired of it if I could show a better account of my stewardship," and in the very last year of his life, he writes out of desperate mortal illness, "I don't bother about Death, but shan't be sorry if he delays as long as he honestly can."

Of course these expressions are colored by his moods, and many letters, to Norton especially, complain of being out of sorts, mentally as well as physically: "I have not been well all winter and at the time I wrote was at my climax—with my head a little confused, I fear. I had a week or two of very unpleasant cerebral irritability, and all the worse because I was corked up too tight." Many years later he apologized to Lily Norton for not having written to her sooner: "I have been for a couple of days in one of my *hazes*, during which everything is dreary, and time ceases to exist. . . . 'Tis as if I had taken of the insane root." And he goes on to explain that "my laziness is like the effect of an opiate that does not fully operate, that is all. It makes things dreary and unreal to me and time goes without my knowing it."

He had his views as to the source of all this in "the drop of black blood I inherited from my dear mother and which is apt

to spread itself over the pupil of my eye and darken everything," and once he says frankly that he has sometimes suspected
in his sensibilities a trace of "my dear Mother's malady." No
doubt this fear often crossed his mind even when he did not
mention it, and the tension under which he lived cannot be
understood without taking this into account. Even Mabel could
not be "languid and drowsy" during a childish illness without
stimulating "the most horrible apprehension of some attack on
the brain, which we have cause enough to dread." It would be
too much to say that he never indulged his "blue" moods (it is
the artist's peculiar temptation that he is always inclined to
relish sensation qua sensation), but his theory, and in the main
his practice, in the matter was sane and wholesome.

The extreme form of insanity expresses itself in the urge to
destroy others and/or oneself, and Lowell was probably the
only one of the "classical" New England writers who was ever
in serious danger of suicide. Norton seems to have been the
most frequent recipient of his confidences along this line, though
it was to Briggs that he described how he would lie awake at
night and think about his razors after Maria died. In 1866 he
wrote Norton that when he was only twenty he had held a
cocked pistol to his forehead and been unable to pull the trigger,
and twenty years later he sent what might almost be called a
case history.

I hate to remember how many times in my life I have been haunted
with velleities of suicide. . . . But this is my reason for never buying
a revolver. Once in Madrid, twice in London and once here, had I
owned one, I should not be writing to you now. Then I could have
accounted for my depression, but oftenest it springs upon me without warning from an ambush. The only word for it is heaviness of
heart.

Two days later he is all right again:

. . . it always begins with suddenly wetting me through. It hits me as unexpectedly as the falling limb of a tree. I remember particularly being so hit once just as I was crossing Mrs. Craigie's brook on my way to my lecture. No warning, but suddenly I was bathed in a cold sweat and filled with indefinable apprehensiveness of evil to come.

Three years later, which was only three years from the end of his life, this kind of thing was still going on:

There was one day last week when if I had had strychnine in my pocket so that I could have walked off quietly and seemed to die of an honest apoplexy, I shouldn't be writing to you now. I am glad now that I hadn't.

All this would seem to come pretty close to what students of the Jameses have called a "vastation." This kind of thing is almost as difficult to explain to those who have never experienced it as mystical rapture. But surely nobody can hope to understand the state of mind in which suicides are committed without comprehending it.

VI

Such were the conditioning forces brought to bear upon Lowell as a man. But, as we have already had occasion to remind ourselves, he was also an artist; otherwise, we should not be interested in him now. And his being an artist introduced a whole new set of conditions. Artists expend a good share of their time and energy in storing the well of creativity and a great deal more in drawing out from it. But what they draw out is not what they have put in but a kind of distilled essence thereof. Both these processes must be examined by those who would search for Lowell's figure in the carpet.

CHAPTER THREE

STORING THE WELL

But with whatever drawbacks in special circumstances, the main interest of biography must always lie in the amount of character or essential manhood which the subject of it reveals to us, and events are of import only as means to that end.

JRL, 1867

I

For nineteenth-century poets in general there was no more important source of material for poetry than nature. For many it was invested with a religious significance. It is entirely suitable, therefore, that this chapter should begin with the consideration of Lowell's attitude toward nature and his use of materials derived from nature.

The Cambridge of his boyhood gave him much closer contacts with nature than he would have there today; besides this, he often went with his father on drives into the country when the latter was preaching in country churches. But he had nature about him even when he was confined to his room:

In winter I can see the sunset, in summer I can see it only as it lights up the tall trunks of the English elms in front of the house, making them sometimes, when the sky behind them is lead-colored, seem of the most brilliant yellow. When the sun, toward setting, breaks out suddenly after a thunder-shower and I see them against an almost black sky, they have seemed of a most peculiar and dazzling green tint, like the rust on copper. In winter my view is a

52

wide one, taking in a part of Boston. I can see one long curve of the Charles, and the wide fields between me and Cambridge, and the flat marshes beyond the river, smooth and silent with glittering snow. As the spring advances and one after another of our trees puts forth, the landscape is cut off from me piece by piece, till, by the end of May, I am closeted in a cool and rustling privacy of leaves.

Later, when as editor of the *Atlantic*, he had to walk to his office of a morning, he found

a little foot-path which leads along the river-bank, and it is lovely; whether in clear, cold mornings, when the fine filaments of the bare trees on the horizon seem floating up like sea-masses in the ether sea, or when . . . a gray mist fills our Cambridge cup and gives a doubtful loom to its snowy brim of hills, while the silent gulls wheel over the rustling cakes of ice which the Charles is whirling seaward.

"An Indian Summer Reverie" shows Cambridge and the Charles in some detail through the changing seasons. But Lowell found such things wherever he was, because he looked for them, even in London ("I have only to walk a hundred yards from my door to see green grass and hear the thrushes sing all winter long"), and his early attitude toward them never changed. In 1856 he wrote Norton after returning from a walk to Fresh Pond:

I really think that it is bad for our moral nature here in America that so many of the links that bind us to our past are severed in one way or another and am grateful for anything that renews in me that capacity for mere delight which made my childhood the richest part of my life. It seems to me as if I had never seen Nature again since those old days when the balancing of a yellow butterfly over a thistlebroom was spiritual food and lodging for a whole forenoon. This morning I had it all over again.

These were no isolated expressions of delight. Lowell prided himself on his knowledge of nature and his friendship with her,[1] which was increased by his farming activities at Elmwood and nurtured by his reading in such writers at Walton, Cowper, and Gilbert White. He once corrected an error in one of Longfellow's nature poems, declaring pertly that nobody except himself knew anything about nature, and he counted "no fairer boon" in his life as he grew older

> Than that what pleased him earliest still should please.

The spring passage in "The Vision of Sir Launfal" deserves its fame, but

> June is the pearl of our New England year

in "Under the Willows" should be quoted more often than it is, and more wonderful still is the longer passage in "Sunthin' in the Pastoral Line" where spring "gives one leap from Aperl into June." Actually, Lowell delighted in the "four jewels rare" of all four seasons:

> Pearl winter, summer's ruddy blaze,
> Spring's emerald, and, than all more fair,
> Fall's pensive opal, doomed to bear
> A heart of fire bedreamed with haze.[2]

It may be, as Norman Foerster says, that Lowell was attracted especially by the softer and quieter aspects of nature, for she was not spectacular in Cambridge, and, as he himself says, he did not require her "to be always on her high horse and with her tragic mask on."

> For nature with cheap means still works her wonders rare.[3]

"To a Dandelion," one of his most satisfying poems, would alone suffice to establish this point.

Yet Lowell was not limited to this aspect. The savage aspects of nature are nobly celebrated in "Pictures from Appledore," and there is a fine description of a thunderstorm and its aftermath in his letters.[4] He "feared to stay" at Trenton Falls; "there was such an impulse to leap down." He disliked the monotony of the sea, but he appreciated the part it had played in the development of New England. Though he did not pretend he enjoyed being cold, "A Good Word for Winter" is perhaps the most cogent that has been entered in behalf of that potentate, and there is one passage in his letters in which winter blends with the love of moonlight by which all romantic souls are enslaved. ("She 'comforts the night,' as Chapman finely says, and I always found her a companionable creature.") "It has stopped snowing," he once wrote Norton. "I looked for a good *blinder* to take my walk in."

Animals are a part of nature, and in "Rhoecus" it appears that tenderness toward animals is a religious duty. When Lowell was ambassador to Spain, he attended one bull-fight "officially, as a matter of duty, and escaped early," all his sympathies being with the bull. Though he calls Mabel "my dearest little pussy," he has very little on cats, and I cannot believe he cared much for them, but he was devoted to his dogs, interested in describing their behavior, and convinced of their devotion to him. One he always "reckoned" among his grandchildren. They were not always wholly amiable, however. Sometimes they killed his chickens, and when he punished them for it, he suffered more than they did. At least one disdained the doormat to wipe the mud off on his master's knees. Lowell loved the Elmwood squirrels, though I think he loved the birds more; birds and trees, I should say, were his two great passions in nature. He seems at least half serious in imputing consciousness to trees—"A horse-chestnut, of which I planted the seed more than fifty years ago, lifts its huge stack of shade before me and loves me with all its leaves."

He thought planting a tree about as good an act as a man could perform, and when the Darwinians suggested that man was descended from ape rather than Adam, he wondered whether he might not have a tree "among my far progenitors."

What landmark so congenial as a tree,

he exclaimed when he read "Under the Old Elm" at the hundredth anniversary of Washington's having taken command of the Continental army there, and he loved the maple when she "puts her corals on in May" and when "the blood of Spring" burned in her veins through the splendors of autumn.

Almost his earliest recollection as a child was that of putting crumbs outside the window during a snowstorm for the robins which did not come. In those days anything which flew was ecstasy to him, and it was not much different when he was old. The screech-owl terrified him in childhood, "and even now I don't feel quite secure in the silenter watches of the night." According to Foerster, forty-one varieties of bird are mentioned in "My Garden Acquaintance" and forty-two in the poems. During his last illness he reported to Child having heard and seen robins from his bed, though his visitor, who had been out and about, had seen none as yet. After the death of his little daughter Blanche, the singing of the song sparrows comforted him on a dreary March day. "I know you think such things foolish," he tells Leslie Stephen, "but I can't believe anything so that comforts." He humanizes the birds but he does not sentimentalize them, and he yields to them—and to squirrels too— upon occasion. "With shame I confess it, I have been bullied even by a hummingbird." And, unlike many non-scientific writers, he is reasonably careful about drawing inferences from insufficient data.

The most important thing to remember about Lowell's love

of nature, however, is that, like Longfellow and like Whittier, he escaped the Romantic fallacy and cleaved to the tradition of Christian humanism. Individual passages, to be sure, might seem to deny this. There are poems in which nature stands opposed to book learning in quite the Wordsworthian manner.[5] In "The Beggar" nature is a source of spiritual strength; in "The Oak" it becomes a model for man. The stars "look down and love me" in "Bellerophon." In "A Legend of Brittany" nature comforts Margaret in her sorrow, and in the early "Love-Song" there is a prayer to "kindly" and "lovely" nature to take the poet "inward to thy heart." Nature's being, we learn here, is warmed by truth, majesty, and earnestness, while littleness and dead-cold forms are unknown to her. As an expression of youthful exuberance, this is not surprising in a nineteenth-century poet, but one raises the eyebrows a little when it survives in a long passage in so late a poem as "Under the Willows," which seems to point the way toward both Whitman and the Edna St. Vincent Millay of "Renascence."

But these are only aberrations in Lowell's poetry as a whole. Even in "The Oak" itself, there is a turning away from nature at the end, toward God Himself, and an 1866 letter presents the same point of view with wry humor. "Last night, the moon was as good as a moon on the stage. It was *too* bright to be natural, and the leaves shone as they always do in the stereoscope." So he went out at ten o'clock without his hat to see to his dogs, and came in with a chill. "This is the beauty of Nature!" He cannot discuss the pastoral (for which he had no great love) without rejoicing that "we have at last got over the superstition that shepherds and shepherdesses are any wiser or simpler than other people." He loved nature, he valued her, but he was a humanist at heart, and, both as a poet and as a man, he feared overrating her or endowing her with powers she did not possess. In "The Cathedral" he denies her healing power altogether; she

> Lets us mistake our longing for her love,
> And mocks with various echo of ourselves.

In "The Search" pantheism is rejected in favor of a search for God in the service of the humble. It is true that even in "The Vision of Sir Launfal" nature *sympathizes* with goodness, but the good life can be lived only by one who learns self-denial and disciplines his will in obedience to the commands of a spiritual ideal which lies outside of nature.

All in all, Darwin would not seem to have been at his most perspicacious when he declared that Lowell was born to be a naturalist. Like his own Fitz Adam, he loved

> Nature much as sinners can
> Love her where she most grandeur shows,—in man,

and he never doubted that man, not nature, was the most important subject of poetry. He believed that "those who have most loudly advertised their passion for solitude and their intimacy with Nature, from Petrarch down, have been mostly sentimentalists," and this was at least one reason for his imperfect sympathy with Rousseau, whose "Nature-mania" he saw breaking down as early as 1863,[6] and also with Thoreau. In 1884 he told the Wordsworth Society that the greatest poets had always "considered nature as no more than the necessary scenery, artistically harmful if too pompous or obtrusive, before which man acts his tragi-comedy of life." And in his essay on Thoreau, which is certainly unfair as a whole, he longed to meet a man who was "as superbly indifferent to Nature as she is to him." [7]

II

If man is nature's masterpiece, and even more if man is the child of God, then man's masterpieces must inevitably have more relevance to man—and especially to man as artist—than trees and clouds and birds and squirrels. There is not a great deal to say about Lowell's interest in architecture, yet what there is illuminates his spiritual nature. He disliked both the giganticism of Rome ("the characteristic of Roman architecture is ostentation, not splendor, much less grace") and the nondescript character of the buildings in the Harvard Yard; the detailed suggestions which he sent Judge Hoar concerning desirable architectural improvements at Harvard [8] are eminently sensible and, outside "The Cathedral" at least, they constitute Lowell's most significant architectural passage. His great architectural love was the Gothic.

The Moorish architecture is the lyrick, the Greek the epic, and the Gothic is no form of poetry but poesy itself. It is like a flame. It soars up and up and ends nowhere and yet everywhere.

Thus he declared in one of his writing books. And in a commonplace book we read:

Grecian temple represents creation completed and an object of contemplation. Gothic as creation forever renewing itself—something onward—striving and unfinished. Hence the relation between music and architecture.

As he saw it, a Gothic church was one, not many, despite all its marvelous surface variety.

> Through gorgeous windows shone the sun aslant,
>   Brimming the church with gold and purple mist,
> Meet atmosphere to bosom that rich chant,
>   Where fifty voices in one strand did twist
> Their varicolored tones, and left no want
>   To the delighted soul, which sank abyssed
> In the warm music cloud, while, far below,
> The organ heaved its surges to and fro.[9]

In "The Unhappy Lot of Mr. Knott" Lowell makes fun of the "unhappy elf" who, having "retired with pelf," sets out to build himself "a mediaeval mansion." But he would give no quarter to Briggs's idea that Gothic buildings as such were out of place in America.

You think it absurd to bring back the architecture of a "Barbarous Age," as you call it. The age which produced those buildings was not barbarous. That which produces Trinity Church [in New York] is, because it is an abortion, because the conception of the edifice was never clear in the mind of the builder. The Gothic style is just as fit for a church (meeting-house) as ever; the difficulty is that The Church has shrunk so as not to fill the ancient idea. Gothic church-buildings are dark because they are no longer irradiated with the faith and piety which formerly lighted them up like Alloway Kirk.

All this, to be sure, is more impressionistic than analytical, but both these passages and "The Cathedral" make it clear that Lowell grasped the basic idea that the perfect, finished Grecian temple, hugging the earth, was ideally adapted to the needs of an essentially this-worldly religion, while the unfinished, imperfect, but inexhaustible spired Gothic guided the mind away from this earth-plane to a more spiritual realm, where alone man's soul can find total fulfillment.

> The Grecian gluts me with its perfectness,
> Unanswerable as Euclid, self-contained,
> The one thing finished in this hasty world,
> Forever finished, though the barbarous pit,
> Fanatical on hearsay, stamp and shout
> As if a miracle could be encored.
> But ah! this other, this that never ends,
> Still climbing, luring fancy still to climb,
> As full of morals half divined as life,
> Graceful, grotesque, with ever new surprise

Of hazardous caprices sure to please,
Heavy as nightmare, airy-light as fern,
Imagination's very self in stone!
With one long sigh of infinite release
From pedantries past, present, or to come,
I looked, and owned myself a happy Goth.

It has been said of Lowell by respectable writers that he does not often refer to the arts or take them seriously, and that his Italian letters "make almost no mention of the art treasures which surround him." The only thing one can say about these statements is that they just do not happen to be true. It *is* true that he once wrote, "As for pictures, I am tired to death of 'em, and never could enjoy them much when I had to run them down," but this is the typical utterance of a tired tourist. It is also true that critical cant disgusted him, as it did Mark Twain, and that he once said most sculpture was bad.

I think that more than half the sculptors that have risen
Should hammer stone to some good end, sent all to Sing Sing prison;
I'm sick of endless copyings of what were always bores,
Their dreary women on one toe, their Venuses by scores.[10]

(If the right foot was forward they called it a "Greek Slave," if the left, a "White Captive.") Lowell believed that if a man did not like the Venus de Milo he had better say so frankly and not "fret" about it, "for he may be sure she never will." [11] Nor did he like illustrated books, doubting that even Michelangelo's copy of Dante "was so great a loss as has sometimes been thought." [12] Yet he himself had tried to learn woodcutting in his youth, "and really succeeded about as well as, if not better than, 'old Caxton.'" Despite such pertness, he recognized his need of training in viewing pictures and conscientiously attempted to supply it to himself.

I make it a rule now on entering a gallery to endeavor to make out the painters of such pictures as I like by the internal characteristics of the works themselves. After I have made up my mind, I look at my catalogue. I find this an exceedingly good practice. Of all the more prominent painters, I can now distinguish the style and motive almost at a glance.

Were either Brownell or Reilly, one wonders, capable of a comparable humility? [13]

It is true, of course, that Lowell approached both art and music as a man of letters. That is what he was. But it is not always dead loss to perceive the fundamental unity of the arts and the resemblances which exist between workers in different fields.

There is something of Lucan in Michelangelo. . . . Again I can never think of Dryden without recalling Rubens, and the association, involuntary as it was at first, led me to discover the singular merit of Dryden as a rapid colorist in words. It is curious, also, but as natural as it is curious, that Pope, who was a disciple of Dryden, should have a certain analogy with Vandyke, the pupil of Rubens. . . . In the same way, I make Mendelssohn help me to criticize Tennyson, and I see that the same causes which produced Euripides in Greece produced Verdi in Italy.

As for specific judgments and reactions, Lowell called Titian the greatest of painters and the Uffizi the greatest of galleries. He thought the head of Christ in Titian's Tribute Money picture the noblest he had ever seen, and he also greatly admired the pictures showing the Presentation and Assumption of the Virgin. "Sacred and Profane Love" inspired a long poem, "Endymion." In Venice, Tintoretto's picture of the Annunciation took him "by assault," and he greatly admired the Cimas and the Bellinis and the Carpaccios also. Except for his Magdalen, Correggio seems to have disappointed him. He calls himself an admirer of Botticelli without specificities as to what he admires. The expression of the faces in the "Sistine Madonna" he thought "almost divine," but the color was "dry and thin"; Rubens carried off the palm on that score. He was chilly toward Michelangelo, whom he obviously thought grandiose, yet he thought he saw his influence, and Blake's too, in Burne-Jones, whom he greatly admired. He placed Rembrandt next to the great Venetians for his portraits, and he achieved a stimulating description of "Jacob's Dream." Of the Dutch painters in general he once declared that they possessed "admirable powers of expression with nothing to express," and he cited Hogarth, for whom his enthusiatisc admiration ("one Shakespeare, one Hogarth") may seem a little surprising in view of the subject matter of many of Hogarth's pictures, as having achieved superbly what the Dutch were only trying to do. Among French painters he liked Rousseau, Poussin, and Couture, and he was greatly excited by his own discovery of Hamon's Théâtre Guignol picture. "I think it a very remarkable work—full at once of poetry and sarcasm like life itself. . . . It is the first time in which German meaning has united itself with Gallic fitness in a French picture." Once he praised Howells by crediting him with a Dutch fidelity to nature plus "a higher sentiment, a more refined humor, and an airy element that recalls the better moods of Watteau." He wrote a poem about "Turner's Old Téméraire." Among modern black-and-white artists he was very fond of Tenniel and du Maurier.

He considered his father's friend Washington Allston the greatest American painter and Horatio Greenough the greatest American sculptor. Where "gentle Allston lived, and wrought, and died," the "street and shop" were transfigured with his "Illumined gaze," and when one of his pictures, hanging in a ballroom, overlooked "with its serene and steadfast eyes the butterfly throng beneath it . . . seeming to gaze from these narrow battlements of time far out into the infinite promise of eternity," one saw "the free, erect, and perfected soul." Once he declared that Allston's only peer was Raphael. He was well acquainted with at least one fine painter, William Page, who painted portraits of both him and Maria, and at least one important sculptor, William Wetmore Story, whose work he praised intelligently.

Musically, Lowell began, as most children did in his milieu, with the kind of songs children and young people sing together. His mother loved his whistling, but he had little or no musical training; in later years, he regretted this. We are told that, in the days of "The Band," his favorite song was "The Battle of the Nile," whose text consisted of only two verses,

> The battle of the Nile,
> I was there all the while

in endless variation, sung to a low, droning tune. James would begin in a lifeless, indifferent manner, hardly raising his head, while the rest listened quietly. Presently a deep bass would join him, then a clear soprano and tenor, and so on until in the end the whole circle would be on their feet singing at the top of their voices.[14]

We may be pardoned if we do not find this very impressive musically, yet H. T. Henry has argued cogently that though Lowell was not a musician like Browning, nor even a musical amateur, he was familiar with musical terms and far more sensitive to music and to musical harmonies in verse than he has commonly been given credit for.[15] It is also worth remembering that though both musical criticism and art criticism were neglected in the America in which young Lowell lived, when he established *The Pioneer*, he used W. W. Story (as "I. B. Wright") on art and John Sullivan Dwight, who, in Frank L. Mott's view, was to develop into the best of contemporary music critics, on music.

The poem "Remembered Music" is an interesting appreciation, developed in terms of a series of similes, and everybody who has read a line of Lowell's will remember the musing improvising organist at the beginning of "The Vision of Sir Launfal." In 1839 he wrote a poem about "Donnazetti" (his spelling). There is a great deal about music in his "Rhymed Lecture," "The Power of Sound"—[16] German music and Italian music; Bach, Handel, Haydn, Mozart (*Don Giovanni*), Gluck (misspelled Glück), and Beethoven (whom Lowell may have learned to care for at the Nortons'); Negro minstrelsy; and the singing in New England churches. Vocal music is praised first.

> What like the human voice can soothe or stir,
> The voice, and Music its interpreter?

Language is "man's highest prerogative" and has been from the beginning. "Yet by mcrc words the soul's but half released," and spoken utterance craves the completion of music. And then, having said these things, Lowell pulls himself up sharply:

> But am I partial? Hath not Music flung
> Her charm o'er other organs than the tongue?

from which he goes on to the organ and the orchestra.[17] He liked Palestrina, whose "dainty unexpectedness" he compared to an Aeolian harp. Jenny Lind, whom he planned to hear, is the only celebrity artist I have found mentioned, but among operas he speaks of *Fidelio, The Magic Flute*, and *Der Freischütz*. There is an early letter to G. B. Loring in which he renounces noisy music for that which, as Tennyson says,

> gentlier on the spirit lies
> Than tired eyelids over tired eyes.

Wagner, whom he thought noisy, was probably the only great composer he rejected; *Lohengrin* "perplexed" him as late as 1887. In *A Fable for Critics* he declares that

> one can't bear [Johann] Strauss when his nature is cloven
> To its deeps within deeps by the stroke of Beethoven.

On the other hand, a whole concert of Bach was a bit too much for him, and an evening of Mendelssohn was "a little vague and cloudy—beautiful clouds, rose tinted and—indefinite. I longed for a good riving flash of Italian lightning."

I first suspected Lowell's comparative indifference to the theater from the fact that he writes about Shakespeare almost wholly as a poet, practically ignoring his dramatic, and especially his theatrical, aspects. He preferred reading *Hamlet* and *Lear* to seeing them acted. In his old age he told Howells that he went to the theater as seldom as to church, and as early as 1855 he wrote his sister from Paris that during three weeks in that city he had seen only three plays. Once, in a speech delivered at an affair given in honor of American actors, he said that he was not an habitual theater-goer because he had always lived in the country!

His theatrical experience began with Fanny Kemble, but he was much more impressed by "the perfection of art" shown by her father, who appeared with her.[18] Many years later, when he saw her in a private production as Mrs. Malaprop, he thought her "exaggerated, like a turkeycock in a back kitchen," and illustrative of "the crying fault of modern art—the mistaking emphasis for expression." He seems to have admired Ellen Terry but not Sir Henry Irving, and he hated Sarah Bernhardt, though he admitted she was "diabolically effective in certain rather unpleasant ways." He added, "I used to forget who and what Rachel was, but can't divorce Sara [*sic*] from her loathsome self. Whom the Devil hath joined together can't be put asunder." Dion Boucicault, who he met in 1854, he considered "a conceited cockney Irishman."

The theater was better in Europe than here—

We spoke of French acting and actors,
And their easy, natural way—[19]

but, as we have seen, he neglected the theater even in Paris. And here too he qualifies. He praised Bouffé as the Abbé Galant, but in *Femmes Savantes* he found the young actresses playing to the audience and thus destroying the illusion. All in all, the German theater pleased him most.

For historical accuracy in costume and scenery I have never seen anything comparable. An artistic nicety and scrupulousness extends itself to the most inconsidered trifles in which so much of illusion consists, and which commonly are so bungled as to draw the attention instead of evading it by an absorption in the universal.

It was amusing, then, that the greatest actress he saw in Germany should have been an Italian, Ristori, whose speech he found so beautiful that it kept him awake at night, and he bitterly criticized the Germans for staying away from her performances because she was a foreigner playing at advanced prices.

Lowell's lack of interest in the theater probably reflects itself in the generally undramatic character of his poetry. Yet there are dramatis personae in *The Biglow Papers*, at least one of whom, Birdofredum Sawin, has been called a developing character. It is interesting too, if not quite consistent, that he should have caused the Reverend Homer Wilbur, who certainly cannot be supposed to have been a better theater-goer than his creator, to use a theatrical figure:

Wonderful, to him that has eyes to see it rightly, is the newspaper. To me, for example, sitting on the critical front bench of the pit, in my study here in Jaalam, the advent of my weekly journal is as that of a strolling theater, or rather of a puppet-show, on whose stage, narrow as it is, the tragedy, comedy, and farce of life are played in little.

But it is even more interesting, and not a little ironical and amusing, that Lowell himself should have had theatrical opportunities which have never come the way of many really stage-struck literary men. In Rome, in 1852, he played Bottom in a private production of a cut version of *A Midsummer Night's Dream,* composing a prologue of some thirty lines, which he himself recited. "This, to me," he writes naïvely, "was the plum of the evening's entertainment." And many years later, in London, he read Romeo's lines in the Balcony Scene to the Juliet of no less distinguished an actress than Mary Anderson.

III

Since Lowell was a writer, literature naturally was more important for him than any of the other arts, but since he was also a professional scholar, a teacher, and an editor, we must do rather more at this point than simply survey his reading. When we speak of him as a learned man, it is desirable that we should know exactly what we mean. "To certain branches of study," says Underwood, "especially to mathematics, he had an invincible repugnance." He has been accused of ignorance of science also, but William White has shown[20] that he read more science than he has often been given credit for. He has also been accused from time to time of ignorance of history, and he plays into the hands of his critics here with his unbelievable statement of 1845 that he has read books about magic and astrology, "and yet never looked into a history of England." Certainly Lowell's reading was not strictly systematized—this is not true of any real booklover of imagination—and certainly he did out-of-the-way reading when it attracted him. Nevertheless he read many learned works. In a single letter to Norton he mentions reading Pictet's *Les Origines Indo-Européennes;* Renan's *Sur l'origine du langage;* Grimm's *Über die Ursprung der Sprache*; and Haldeman's *Analytical Orthnography.* Elsewhere he speaks of Buckle and of Gobineau's *La Philosophie et les Religions de l'Asie Centrale.* The anonymous author of "Conversations with Mr. Lowell" in the *Atlantic* found him very conversant with the period of the French Revolution and possessed of "views" concerning it, and Henry James was impressed by his knowledge of English history. Robert Morss Lovett carefully exempted from his presumed historical ignorance or indifference the history of New England and that of the Puritans on both sides of the ocean.[21]

Said Bliss Perry, speaking at Harvard's centenary celebration of Lowell's birthday in 1919:

> It is quite possible that the university possesses today a better Dante scholar than Lowell, a better scholar in old French, a better Chaucer scholar, a better Shakespeare scholar. But it is certain that if our Division of Modern Languages were called upon to produce a volume of essays matching in human interest one of Lowell's volumes drawn from these various fields, we should be obliged, first, to organize a syndicate, and second, to accept defeat with as good grace as possible.

Since this statement was made in the presence of persons who may well have considered themselves the "better" scholars Lowell was talking about (George Lyman Kittredge may have thought himself several of them), the thrust involved was both bravely and neatly made. But perhaps John Livingston Lowes's comment was more conclusive. Anyone who doubted Lowell's accomplishments as a scholar might well, he thought, spend a few hours in the Harvard library "over the margins and fly-leaves" of his French, Italian, and older English books or his own notebooks. Admitting that Lowell neglected what is now the accepted apparatus of scholarship, Lowes declared that "his daemon sometimes runs riot through the groves of Academe; usually, however, one is chiefly conscious, as one reads, of an amazingly vivifying reagent upon various valleys of dry bones." [22]

When it comes to linguistics, Lowell's knowledgeability has never been denied. "A philologist of national repute, one of the founders of the American Dialect Society, first president of the Modern Language Association, and the holder of a Harvard chair of language and literature, he knew linguistics as a scholar." [23] He would study ten to twelve hours a day even during vacation periods, and he makes the statement, odd for a creative writer, that "if Ovid, instead of sentimentalizing in the *Tristia*, had left behind him a treatise on the language of the Getae which he learned, we should have thanked him for something more truly valuable than all his poems." Even here, however, Lowell's methods were quite his own. He had no use for formal grammar, in either English or foreign languages. He was an indefatigable note-taker, and he had a phenomenal memory. Once, when President Eliot, asked him about an obsolete word, he got up and reached down a seventeenth century book from the top shelf of his study. "It is many years," he said, "since I have had that book in my hand or have heard that excellent word." [24]

Lowell knew that there was an "American language" long before Mencken made the term famous, though he keeps free of Mencken's idiosyncrasies in considering it. He knew that "formal logic can never be applied to language, which has a logic of its own of more than feminine nimbleness, and verbal critics should learn their own tongue before they meddle with others." He distinguished sharply between dress and undress occasions in speech ("boys and blackguards have always been my masters in language"), but it would be too much to say that he was always consistent. He burlesqued Latinate diction in *The Biglow Papers*, but he was quite capable of using it seriously, and Dr. Johnson himself could not have surpassed in kind his reference, in his essay on witchcraft, to "broomsticks, spits, and similar utensils" as "the canonical instruments of . . . nocturnal equitation." He could be pernickety in his criticism of the language

of others, but he could also permit himself the use of such atroc-
ities as "undisprivacied" and "disnatured." He often discerned
linguistic vitality and "poetry in the egg" in extravagance. Certainly nobody—not even Mark Twain in *Huckleberry Finn*—
ever demonstrated better than Lowell did that dialect can be
used convincingly in first-rate literature, and it is exciting too
when nobility takes over in such passages as this:

> O strange New World, thet yit was never young,
> Whose youth from thee by gripin' need was wrung,
> Brown foundlin' of the woods, whose baby-bed
> Was prowled roun' by the Injun's cracklin' tread.

Here, as in so many areas, Lowell did more pioneering work
than he is often given credit for, but here too he often gives the
impression of being unwilling to trust his forward-looking impulses or whole-heartedly commit himself to them. Thus he
praises Lincoln's English "not because he learned it in Illinois,
but because he learned it of Shakespeare and Milton and the
Bible," and he always seems pleased when he can prove that
what has hitherto seemed a distinctively American turn of speech
is actually not a coinage but a survival, forgotten by modern
Englishmen but preserved in America.[25]

Lowell's training in Latin, like the medieval scholar's, started
as soon as he went to school (Greek began later). There would
not seem to be much question concerning his competence; he
sometimes wrote Latin notes in his Latin texts, and the macaronic
verses, "Kettelopotomachia," [26] could only have been produced
by a good Latinist. He made no pretentious claims for himself
as a classicist, however. He was "so poor a Grecian" that he
missed "three quarters of what was most characteristic" in Aristophanes, and much of that came "through the fog of Latin on
the opposite page." As late as 1886, he told Norton that his Greek
came easier through the ear than through the eye. His classical

allusions, though not always accurate, are numerous and could be pedantic, but inaccuracy in quotation does not, with Lowell, necessarily imply lack of close acquaintance. He could ascribe a saying of Frederick the Great's to Bacon and attribute a quotation from Pope to Swift; he even makes mistakes when quoting from the Bible. (He told James T. Fields that he nearly always quoted "provisionally from memory with an intention to revise," but the revision was not often made.)

As for the modern languages, in 1866 Lowell claimed to be able to speak four of them like a native—of Cambridge! Once, in Paris, he found himself talking English to one person, French to another, and Italian to a third, and being somewhat impressed with his feat. In 1855 he reported to Story that his French was "(for a professor) to tell the truth, in rather a lamentable condition," but by 1858 he was translating the article on Béranger which Sainte-Beuve had sent him for the *Atlantic*.[27] By 1873 he could talk French with reasonable fluency and maintain his part in table conversation without trouble, and the next year he writes Norton, "You would be amused at my eloquence in the French tongue now and to hear me discussing politics with 'em." [28] Old French, like Old English, he studied diligently for his teaching, and mastered.

His first concentrated study of Spanish seems to have been in 1859, when he was forty, and he found that he learned it fast. But when he got to Spain as ambassador, he had a problem. Previously he had never been primarily concerned to learn to *speak* the language, but now he insisted from the beginning on conducting all his official business in the language of the country, and found his previous knowledge a handicap in learning Spanish *by ear*. He also found both his Italian and his French getting in his way, but he worked hard, and after a few months, he could say, "I can talk now with comparative ease and write notes without fear of scandal." In 1878 he wrote Child from Spain that he had lost all his Italian. "When I first got here I kept mixing it with Spanish and now *that* has crowded it all out, so that I have to think five minutes to recall the forms of a verb." William Roscoe Thayer thought Lowell read Italian fluently but spoke it like a foreigner. "He was too scrupulous in pronouncing each syllable, as if it stood alone, instead of letting syllables and words melt into each other, as the Italian does."

German, of course, was in a different class. He called it the "Open, Sesame" to a larger culture, and in 1875 he advised Mrs. S. B. Herrick to read a little every day, "and you will be surprised to find how soon it grows easy to you." In the light of his own experience with the language, this advice seems a little cavalier. In 1850 he called German worse than the black tongue and described himself as "rapidly sinking under a determination of irregular verbs of the head and a compound fracture of the larynx," and five years later he was sure it had been the original language, and that Babel came into being when those patriarchs who had not been able to master it by the age of 150, set off on independent lines. This year, 1855, seems to have marked his most concentrated study of German, and consequently is most marked by his cries of distress. "How long did it take you," he asks Longfellow, "to learn to drive this four-wheeled chariot of the German auxiliary verb with its half dozen long-tailed steeds of sentences—like one of our monster sleighs—and to get comfortably round corners?" He told Norton that "German is long and life is short," and that he expected to die of "der, die, das," not because he caught them but because he couldn't. Yet he was pleased when Dr. Reichenbach found his progress "*ungeheuert*," and before the end of the year he was speaking German as easily as French. But it was still "this horrid jabber," and G. W. Smalley says he read it to the end "with a kind of protest." When he was in Germany again in 1881, he found his disused German coming back to him, though when he was spoken to suddenly in that language, he was quite likely to answer in Spanish.[29]

Lowell began his teaching at Harvard in 1856 and continued until 1877. He resigned in 1874, when he was refused a leave of absence on half pay, but President Eliot brought him back into the fold. His ideal of what the teacher should be and do was very high.

He must unite in himself elements as seemingly incompatible as fire and water. He must have in him something of the fervor of youth and something of the judicial coolness of age; he must know both how to inspire wholesome and how to moderate unhealthy enthusiasms. He must have a fund of life in him ample enough to understand and survive such discouragements as few other callings have to cope with. He must work mainly in an unwilling or even refractory material. Even his success must be largely posthumous and his consolations mainly borrowed of the future.

But he was far from believing that this ideal had been embodied in himself. Eliot thought he had "no natural inclination" toward teaching, and Lowell quite agreed. If he had had no other disqualifications, he thought his inability to remember names and dates ought to have been enough to wreck him. All his nightmares were of lecturing, and while the "Old Man of the Sea" of his lectures was on his mind, he could think of nothing else, and especially not of poetry. In 1869, having agreed to lecture at Cornell, he humorously wrote his daughter that "after meditating flight, suicide, and various other temporary remedies," he had at last decided that if his hearers could stand his lectures, perhaps he might be able to do so. He disliked the mechanical, routine side of a teacher's life, and when John Fiske had the measles in 1863 and was absent for six weeks, he not only continued to mark him absent after his return, but forgot to change the records after his error had been pointed out to him.[30] He is quoted as saying that there was more bad weather in Cambridge on Monday nights, when faculty meetings were held, than at any other time. "He rarely spoke in conclave, and when the question came up in response to the suspension of students he often declined to vote."[31] Possibly he felt that his own experiences as a student had disqualified him here.

If reports may be believed, Lowell's actual performance as a teacher was somewhat at the mercy of his moods. He could be bored, routine, even curt, or he could strike a flash of inspiration, and then, as Sarah Bernhardt would say when she gave a performance that really satisfied her, "God was there." He has been accused of mumbling and of indulging his whimsies to such an extent that his students sometimes found it impossible to discover what he was talking about. A dull class could always be counted upon to take the life out of him, and he simply did not have the patience to adapt himself to the sluggard's pace. Julian Hawthorne says that when Lowell perceived he was not getting much out of his private German lessons, he

gracefully adopted the only course practicable: he would assign me a passage from the poem, courteously assume at our next meeting that I had mastered it, and would then proceed to read-out and construe it himself, giving me the benefit both of the great poet's visual, and of his own eloquent, comprehension of it.[32]

Naturally, he was more often bored when he had to handle routine elementary language classes than when he could interpret the literature he loved, and his best teaching seems to have been done in his Dante classes, often held in his study at Elmwood. In spite of his own tremendous interest in the ways of words, he despised courses which focused on grammar and philology; for him language was valuable only as the vehicle of literature. Students like Barrett Wendell and Robert T. Lincoln remembered his Dante course as the best they had had in college,[33] but it certainly made no wide appeal; at one time only three persons were enrolled in it. When Lowell was seventy, Wendell tried to tell him what he had meant to him as a teacher. "I'm glad you said that," he replied. "I've been wondering if I hadn't wasted half my life."

His editorial work naturally made less direct use of his scholarship than his teaching did. But Frank L. Mott, the foremost authority on American magazines, calls his brief and ill-starred *Pioneer* "a magazine of higher literary tone than any which had yet appeared in America." His editorship of the *Atlantic* has been criticized on the ground of his practical ineptitude, and in view of the fact that he kept on finding manuscripts in his study after he had stopped editing it, there is some justice in these charges, but Lowell, who sometimes worked a fifteen-hour day, had no staff, and no modern editor would dream of facing all the editorial chores which he assumed. He took care that his contributors should not offend the religious press, in whose eyes the *Atlantic* was highly suspect, and once he had to renege on a piece he had accepted because Fields objected to its publication on moral grounds. Beyond that, he aimed to keep himself and his opinions out of it, except to emend obscurity and rule out bad taste and bad grammar. Of course he was not always wholly consistent in such matters, and when he felt that Parke Godwin had not gone far enough in his analysis of Buchanan, he himself added to his article on the subject, thus making the contribution in question neither Godwin's nor his own. (It must, of course, be remembered that at this time all *Atlantic* contributions were unsigned.) All in all, however, Lowell went as far as any editor could have gone in his time to make the *Atlantic* a national, not a regional, magazine, and he printed a large number of articles showing a high degree of social awareness.

IV

We have come at last, then, to Lowell's reading, considered as a preparation for his own writing. An exhaustive investigation here would be a subject for a book in itself. Since our purpose is portraiture and characterization, we must confine ourselves to choices which reveal significant tastes and indicate influences. Lowell called himself "one of the last (I fear) of the great readers." "Last," like "first," is nearly always ill-advised in such statements, but this time "great" surely applies. He was, as he said, a "bookman." He had the good habit of reading through the authors he especially liked, but he also confessed feeling some force of the stupid compulsion to finish any book he had begun, which is surely to assume that men were made for books, not books for men. He was capable of advising others to concentrate on solid historical works or to confine themselves to the best writers and read them thoroughly, but his practice was more liberal than his theory. On the other hand, he knew the disadvantages of wide and desultory reading, and how it has "taught men to depend on their shelves rather than on their brains."

Pritchard counted 1300 references to classical authors and their writings in Lowell, 300 more than to the Bible. These indicate especially his indebtedness to Aristotle and Horace. "It is not too much to say that Lowell's important position in American letters and criticism is based largely upon his knowledge of the principles advocated by Aristotle in the *Poetics* and his adherence to them." [34] Apparently he thought Homer the greatest classical writer; at any rate, he was the only ancient whom he placed with Dante, Cervantes, Goethe, and Shakespeare in his *Century* article on "The Five Indispensable Authors." [35] In the *Conversations* John preferred the *Odyssey* to the *Iliad*, and it seems likely that Lowell agreed with him. He told one of his Lowell lecture audiences that if Shakespeare could not read Homer, Homer could not read Shakespeare either, and that Homer's loss was the larger of the two. He fell in love with Euripides when he read him through during the winter of 1868–69, though he thought Aeschylus had more imagination and Sophocles more strength. He cited Aristophanes, the "highest type of pure comedy," as, above all other writers, expressing the spirit of Greek nationality, but doubted that he could hold the stage today.

In comparison, Roman art, despite the "supreme elegance" of Virgil, was "derivative and superficial." The Romans "stole everything. They stole the land they built the Eternal City on, to begin with. Then they stole their wives, then their religion, then their art." Cicero "used to twaddle about Greek literature and philosophy, much as people do about ancient art nowadays." But of course the Latin writers meant more to Lowell than such utterances, taken by themselves, would indicate. In 1866 he was reading Lucretius: "I don't quite *taste* him yet, but I see clearly that he beats all the Latin poets in poetic beauty of phrase." Seneca captured him, though with reservations, when he returned to the *Medea* after forty-eight years in 1887, and in 1890 he reports having read Terence through again. But perhaps his most interesting comment on a Roman writer is what he says of Plutarch, to whom he attributes almost the spiritual sensitiveness of Plato.

Not a man of genius or heroism himself, his many points of sympathy with both make him an admirable conductor of them. . . . Few men have so amicably combined the love of a good dinner and of the higher morality. He seems to have comfortably solved the problem of having your cake and eating it, at which the ascetic interpreters of Christianity teach us to despair. He serves up his worldly wisdom in a sauce of Plato, and gives a kind of sensuous relish to the disembodied satisfactions of immortality. He was a better Christian than an orthodox divine.[36]

The most interesting thing, however, is the way Lowell rebels against the classics even while he accepts; it was no accident that he never devoted one of his critical essays to a classical writer. He quotes Goethe's statement that destructive criticism is easy, since "one has only to set up in his mind any standard, any model, however narrow," and at this point Lowell boldly interpolates, "let us say the Greeks." The reasons for the apparent contradiction are clear enough:

> Greek art at its highest point is doubtless the most perfect that we know. But its circle of motives was essentially limited; and the Greek drama in its passion, its pathos, and its humor is primarily Greek, and secondarily human.

Moreover, Lowell was a Christian, and the fact that the Greeks and the Romans were pagans set up a barrier between him and them. It was for this reason, among others, that he felt closer to medieval writers, and outstandingly of course to Dante. He never had any sympathy with those who imitate Greek forms, as Swinburne did, for this is to be derivative where the Greeks were direct. "No effort to raise a defunct past has ever led to anything but just enough galvanic twitching of the limbs to remind us unpleasantly of life." This interesting statement is commended to the attention of those who think of Lowell as a wholly backward-looking figure in American criticism.[37]

Among French writers, Lowell speaks with relative frequency of Rabelais, Montaigne, Voltaire, and Rousseau, but Rousseau is the only one who gets an essay, and Lowell was perhaps wholly en rapport only with Montaigne, whom he calls "the first modern writer." He had no sympathy with Voltaire's inclination to "scoff at God for an antithesis," but he paid him a well-deserved tribute when he marked that "we owe half our freedom now to the leering old mocker." He considered French poetry "purely artificial," kept from decay only by its high polish, and called

Corneille and Racine "sham-classic pastures . . . where a colonnade supplies the dearth of herbage." Dumas had no more grace
of style than a kangaroo, yet his stories were enthralling. Unlike
Fielding's coarseness, which was incidental and the result of his
having lived in a coarse age, Zola's was unpardonable because a
matter of deliberate choice. In 1888 the comedies of Labiche en-
tertained Lowell greatly through a fierce attack of gout. Sainte-
Beuve he greatly admired, but one wonders what the French
critic thought when Lowell wrote him that his style had "all the
grace and *esprit* so peculiar to your countrymen" in combination
with "a truly English solidity and good sense." [38]

In Italian literature, Dante was of course one of Lowell's
specialties, though there is an 1849 letter in which he says,
surprisingly, that Dante, Ovid, and Boccaccio make up "the
best part of Italian literature," and that Boccaccio was "probably the best man of the three." We should expect Petrarch's
name where Ovid's occurs, but Lowell elsewhere calls Petrarch
the first great sentimentalist. He also tells us, however, that it
was *The Divine Comedy* which lured him into learning, and in
1884 he called the conclusion of the "Paradiso" "the sublimest
reach to which poetry has risen."

Among the Spaniards, Lowell had two great favorites—
Cervantes, the world's greatest humorist, as Don Quixote was
"the most perfect character ever drawn," and Caldéron, who
"always entertains and absorbs me after everybody else has given
it up." Caldéron came to his aid in illness in 1875, when he
wrote "The Nightingale in the Study," and again after the death
of his second wife.[39] Lope de Vega touched no such depths in
Lowell, but he thought him wonderful in his way, and he once
defended his moral tone against Henry James.

Lessing, whom Lowell greatly admired as a man, is the only
German who gets a full-length essay. Heine he considered a
sentimentalist turned cynic. On Goethe, "the Louis XIVth of

literature" and "the last of the *great* poets," various opinions
are expressed, but Lowell never placed him as high as Dante,
Cervantes, or Caldéron.[40] He shows some interest in Scandi-
navian sagas, but Russian literature seems to have been a blank
to him, and his refusal even to look at the great Russian novelists
is perhaps the blot on his critical record which many moderns
find most difficult to forgive. He was also indifferent to the
Spaniards Valdés and Galdós, by whom his friend Howells was
so greatly enthralled. One might certainly have expected him
to care for the Gallicized Russian Turgenev, but there is an
undated letter in Higginson's *Part of a Man's Life*,[41] in which
Lowell says that, though he has met Turgenev, he has never
read one of his books.

V

Chaucer, to whom he devoted one of his principal essays,
was the only pre-Elizabethan English writer whom Lowell considered at length. He was "second only to that English poet to
whom all other poets are second." Lowell took a dim view of
Anglo-Saxon literature, and I suspect knew little about it. He
enjoyed reading in old books like Hakluyt and Purchas, but
he detested Gower, and he was cold to Wyatt and Surrey. He
found a "manly, trustful, and tender" heart beating through
Piers Plowman, but judged it, after all, a sermon rather than
a poem. He preferred the popular ballads to the metrical romances because there was much less "stuff" in them.

In Shakespeare the "most rhythmic genius," the "acutest intellect," the "profoundest imagination," and the "healthiest understanding" of the English race was happily combined in a
single man. Not so untutored as commonly conceived, he was
essentially a Goethean observer, not (like Milton) a reformer.
Shakespeare gave Lowell standards for the evaluation of other

writers, thus serving him well, though there are times when he falls captive to what Bernard Shaw was to call "bardolatry." Thus the First Folio

should be deferred to as authority in all cases where it does not make Shakespeare write bad sense, uncouth metre, or false grammar, of all which I believe him to have been more supremely incapable than any other man who ever wrote English.

Assume Shakespeare's perfection in such terms, and you will soon come to the place where, whenever you find anything in one of his plays that you do not like, you must reject it on the ground that Shakespeare could not possibly have written it. Some editors have operated upon this assumption, but they have not enriched our understanding of Shakespeare nor contributed to the establishment of a standard text. Lowell had too much sense to go quite that far; he did admit momentary lapses and concessions to the groundlings. Nevertheless he is on the edge, and he denies *Richard III* to Shakespeare basically because he does not think it good enough for him. There is one interesting passage in which he suggests the study of Shakespeare's imagery which Caroline Spurgeon and others have made in our own time,[42] and there is one highly imaginative reference to *King Lear* in *Under the Willows*, where, discussing the "pious fraud" or "ghastly parody" of "real Spring" that May is in New England, he writes,

> And Winter suddenly, like crazy Lear,
> Reels back, and brings the dead May in his arms,
> Her budding breasts and wan dislustred front
> With frosty streaks and drifts of his white beard
> All overblown.

On the other hand, he labors the too-too "psychological," Coleridgean or Goethean notion of an irresolute Hamlet, though admitting frankly that he may be reading something in, and, in view of his own dislike of allegory and general determination to ignore it, even in Spenser, where its presence is undeniable, it is surprising that he should go off the deep end as he does when he interprets *The Tempest* as an allegory, with Prospero as the Imagination, Ariel as Fancy, Caliban as Understanding (what does he understand?), and Shakespeare himself as the Poetic Imagination.

Though he dismissed the pre-Elizabethan dramatists with a wave of the hand, Lowell wrote about Shakespeare's contemporaries at some length. Jonson impressed him more as critic than as either poet or dramatist, but he responded with some enthusiasm to the imagination of Chapman.[43] In 1885 he wrote Lady Lyttleton that he was reading Beaumont and Fletcher again, "with mixed feelings of delight and disgust." But more important than any dramatist was Spenser, who enthralled him from early childhood and influenced the imaginative and idealistic side of his character as no writer can influence any reader of mature years.

The seventeenth-century giant, of course, is Milton. Lowell knew him well by the standards of his day and wrote one of his most famous essays about him, but though his penetration here and there is illuminating and suggestive, his performance as a whole is not very impressive. He grasped—and expounded —the difference between the Miltonic and the Shakespearean imagination,[44] but he calls him a Unitarian and anticipates the ultra-Romantic view that because Satan was a foiled rebel, Milton could not help sympathizing with him. Since "we feel no interest in Adam," Satan must be the hero of *Paradise Lost*, but he is not a satisfactory hero because, knowing that he has no chance, he cannot really struggle against fate. But Lowell was not satisfied to anticipate the Romantic rebels; he had to anticipate T. S. Eliot and his school also. Milton left no impress upon thought; his pamphlets were occasional; he was harmonist rather than melodist and more rhetorician than thinker. Thomson was "well-nigh ruined by him," Wordsworth "encumbered," and Cowper "only saved by mixing equal proportions of Dryden in his verse, thus hitting upon a kind of cross between prose and poetry."

Some consider Lowell's essay on Dryden his finest critical achievement. He did not think this "Englishman who forever dabbled his French ruffles in beer" a great poet in the higher sense of the term, but his was a "large and benignant nature," never "wholly subdued to what it worked in," and forever throwing out hints of something "finer than anything he has done." To the end of his life, "his mind was growing" and "his judgment widening and deepening, his artistic sense refining itself more and more." On Donne he ran the gamut, the extremes being marked by an unsupported heading in one of his notebooks—"Donne's subternatural poetry"—and by George Smalley's statement that when he presented Lowell with a copy of the valuable second edition of Donne, the recipient took it into his hand with the gesture "of one who is performing a religious act, reverent and tender." The notebooks and manuscripts contain other derogatory comments on Donne:

Donne worked underground among the very roots of thought—but poetry is the flower of thought and feeling.

If weight of thought or pithiness of phrase were all, Donne would be one of the greatest of poets, whereas he is only one of the oddest of versifiers.

He solves problems in rhyme, that is all. A demonstration in verse is an absurdity; in poetry it is an impossibility, for a poem is always its own demonstration.

Yet Lowell can also write of "As virtuous men pass mildly away,"

The poem, to my feeling, is a truly sacred one, and fuller of the soul of poetry than a whole Alexandrian library of common love-verses. . . . The meaning of it is so pure and holy and profound, that I can fancy it was written under the immediate inspiration of St. Joseph, the patron saint of the Joiners' Craft.

Samuel Butler, "the greatest wit who ever wrote English," got a whole lecture in the 1855 Lowell Lecture series. On the other hand, Lowell says nothing noteworthy about Herbert, Vaughan, Herrick, or Marvell, though he appreciated Herbert's exaltation and calls Marvell a "great favorite of mine." In *Conversations* Philip calls a passage from Crashaw "the best music in words I ever read."

Lowell understood Bunyan's power as a mouthpiece of the Puritan spirit, but he did not give him an essay as he did Walton. Nor did he write an essay about Sir Thomas Browne, "a man who gives proof of more imagination than any other English-man except Shakespeare." Poor Mrs. Behn only gets a place in the "kennels of literature," though Lowell recognized her ability. He relished Pepys and the less familiar letters of James Howell, to which he refers several times.

In the eighteenth century, Pope gets an essay in which his virtues and his shortcomings are weighed in typical Romantic fashion. Gray is the only pre-Romantic who gets a whole essay; Young's *Night Thoughts*, Lowell confesses, gave him "as many hearty laughs as any humorous book I ever read." He liked Cowper. But the eighteenth-century poet who meant most to him was Burns, whom he revered, as Whittier did, as a kind of patron saint of the unspoiled human heart at its best.

Dr. Johnson's *Lives of the English Poets*, like his other works, has "all the values which can belong to a criticism of poetry whose point of view is restricted to the understanding alone." Johnson's judgment was always "that of the thumb and fore-finger"; he was better qualified "to reckon the quantity of a man's mind than the quality of it," and when he had a subject with whom he could not sympathize, he failed, as he did with Swift. Yet Lowell himself, who saw Swift as a cynic, had no more relish for him than Johnson had had. As for Boswell, there was "something half-comically beautiful in the poor, weak creature, with his pathetic instinct of reverence for what was nobler, wiser, and stronger than himself."

The eighteenth century, too, brought Lowell face to face with the English novel, and though he has been accused of comparative indifference to fiction, this does not seem to have been the case. At the end of his life he called the reading of novels "a new habit with me," but some of his interpreters have taken this too literally. Being a man of taste, he was inevitably painfully impressed by the limitations of much popular literature, and most popular literature in his time was fiction. He believed that the novel had begun to replace the epic as far back as Fielding, and he defended the reading of fiction against the charge that it was a waste of time when it still needed such defense: "Let us not go about to make life duller than it is." He certainly wrote less about fiction than he did about some other forms of literature, and Scott and Cervantes, alone among novelists, can be placed in the front rank of his reading passions, but he did not lack experience with the form.

Among the eighteenth-century novelists, he recognized Richardson's ability, but I do not believe that *Clarissa* meant much to Lowell; when he wanted sentiment, he got it better from Goldsmith. Defoe was another matter, and when Mabel was just begnning to have *Robinson Crusoe* read to her, he wondered what he, or any other grown man, could have left in life to match that. Smollett's novels he valued mainly for their historical interest; they could "neither warm the heart nor impregnate the imagination," and their coarseness, unlike Fielding's, was the index of an essentially coarse mind. The lecture on

Sterne reported after Lowell's death in *The Harvard Crimson*
(May 4, 1894) hedges a bit, for we are told that Sterne's humor

> seems to be entirely aimless, and we should be inclined to say he
> had no conscience at all. He is an exceptional character—a humorist
> without depth of nature. But . . . if he is one of the greatest of
> humorists, he is also one of the most artificial.

Yet he understood Sterne's genius, for he speaks of "the living
reality of Walter Shandy and his brother Toby, characters
which we do not see merely as puppets in the author's mind,
but poetically projected from it in an independent being of their
own," and Leon Howard feels that if Lowell had ever written
his projected novel, it would have been Shandean in character.[45]

Fielding was Lowell's candidate for the title of greatest English novelist, yet Fielding is the novelist on whom he hedges
most. He calls him "the greatest creative artist who has written
in English since Shakespeare"; he gives Amelia a place with the
great characters of literature; and G. W. Smalley says he read
Tom Jones through once a year. Yet his performance when he
delivered an address at the unveiling of a bust of the author at
Taunton, in Somersetshire, in 1883, was very curious. Though
he put Squire Western with Falstaff and Don Quixote (surely
an extravagant estimate), he insisted that Fielding's imagination
was of the "secondary order," lacking "tragic power or passion,"
and incapable of "ecstasy of conception." "He has the merit,
whatever it may be, of inventing the realistic novel, as it is
called." Since Lowell cannot praise Fielding by comparing him
to the great poets, he gives him credit for being unlike modern
French realists, for whom he suggests a motto from an old
tavern sign—"Entertainment for Man—and Beast."

Of the Romantic poets, Wordsworth was the one who gave
Lowell most trouble, pulling him uncomfortably in two direc-

tions at once, so that he excoriated him for his defense of capital punishment—

> And always 'tis the saddest sight to see
> An old man faithfuless in Humanity—

less than a year before he wrote the tribute beginning "Poet of the lofty brow! far-sighted seer!" which is preserved in Smith's *Uncollected Poems*. Certainly he omits little in his account of Wordsworth's shortcomings as either poet or thinker. Wordsworth's sympathies and his experiences were both narrow. He was self-centered and he confused originality with eccentricity. He lacked both humor and spontaneity, becoming not only the partisan of a system but of himself as its representative. He lacked both narrative and dramatic power, and he was too didactic. He had vision but lacked craftsmanship. In meter he was the least original of writers, imitating every conceivable master in turn. The meter of the *Ecclesiastical Sonnets* was as monotonous as the movement of the sea. When inspiration failed him, he "watered" his thought with "gallons of poetic diction."

One might not expect this from Lowell's statement that "whoever values wisdom, profound insight, breadth of thought, and sustained flow of passion . . . will hold Wordsworth to be the greatest man who has written poetry in modern times." Insofar as Lowell's attitude toward Wordsworth admits of summary, he achieved it when he denied him "that shaping imagination which is the highest criterion of a poet." His "insight and utterance" were "piecemeal"; his imagination was "feminine, not masculine, repetitive, and not creative." Not technically a great poet, he was yet, at his best, "greatly inspired." Though his "general output" did not equal Dryden's, "he dwelt habitually in an ampler ether, a diviner air, and alone of modern poets, renewed the holier faith that made poet and prophet interchangeable terms." [46]

Lowell says much less about either Coleridge or Shelley (Gay Wilson Allen thinks Shelley an important influence on Lowell's prosody), but we know that he read Coleridge with avidity, in the 'thirties at least, and that "The Rime of the Ancient Mariner" was for a time his favorite poem. In his essay on Keats, he mentions Wordsworth, Keats, and Byron as having brought English poetry back "from the sandy deserts of rhetoric," but he says nothing of Shelley. Byron he here oddly judges as "more intellectual" than either Wordsworth or Keats, but this is not supported by his introduction to Shelley's poems, in which he finds Shelley's radicalism "a matter of nature as well as conviction" and Byron's "an affair of whim" which "cost him nothing." (It would seem, in the last analysis, to have cost him his life.) In his youth he liked the kind of poetry that "sends a cold thrill through one," like Byron's and Campbell's, but this appeal apparently declined with maturity. In 1869, however, he took his stand with Mrs. Stowe's critics after she had accused Byron of incest in her sensational, circulation-wrecking *Atlantic* article in defense of Lady Byron. Lowell not only disbelieved the story, but was ungenerous and, I think, unconvincing in his analysis of Mrs. Stowe's motives.[47] In view of what he wrote about him elsewhere,[48] the essay on Keats in *Among My Books* is curiously cool.

Lowell accepted Tennyson less wholeheartedly than many of his contemporaries did, considering *Idylls of the King* mere clever fake-medievalism, but being greatly moved by *Maud*.[49] Browning's obscurities troubled him, and once he rejects the dramatic monologue as a form on the ground that "people don't cross-examine their motives and dissect the nerves of their character in this fashion" (surely Lowell must have accepted conventions in others forms of literature), yet he discovered Browning early in his career and praised his genius in *Conversations*, and his 1848 essay[50] is both understanding and discriminating.

In 1842, when he was soliciting material for *The Pioneer*, he told Mrs. Browning-to-be that she had "shown more true poetic genius than any poet of her sex"; later he disliked *Aurora Leigh* for its "hectic flush and the tendency to over-intensity; pushing expression to an unpleasant *physical* excess." [51] Lowell's notion that Arthur Hugh Clough achieved "the best utterance in verse of this generation" seems quite extravagant; perhaps he was prejudiced by his friendship with Clough, developed during the period the English poet lived in Cambridge. He is more reasonable when he looks forward to Clough's poetry being considered a century hence "the truest expression in verse of the moral and intellectual tendencies, the doubt and struggle toward settled convictions, of the period in which he lived," but most will feel that even this distinction belongs more properly to Matthew Arnold, of whom Lowell says nothing of significance. Nor had he much to say about the others. Though he gave Swinburne a long review article, he had no love for him, and he was doubtful about Rossetti. In London, in 1881, he gave Oscar Wilde, who had evidently made a very good impression upon him, a letter of introduction to Oliver Wendell Holmes, all unaware, we may be sure, of the portent before him.

Although he gave Walter Savage Landor two papers[52] as against Carlyle's one, the latter was the Victorian non-fiction prose-writer with whom Lowell would seem to have been most concerned. Carlyle, in his view, lacked the plastic imagination, he had "no artistic sense of form or rhythm, scarcely of proportion," and his feeling for structure was slight. Lowell took off his style amusingly in the extract from the "World-Harmonic-Aeolian-Attachment" prefixed to the first series of *Biglow*. He thought him "sweet and gentle" when they met, but Mrs. Carlyle's *Correspondence* struck him as "a very painful book." Carlyle, he once wrote, was "like a seventy-four gun ship on fire. As the fire spreads he fires his shot in every direction."

Lowell thought Carlyle's fondness for dictators a sign of moral weakness, but after his death he judged him a sentimentalist whose "bursts of humorous brutality were the protests of his consciousness against this innate weakness."

Scott is the one novelist one can always count on Lowell's praising. References to him begin as early as 1828, when he wrote his brother Robert that "I have read Waverly [sic] through," to 1888, when he urged his daughter to have her sons read Scott for his "wholesomeness and manliness," and 1890, when Oliver Wendell Holmes visited him in his final illness, and was greeted by, "Oh, I suppose I'm in pain; I always am more or less, but look here, I've been reading *Rob Roy*. I suppose it may be for the fortieth time, but it is just as good as when I read it first." In his essay on Dante, he placed *The Heart of Midlothian* and *The Bride of Lammermoor* with the work of the great poets, and he did not deny that Jedediah Cleishbotham had served as the model for Parson Wilbur.

Dickens, however, draws a much larger number of references, though Lowell, amazingly, records not having read *David Copperfield* until 1887. He met the novelist and had a hand in entertaining him on both his visits to Boston;[53] in 1853 he thought him rather vulgar-looking, but in 1867 he found him "a very delightful man of genius . . . —simple, sweet, and natural—and so used to being a lion that he might lie down with Charles Lamb without scaring him." He defended *American Notes* (in whose favor he was, of course, prejudiced by its strong anti-slavery tone) and excoriated those of his fellow-countrymen who imagined that because they had admired Dickens's novels, he was obliged to admire them; though not a profound book, it was the work of "the keenest and shrewdest observer of his time" and "a man of genius" who belonged as much to America as to England. When Dickens died in 1870 to the accompaniment of considerable posthumous snarling by the scandalmongers, Lowell was indignant in the extreme. "I can stand it no longer! If Dickens is to be damned, the rest of us might as well fling up our hands." And he sent Fields a sonnet:

> A man of genius, simple, warm, sincere,
> He left a world grown kindlier than he came;
> His hand the needy knew, but not his name;
> Dumb creatures snuffed a friend when he drew near,
> And the strange dog pricked one suspicious ear,
> Then couched his head secure. Safe be this fame
> From critics' measured praise or close-picked blame—
> He loved God's gentler face, and made it dear.
> Was then Stylites' post the better way,
> Or mingling with his kind, a man with men,
> Like Him that was and was not such as they?
> I judge ye not, but to my simple ken,
> If on your guideboards the right name be kept,
> Some foe hath changed their places while ye slept.

Ten years later, after Charles Dickens the Younger had proposed a toast to him at the Savage Club in London, Lowell paid his tribute to the dead novelist by quoting (inaccurately) from *In Memoriam:*

> Oh, for the touch of a vanished hand!
> Oh, for a voice that is still!

Yet Lowell was far from being an unqualified admirer of Dickens. It is true that as early as 1847, in a paper on Disraeli in which he complained bitterly of the decline of the novel in England (which he attributed to its rejection of imagination, indifference to art and beauty, and determined didacticism), he admitted that

Dickens, with his many egregious faults of style, his mannerisms, and his sometimes intolerable descriptive passages, is yet clearly enough a great genius, a something necessary to the world, and the figures upon his canvas are such as Emerson has aptly termed *representative*, the types of classes, and no truer in London than in Boston.[54]

The faults alleged here are explained and enlarged upon elsewhere. Dickens views the world "from the reporters' bench in the police court." He creates "either unnatural men or the oddities natural only in the lowest grades of a highly artificial system of society" (in later years, when he knew London better, Lowell was much less sure that Dickens was a caricaturist). He was sentimental and affected, and he forced the tragic note and made a mess of it. Lowell compared him to his disadvantage to Fielding (who had much more *conception* of humor though less observation), to Cervantes, and (for once accepting the realism he generally seems to dislike), to Thackeray. Even when reading *Great Expectations*, he feared the melodrama was just around the corner. He greatly disliked Forster's biography of Dickens, and this did not endear its subject to him. Shortly before his death, he was reported as having told an interviewer: "I have been dipping into Dickens . . . but I don't like him as well even as I used to, and he never was a great favorite of mine. His humor always struck me as being forced, and his style was not always as refined as it might have been." [55]

I find nothing of significance on the other Victorian novelists, nor, for that matter, on Jane Austen, though he once went to a ball in Yorkshire for her sake! He met and dined with Trollope, whom he described to Norton as "a big, redfaced, rather underbred Englishman—of the bald-with-spectacles type. A good roaring positive fellow who deafened me . . . till I thought of Dante's Cerberus." I have found one reference to Mrs. Gaskell but none to George Eliot, though she speaks of Lowell. In his last illness he read both *Armadale* and *The Moonstone* by Wilkie Collins, finding no such "breakneck interest as Reade's, where one follows the scent of the plot headlong as that of a fox in the hunting-field, but still with an interest keen enough for that of the armchair." The Brontës fare a little better but not much. *Jane Eyre*, though it had "real power," was "unreal," and *Wuthering Heights* (Lowell carelessly calls Rochester a character in it!) is like "looking at nature through a crooked pane of glass." He once read Charles Lever's novels on shipboard, and he refers to G. P. R. James and his solitary horsemen in one of his political papers. I am amazed at his statement that he could not read *John Ingelsant* by Joseph Henry Shorthouse. His own mystical sensitiveness being what it was, I should have expected him to love that beautiful book, but possibly anti-High Church prejudices affected him here. At the end he recognized Kipling's power and was much taken with the novels of the now-forgotten William Edward Norton. The last letter in Norton's collection finds Lowell looking forward eagerly to the publication of a new one, which it is sad to remember, he probably did not live to see.

VI

American literature for Lowell was contemporary literature, with a large share of the New England writers his personal friends. He mentions Joel Barlow and Cotton Mather, but he did not admire them, though he gives Mather high rank as an unconscious humorist.

Among the poets, Emerson presented a problem. He was kind to Lowell when the boy was rusticated to Concord, but, shocked by what seemed to him the irreverence and muddleheadedness of the Divinity School Address, Lowell first attacked Emerson in his Class Poem, then apologized in a private letter which has a curiously independent sound. Lowell could not think Emerson so "small" as to think less of him for holding up his head and speaking the truth or imagine that he had willfully maligned "a man whose salt I had eaten, and whose little child I had danced on my knee" (why, then, was an apology called for at all?). Actually, however, Lowell did not mean to apologize. He wanted to be "*acquitted* of all uncharitableness," but he did not think there was anything "to *forgive* or *pardon*." Emerson responded graciously, and their relations were never disturbed thereafter. Maria White passionately admired the Sage of Concord, and after their marriage, she and Lowell were quite at one in this.

It is true that the lines on Emerson in *A Fable for Critics* discriminate carefully. He is "a Plotinus-Montaigne," "a Greek head on right Yankee shoulders," whose "prose is grand verse" but whose verse is not always even prose. "He never leaves a doorway to get in a god" to his "glorious temples," and he has a way of talking about things "as if they were dead," and reducing "life, nature, love, God, and affairs of that sort" to ideas.

But almost all Lowell's private references to Emerson are reverential in the extreme,[56] and as editor of the *Atlantic* he was, for the most part, almost fulsomely deferential toward him. "I am gratefully and affectionately your liegeman" is a typical complimentary close to a letter. "Emerson awakened us, saved us from the body of this death" is the great tribute he paid him in his essay on "Emerson the Lecturer." Some natural scenery, some cathedrals had stamped themselves upon his mind as Emerson did, but no other man, and he grew "sweeter if possible" as he grew older. All in all, Lowell had "never known a character on the whole so beautiful, so high above self, and so kindly a mixture of strength and gentleness." [57] When one saw him, the Fall of Adam seemed a false report. In his lecture on "Democracy" he placed him with Lincoln, and after Emerson's death, he told his daughter that he had never known a man so much revered who was also so much loved. Even when he was forced to recognize Emerson's shortcomings, he tended to turn them to his advantage, as in considering his lectures, for instance:

It was as if, after vainly trying to get his paragraphs into sequence and order, he had at last tried the desperate expedient of *shuffling* them. It was chaos come again, but it was a chaos full of shooting stars, a jumble of creative forces.[58]

Longfellow put the Christian charity of all his brother poets to another kind of test, for he was so much more popular than any of the others that they must have had his own angelic disposition not to resent it. As Lowell himself once wrote Norton from England, "Give my love to Longfellow, and tell him that to know him is to be somebody over here. As the author of various esteemed works I am nothing in particular; but as his neighbor—it is as good as knowing a lord." He was humorously outraged when an artist whom he found sketching in one of the places he loved best told him that it was a favorite walk of Mr. Longfellow's. What hurt most was to have it given to a "rival" who seldom walked farther than to the post office. "I did not know what a jealous creature I was before." As for Longfellow himself, his brother tells us that Lowell and Hawthorne were the two writers of whom he most often spoke, and that he said of Lowell, "He is one of the manliest and noblest men that ever lived." [59]

Lowell reviewed both *The Courtship of Miles Standish* and *Tales of a Wayside Inn.*[60] Though he did not like the measure of *Standish* (which is also that of *Evangeline*), he praised the poem. Longfellow is "our Chaucer." He moralizes too much and falls "short of the highest reaches of imagination," but he is "a master within his own sphere." Lowell was careful not to overpraise Longfellow for his *Poems on Slavery*, but he defended him when the abolitionists criticized him for not doing

more, and nobody ever better understood the older poet's
ability to retain his sweetness of temper in the face of some of
the terrible blows which life dealt him.

> Some suck up poison from a sorrow's core,
>   As nought but nightshade grew upon earth's ground:
> Love turned all his to heart's-ease; and the more
> Fate tried his bastions, she but forced a door
> Leading to sweeter manhood and more sound.[61]

In a review of Bayard Taylor's *Picture of St. John*,[62] Lowell
calls Longfellow's *Golden Legend* the only other long American
poem of evenly sustained power, which, though a compliment
to the *Legend*, is none to *Evangeline* or *Hiawatha*. He seems
to have hurt Longfellow's feelings by not liking *The New England Tragedies* and being indifferent to the impending appearance of *The Divine Tragedy*, and Longfellow himself told Mrs.
Fields that Lowell was "constituted to like few things and
those of a peculiar class." Since he disliked parodies, Longfellow probably would not have enjoyed the take-off on *Hiawatha* which Lowell scribbled in some verses to Norton on the
subject of lending and borrowing books, nor yet the fact that,
even while complaining about Poe's treatment of Longfellow,
Lowell should find it necessary to add, "I have no doubt that
Poe estimates Longfellow's poetical abilities more highly than
I do perhaps." But he would have been pleased by Lowell's
calling his translation of Dante the best that had been made and
his comparing him to Gray when speaking at the dedication of
the Longfellow memorial bust in Westminster Abbey:

There was the same love of a certain subdued splendor not incon-
sistent with transparency of diction, there was the same power of
absorbing and assimilating the beauties of other literatures without
loss of originality, and above all there was that genius for sympathy

with universal sentiments and power of expressing them, so that they come home to everybody both high and low.

Lowell reviewed three of Whittier's books: *Home Ballads and Poems, In War-Time*, and *Snow-Bound*.[63] Though well aware of the Quaker poet's technical limitations, he is fair in his assessment of his merits; in the Civil War poems, he thought him faithful to the New England rather than the Quaker aspects of his heritage. Not only did he praise Holmes warmly in the seventy-fifth birthday poem, he made his editorship of the *Atlantic* contingent upon Holmes's agreeing to contribute to it, and since *The Autocrat of the Breakfast Table* turned out to be the great hit of the early *Atlantic* years, this was uncommonly perspicacious on Lowell's part. He found "good stuff" in Julia Ward Howe's *Passion Flowers*, of which many others were critical, but he was obviously shocked by her Italian romantic tragedy, *Leonora*.[64] He enjoyed the New England flavor in J. G. Holland's *Bitter-Sweet*. "We read ourselves gradually back to boyhood in it."[65]

Of New England's great prose writers, Lowell does best by Hawthorne and worst by Thoreau. Hawthorne was "a John Bunyan Fouqué, a Puritan Tieck," the "unwilling poet of Puritanism," "the rarest creative imagination of the century" and "the rarest in some ideal respects since Shakespeare." The difference between him and Poe was the difference between genius and talent carried to its utmost limit. Lowell was, of course, not so foolish as to consider Hawthorne Shakespeare's equal. Because he was detached from life, beyond almost any other writer of comparable talent, "his characters are apt to be types; his imagination does not enter into them and make them live through sympathy, as those of Shakespeare and Cervantes do." He could have been the greatest poet since Shakespeare if a little had been added to him, but if a little had been taken away, he would have been only a writer of emblems. Lowell cherished him peculiarly because "he bore unstained his loyalty to the orthodox creed of the ideal in art." When *The Marble Faun* came out, he told Fields it was a "great book," Hawthorne's "best yet," and reviewed it in the *Atlantic*. Hawthorne had made art "the interpreter of something profounder than herself."

Lowell's special quarrel with Thoreau was occasioned by the editor's alteration of a sentence in one of his *Atlantic* papers which he feared might offend the orthodox. Thoreau wrote a furious letter, to which Lowell apparently did not respond, and the author sent nothing more to the *Atlantic* until after Fields had become its editor. Lowell had thought Thoreau an amusing ape in Emerson's shadow as far back as 1838, and although his review of *A Week on the Concord and Merrimack Rivers*[66] is much friendlier than the notorious essay in *My Study Windows*, there are uncomplimentary references even here. "Mr. Thoreau is clearly the man we want. He is both wise man and poet," and he persists "in a fine, intelligent paganism." His description of twilight at the river's bottom surpasses Melville's picture of life in the South Seas. But when Thoreau makes his two rivers "run Thoreau or Emerson," he loses Lowell. "We were bidden to a river-party, not to be preached at." He objects also to Thoreau's digressions, his structural deficiences, and his bad rhythm. "If Mr. Emerson chooses to leave some hard nuts for posterity to crack, he can perhaps afford it as well as any. We counsel Mr. Thoreau, in his own words, to take his hat and come out of that." In the later essay, Lowell's charges, generally quite unsubstantiated, are more serious, and Thoreau now becomes the very type of Romantic egoism, eccentricity, and individualism. "Mr. Thoreau seems to me to insist in public on going back to flint and steel, when there is a match-box in his pocket which he knows very well how to use at a pinch." Lowell believed that "a greater familiarity with ordinary men would have done

Thoreau good, by showing him how many fine qualities are common to the race." He adds that "it is a very shallow vice that affirms trees and rocks to be healthy, and cannot see that men in communities are just as true to the laws of their organization and destiny." The statement is true, but Thoreau made no such claim as Lowell attributes to him. "In outward nature it is still man that interests us." It was what interested Thoreau also. He sometimes left himself open to misunderstanding, so that even Emerson once told him that if God had meant him to live in a swamp, He would have made him a frog. Yet Thoreau wrote: "If it is possible to conceive of an event outside of humanity, it is not of the slightest significance, though it were the explosion of a planet." [67]

Though he has references to both Alcott and Brownson, Margaret Fuller is the only other Transcendentalist whom Lowell considers at length. She is, of course, Miranda in *A Fable for Critics*, where she is savagely portrayed, partly, but not wholly, as Howard Ehrlich has now shown,[68] because of her own criticisms of Lowell. He afterwards had qualms of conscience about his treatment of her, and the very next year he praised her for her hospital work in Rome: "Women have been sainted . . . for less." His appreciation of Harriet Beecher Stowe is sufficiently shown in his comments on *The Minister's Wooing*, which he serialized in the *Atlantic*.[69] He calls Lydia M. Child's *Philothea* "a divine book," but in the *Fable* his treatment of this author is somewhat condescending. He relished the New Englandism of Sylvester Judd's *Margaret*,[70] and called Dana's *Paul Felton* "a tale of wonderful depth and power."

Lowell greatly admired Joel Chandler Harris, but of his American contemporaries outside of New England, Poe was by all means the one with whom he had most to do, and at the beginning their relations were much closer and more sympathetic than the rather cruel lines in the *Fable* might indicate:

There comes Poe, with his raven, like Barnaby Rudge,
Three fifths of him genius and two fifths sheer fudge,
Who talks like a book of iambs and pentameters,
In a way to make people of common sense damn metres,
Who has written some things quite the best of their kind,
But the heart somehow seems all squeezed out by the mind.

They tried to work together in *Pioneer* days, but Lowell thought Poe's aesthetic theory too narrow, and he was repelled by his genius for detecting plagiarism, especially in Longfellow, and, as Lowell says, mistaking his vial of prussic acid for his inkwell. After their only meeting, in 1845, when Poe was nursing a hangover, Lowell concluded that though he might possess genius, he lacked character. Poe, for his part, praised "A Legend of Brittany" warmly, but he was angered by the *Fable*; by this time, too, he had made up his mind that Lowell's fanatical abolitionism made it impossible for a Southerner to expect justice from him. Lowell was not wholly consistent in his treatment of Poe (at different times he both gave and denied him genius), but he was never taken in by the slanders of Rufus A. Griswold, whom he considered both an ass and a knave, and he appreciated Poe's creativity, saying that he had "squared out blocks enough to build an enduring pyramid, but left them lying careless and unclaimed in many different quarters." He is penetrating too when he defines Poe's special quality in terms of the odd combination he effected through joining two apparently disparate qualities—"a power of influencing the mind of the reader by the impalpable shadows of mystery, and a minuteness of detail which does not leave a pun or a button unnoticed." [71]

Of the others, Whitman must just be written off; as late as 1863 Lowell told W. L. Gage that he had never looked into *Leaves of Grass* except far enough to assure himself that it was a solemn humbug, and he told Agnes Repplier he saw no reason why Whitman should be called the Good Gray Poet when he himself was quite as gray and good and perhaps even a little better. Lowell's dislike of Whitman was not based wholly upon moral grounds; he also objected to what he considered Whitman's straining after originality and simulated naturalism or barbarism. Yet he did publish one poem, "Bardic Symbols," in the *Atlantic*, leaving three others on hand to the decision of his successor Fields.[72] There are references to Melville's *Typee* and also to "The Encantadas," which Lowell seems greatly to have admired. He grew tired of Cooper's red men, but he appreciated Leatherstocking as "our new Adam of the wilderness" and "the protagonist of our New World epic, a figure as poetic as that of Achilles, as ideally representative as that of Don Quixote, as romantic in its relation to our homespun and plebeian mythus as Arthur in his to the mailed and plumed cycle of chivalry." Here again, however, the *Fable* is more caustic than the prose. No "American Scott," as he has been called, Cooper has copied the same figure over and over, and his women are "all sappy as maples and flat as a prairie." Bryant, too, got pretty rough treatment in the *Fable*:

> "There is Bryant, as quiet, as cool, and as dignified,
> As a smooth, silent iceberg that never is ignified."

Though he stood alone "in supreme iceolation," calling him an American Wordsworth was something else again.

Among his younger contemporaries, Lowell was closest to Howells, whose ability he recognized from the very beginning, and with whom he never quarreled, even when their ideological outlook differed. He detected Henry James's essential modernity and indifference to classical influences as early as "A Passionate Pilgrim," admired *The Princess Casamassima*, granted him the right to prefer European to American settings, and never found his stories too long.[73] He enjoyed the short stories of Sarah Orne

Jewett and Harriet Prescott Spofford, and found "the beautiful simplicity of the old Quaker home" still clinging to Bayard Taylor.

But he also welcomed less traditional writers. Not only did he praise Mark Twain for the "serious and even pathetic beauty" of *The Prince and the Pauper*, but he once read the Blue Jay yarn from *A Tramp Abroad* to the Henry Adamses.[74] And when Bret Harte came out of the West, he was "our Theocritus at last, and from California, whence we least expected him." With "a feeling for what is noble in character, and a faith in the final perseverance of humanity under the most adverse circumstances," Harte

divined the poem that lay hidden in that wonderful border life, Homeric in its simple savagery, in its emphasis of the manlier qualities. It was plain, too, that here was a humorist of no mean quality, perhaps the first who had pushed to its utmost allowable limits that contempt for all received conventions which is the leading characteristic . . . of the purely American type of the humorous.[75]

VII

These things, then, and many others went into the well. But it is now time to turn to what is for us the more interesting matter of what came up out of it.

CHAPTER FOUR

THE CREATIVE LIFE

Be sure and don't leave anything out because it seems trifling, for it is out of these trifles only that it is possible to reconstruct character.

JRL, to James T. Fields, 1871

I

Though Lowell never confined his activities to writing poetry, he still thought of himself as essentially a poet. He chose this goal for himself early in life, even while his father still regarded it as a species of vagabondage, and he planned a course of study in the laws of English verse preparatory to it. In his law office days he wrote,

> They tell me I must study law,
> They say I have dreamed, and dreamed too long;
> That I must rouse and seek for fame and gold;
> That I must scorn this idle gift of song,
> And mingle with the vain and proud and cold.
> Is, then, this petty strife
> The end and aim of life,
> All that is worth the living for below?
> *O God! then call me hence, for I would gladly go!*

And George William Curtis quotes him at twenty-seven:

If I have any vocation it is the making of verse. When I take my pen in hand for that, the world opens itself ungrudgingly before me;

everything seems clear and easy. . . . But when I do prose it is *invita Minerva*. I feel as if I were wasting time and keeping back my message. My true place is to serve the cause as a poet. Then my heart leaps before me into the conflict.

He never really changed his mind about all this, and in later life he thought of his other activities as a kind of infidelity. When Minot J. Savage regretted that he had not given all his time to poetry, Lowell replied, "You have given substantial expression to my own feeling. I have been haunted by the idea that it might have been better if I had devoted myself more exclusively to my literary work." At other times, however, he was not so sure that what was good for the poet would also have been good for the man. Perhaps he was thinking of Goethe's statement that a talent was formed in isolation but a character in the stream of the world.[1]

Lowell wrote rapidly, though often only after long brooding, nearly always on a pasteboard pad on his knee. He began comparatively late for a poet, essentially during his college years. He cherished spontaneity, sometimes even irregularity ("you must write easily," he wrote Henry James, "for you are read with pleasure"), and his writing could be cathartic, for he said he could get rid of something which troubled him by shutting it within covers. His visual imagination was keen ("I always see what I describe while I am thinking of it"), and he wrote, in response to an "inner light," what he "needed" to write, and when he "felt" like it.

He claimed to be able to write verse faster than prose, and in 1838 he told Longfellow he was not going on with poetry for the time being because he could not write slowly enough. The verses in Beatrice Müller's album were dashed off on the spur of the moment in response to her request for an autograph, and he once sent six letter-paper sides of verse to Charles Hazen Dorr, praising the cheese he had sent him.

Yet he could not write to order. For him Dr. Johnson's "setting doggedly about it" just did not work. Though emotional crises could sometimes stimulate him, he often had to wait upon moods and even weather before he could so much as complete an enterprise in hand. Trying to write while serving as ambassador in London was, he said, like trying to be a setting hen who should also have to answer the doorbell. Sometimes he would labor diligently at a composition and be obliged to give it up. Naturally, it was especially hard to try to be humorous to order, and in 1854 he tried to revive *Biglow* and failed. In 1889, having attempted a poem for Aldrich's *Atlantic*, he found that "cold molasses is swift as a weaver's shuttle compared with my wits." [2]

As he grew older, the spontaneity was less and the craftsmanship more,[3] but not even large offers could draw a poem out of him when the inner impulse was lacking. Even when he could write with as great enthusiasm as ever, he would print with less confidence. During forty years he only managed to bring out two collections of verses.

To be sure, happy accidents sometimes occurred. "The Courtin'," certainly one of his finest poems, was originally a six-stanza space filler, of which he kept no copy. He added six more for a later edition of *Biglow*, and ultimately there were twenty-four.[4] With poems like "The Vision of Sir Launfal," "Agassiz," and the Commemoration Ode, it was more inspiration than improvisation, however; at least Lowell was, as it were, rapt clean out of himself, composing at high speed, and in a keen state of excitement which drained his energy and left him limp and doubting afterwards. ("Like a boy I mistook my excitement for inspiration, and here I am in the mud.") He says "The Cathedral" absorbed him to such an extent that it made his wife jealous. To a lesser degree, he depended upon such excitement when he wrote prose also, and he thought his essay on Rousseau second-rate because it had not kept him awake at night. The fullest description of such an experience he achieved, however, in connection with the Agassiz Ode:

I had gone out of myself entirely. I was in the dining-room at Parker's, and when I came back to self-consciousness and solitude, it was in another world that I awoke, and I was puzzled to say which. It was a case of possession but not self-possession. I was cold, but my brain was full of warm light, and the passage came to me in its completeness without any seeming intervention of mine. I was delighted, I confess, with this renewal of imagination-in me after so many blank years. . . . The only part I *composed* was the concluding verses which I suspect to be the weakest part.

And he adds: "I have a respect for things that are *given me*, as the greater part of this was."

Occasionally Lowell cites a source for one of his poems, as Schoolcraft's *Algic Researches* for "A Chippewa Legend," a Breton story of Souvestre's for "The Washers of the Shroud," and Burns's "The Twa Brigs" for the Mason and Slidell piece in *Biglow*. In his early life at least, he considered echoing the old poets he had loved as a tribute he owed them. There is reason to believe that Samuel Worcester Rowse was the model for one of his best characters, Fitz Adam.[5] Once at least he dreamed a poem, and though he says, justly on the whole, that he did not belong with those "that hawk their sorrows in the market-place," he did use family griefs in such poems as "The First Snow-Fall" and "After the Burial." On the whole, however, sources were much less important for him than they were for either Whittier or Longfellow. He understood, and stated felicitously, the conditions under which literary source material may be effectively used: "If a poet take his subject (or plot) from history (or in any other way ready made to his hand), just in proportion to the amount of matter furnished must be that which he supplies out of himself."

Lowell himself said that he liked conceiving a poem but not working it up, and he told Mrs. Herrick that "my temper of mind is such that I never have the patience to read over again what I have once printed." He was, however, much given to suggesting emendations between the acceptance of a poem and its publication. Once at least he revised to avoid the unfair appearance of plagiarism. Actually, revision does not seem to have been a very profitable business for him. When he attempted it conscientiously, as he did with "The Cathedral," which he went over carefully as with a file, he was likely in the end to restore nearly all the original readings.[6]

II

For Lowell, poetry was "made up of Imagination, Experience, Indiscretion, and Art." The first and the third were "the good fairy's gifts." Experience came with years, Art with many years. By Indiscretion he meant "not want of judgment but the faculty of keeping green in despite of Experience." Poetry differed from prose not merely in degree but in kind, and it should concern itself with matters of fact only as they were "embodied by imagination," which was "the everlasting resurrection of the soul from the body." To a prose writer the dictionary was a forest or a quarry, but the poet entered it "like Orpheus" and made "its wild inmates sing and dance and keep joyous time to every wavering fancy of his lyre." And he who possessed an imagination had no need to sigh with Alexander for new worlds to conquer.[7]

Lowell was classical in his insistence upon universal appeal in literature of quality, and this caused him to condemn both the provinciality which is nationalism and the sentimentalism and subjectivism encouraged by Romanticism. As he saw it, the unity of a poem was not "a thing of manufacture like that of a brick" but one "of growth like the rooted and various and waving unity of a tree."

Its shape, its law of growth, its limit, is irrevocably fore-ordained in the seed. There is nothing haphazard in the matter, from beginning to end. The germ once planted, everything then tends simply to the bringing about of one end,—perfection in its kind. The plot which it has to fill out is definite and rigid. The characters and incidents balance each other like the branches, and every part, from the minutest fibre of the root to the last leaf, conspires to nourishment and so to beauty.

Once he seems to be bringing himself within hailing distance of Poe by declaring that the *Odyssey* is the only long poem that will bear consecutive reading, but when he goes on to distinguish between poetic sense and poetic faculty, he parts company from him. In such poems as *The Divine Comedy* and *Paradise Lost*, one recognizes in every verse, even if detached, a part of the whole, much as one may recognize a friend by his walk. "Perfect in themselves," the parts also contribute to "totality of effect." This evidences poetic faculty, or "the shaping spirit," which is what Poe seems to have ignored in long poems. As for Poe's idea that man cannot create but can only combine previously existent materials, this Lowell dismisses as irrelevant nonsense:

Suppose by an exertion of my will I could create a black cat here on the desk, would it be less a creation because black cats were invented so long ago, and every boy has flung his boot at some Romeo of the tribe on a moonlight night? Now if I could by my will give every one of you the impression of one sitting here on the desk, how would you decide that it was not a real Grimalkin? This is the way in which the Imagination creates—by magnetising all the senses till they see, hear, taste, feel and smell only what it chooses.

Like Aristotle, Lowell knew that literature must give aesthetic pleasure. "The first duty of the Muse is to be delightful." He praised Howells for having known from the beginning of his career how to be entertaining, for this, he thought, was generally one of the last things a writer learns, and "without it, a man may have all the cardinal virtues, but they are nothing to the purpose." [8] Moreover, a literary work must be judged as literature, not as a system of law or morality.

However much Lowell might be indebted to classical standards, he was not enslaved by them; neither did he neglect later writers when they had something to contribute to his purpose. He was impressed by Goethe's three questions: "What did the author propose to himself? Is what he proposes reasonable and comprehensible? and how far has he succeeded in carrying it out?" He also responded affirmatively to Milton's demand for poetry as simple, sensuous, and passionate.

It should be simple as being clear, not obvious, as dealing with primary emotions and not with metaphysical refinements upon them; it should be sensuous as not making its appeal to the intellect but to that finer sense to which language is still not the mere vehicle for conveying thought but is a part of it—its very flesh and blood; and it should be passionate not in any sense of wildness or waywardness but simply because [it] can saturate words with all the meaning of its own intenser mood.

Poetry for Lowell was not quite the "pure" thing to which Poe gave his allegiance. Many references scattered through his poems show what he conceived the poet's function to be. His eye is clearer than other men's. He can heal desolate hearts and cause men to hear the songs of the angels and catch golden glimpses of a more glorious future to be. In "The Shepherd of

King Admetus" he serves God's Kingdom on earth even when he appears to be doing nothing. In "An Incident in a Railroad Car" he finds his message in the common heart of humanity, though its ultimate source is God.[9] Humor in poetry, "which consists in a perception of the invincible contradiction between the Imagination and the understanding, between soul and sense," is the result of qualifying Imagination "by the understanding instead of the sense of Beauty." Fancy, which is inferior to the Imagination, combines with sentiment to produce poetry or with experience to produce wit.

Theoretically Lowell realized that a very good case might be made for the thesis that a poet should concern himself only with beauty, but in times like those in which he lived, he believed that in actual practice the poet must also be "a Schoolmaster," a "John the Baptist, a voice crying in the wilderness, preparing for the simply Beautiful, for Art in its highest sense, a wider and more universal reception in a future age." After he himself had served his apprenticeship at making bricks without straw, he wrote Mrs. Horace Mann, he hoped also "to be led to the promised land of Song, and to have my Sinais and my waters from the rock by the way." This was the more important because in the evolution—or devolution—of society, the poet, though not claiming "immediate inspiration," had so largely taken the place of the prophet, "by force of seeing the heart of those mysteries whose shell only is visible to others." [10] The poet, therefore, had become forerunner and prophet "of changes in the moral world." To behold only the "body" of his thought and its "outward grace" was to miss half. Even his lightest fantasies had two meanings—"one of the flesh and of the spirit one." In Lowell's poem about him, Columbus "believed" the poets and thought they spoke for God. Moreover prophetism was one with humanitarianism. "I have made it *radical*," Lowell writes Charles Briggs of "Prometheus," "and I believe that no poet in this age can write much that is good unless he give himself up to this tendency." In *Conversations* he makes Philip say, "You forget that I believe the poetical sentiment and what we call the sentiment of natural religion to be identical. Both of them are life-members of the New England Anti-Slavery Society." He might not have put it quite that way in later years, but his essential point of view never substantially changed.

Lowell judged writers both absolutely, by reference to his own formulated and unchanging standards of what constituted excellence in literature, and relatively, considering the writer's position in the literary history of his country and the special conditions affecting the creation of literature in his generation. Neglect the second criterion, and you will not understand the factors which conditioned his talent nor judge him fairly, but if you neglect the first, you will find it impossible to choose between, say, Milton and Samuel Butler, since both were highly representative figures. A critic must know what he believes and bring his writers to the bar of his own standards, but if he is too rigid and inflexible about this, he will cut himself off from the relish and fair evaluation of many kinds of excellence.

Lowell also insisted that writers must be accepted for what they are. "Because continuity is a merit in some kinds of writing, shall we refuse ourselves to the authentic charm of Montaigne's want of it?" Surely this would be a "schoolboy blunder," for "there never has been a great work of art which did not in some particular transcend the old rules and establish new ones of its own."

A true scholar should be able to value Wordsworth for his depth of sympathy with nature, without therefore losing all power to enjoy the sparkling shallowness of Pope; he should be able to feel the beauty of Herbert's puritanism, the naked picturesqueness of his style, and yet not refuse to be delighted with the sensuous paganism of Herrick.

He adds that " 'In my father's house are many mansions' conveys a lesson of criticism no less than of charity." Even form, which might almost be said to *make* literature, is not absolutely indispensable, for "there have been men of genius, like Emerson, richly seminative for other minds; like Browning, full of wholesome ferment for other minds, though wholly destitute of any proper sense of form."

With such an emphasis as this, the richly sympathetic Lowell inevitably made criticism in large measure a matter of appreciation; as he saw it, the critic's highest function was to think the poet's thoughts after him and not merely to point out where he had failed to express them adequately. Philip of the *Conversations* admitted that "for whatever I love, my delight mounts to an extravagance. There are verses which I cannot read without tears of exultation, which to others are merely indifferent," and he doubted that any really convincing reason for such a passion could be communicated to a mind not already predisposed to share it. Lowell himself disliked disenchantment as a critical function. The critic must not "make war on men's little loves and faiths, but endeavor to show how far, and in what sense, they are justifiable. When disenchantment was necessary, it must always be performed "with a kindly tenderness," for "life is too sad and too serious for one to wish to undeceive those who are so lucky as to be happy by mistake."

He also insisted that there was room in the world for much besides great art.

We cannot breathe the thin air of that Pepysian self-denial, that Himalayan selectness, which, content with one bookcase, would have no tomes in it but *porphyrogeniti,* books of the bluest blood, making room for choicer newcomers by a continuous ostracism to the garret of present incumbents.

If man cannot live by bread alone, he cannot live by spices and stimulants alone either, nor yet by nectar and ambrosia. He must not be told that it is wrong to enjoy Gray or Cowper or Scott because they are not Wordsworth or Shelley. A definition of poetry too narrow to embrace Horace and Crabbe "and whoever else prefers the familiar scenery of life and the habitual to the exceptional motives of happiness and misery would not do." There is a great deal in literature which must be accepted as Mercutio accepted his death-wound: "No, 'tis not so deep as a well, nor so wide as a church-door; but 'tis enough, 'twill serve."

There is far more generous and liberal humanism in these pronouncements that can be found in the official "line" followed by any "school" of criticism nowadays, or, for that matter, illustrated in the practices of many art museums. Yet they have often been attacked as illustrating Lowell's vagueness and uncertainty, his tendency to find his standards in the subject of his essay rather than bringing them to it. This is not altogether unjust. Lowell understood as Keats did—and Keats helped him to learn it—that the poet can *become* that of which he writes, and there are even times when he seems disposed to extend this privilege to the critic. It is hardly unfair to say that he wrote of the Puritans in "New England Two Centuries Ago" not as an historian but as an apologist, and the very title of "A Good Word for Winter" is characteristic of both his method and his type of mind. His criteria for choosing "The Five Indispensable Authors" [11] have some arbitrariness and inconsistency about them, and he is quite capable of today hitting over-subtlety in criticism and the searching out of hidden motives, so that the critic may be glorified by demonstrating that he has been able to perceive something nobody else has ever seen,[12] yet tomorrow he might tolerate those who read their own ideas (if one can call them that) into a book instead of getting the author's out of it, and of thus (to take an extreme example), encouraging the lunatics who find Napoleon, the Kaiser, or Mussolini, or whoever hap-

pens to be the current villain of the moment, in the Book of
Daniel and The Revelation of St. John.[13] When he writes about
Spenser he praises him for his stylistic lavishness ("in poetry
enough is not only not so good as a feast, but is a beggarly
parsimony"), but it never occurs to him that, when he writes of
Dante, he must not feel quite free to praise him for having discovered "the secret of that magical word too few, which not
only distinguishes his verse from all other, but so strikingly from
his own prose."

It would be stupid not to perceive these things, but it is even
more stupid to make more of them that they deserve. Lowell has
a way of being right in both places, as Shakespeare was right
when he ran contradictory time-schemes through *Othello* and
The Merchant of Venice, for this is a much less logical world—
the humanist's world at any rate—than the partisans of most
critical systems are willing to allow. As a matter of fact, Lowell
is much more likely to get into trouble when he does *not* take
his tone from his subject, for then he can be as imperceptive as
he was about Thoreau or as cruel as he was when flogging a
dead horse in his essay on Percival. He applied both historical
knowledge and a formulated set of standards to his subjects;
only a fool could call him an impressionist. But he would be a
considerably bigger fool who should leave his readers with the
impression that Lowell's being an impressionist would have left
his critical writings worthless. For until criticism comes to be
written by machines (and a number of experiments seem to be
under way in this area), the impressionistic element must remain
the life-giving element in the work of any critic, no matter what
he may be called. Of course he must have standards; otherwise
he will have no frame of reference, and his sun may well rise in
the west and set in the north. But unless he manages, even within
the bounds of his "system," to express something which is himself and no other human being, how on earth can he expect us

to continue to read him instead of turning for our fodder to newer and better machines?

III

Much too much has been made of Lowell's alleged dislike of realism in literature. Insofar as this existed, it was based upon sound aesthetic, as well as moral, grounds; he did not believe that the literal reproduction of nature or of fact was possible in a work of art, and he disliked lingering upon physical detail for its own sake as a distraction from the theme under consideration and, ultimately, a confession of unreality.[14] Few of us today could be expected to agree with his classification of Trollope's novels, along with the sculpture of John Rogers, as matter-of-fact rather than real, but we ought not to forget his advice to Harriet Beecher Stowe to "stick to Nature and avoid what people commonly call the ideal," his encouragement, as editor of the *Atlantic*, of a whole host of local color writers who did just this, or the admiration which such writers as Edward Eggleston and Joel Chandler Harris felt for him.

Higginson notes that in Lowell's youth Cambridge families employed hired men from the country, to whom the boys liked to talk. Their conversation was "usually harmless, often profitable, sometimes racy; and every trait of Hosea, or even of Bidofredum Sawin could be matched in them." Lowell hated allegory and literary metaphysics, disliked the melodramatic, overblown, dishonestly glorified heroes and heroines of Bulwer and Disraeli, and tried to consider chivalric graces in the metrical romances from the lamb's point of view. He forgave *Gammer Gurton's Needle* its coarseness and earthiness because the author was "at least a man among men, and not a humbug among humbugs." The hackneyed, "refined," conventionalized poetic diction of poets like Thomas Young he found quite destitute of force and vitality, but Chaucer's Pegasus "ambles along, preferring the sunny vales to the thunder-daunting cliffs," and Shakespeare uses a "low" word whenever he needs it. "His pen ennobled them all, and we feel as if they had been knighted for good service in the field."

What Lowell rejected, in other words, was that same surface realism to which, in their own way, expressionists and other aesthetic revolutionaries were later to take exception. He was sure that "all great poetry must smack of the soil, for it must be rooted in it, must suck life and substance from it." But it must grow out of, not in, the soil, like a pine rather than a potato. Otherwise, it will lack idealism (which is a moral objection), but it will also be parochial (which is an aesthetic objection). Truth to nature is not truth to fact, and "the facts of life" must be distinguished from "the accidental and transitory phenomena of life." Only "art's absolution" can "purge" the "polluting" stain of life and grasp "ideal grace." When Lowell compares the reading of cheap fiction to opium eating, or permits one of the speakers in *Conversations* to declare that "nothing that God has not thought it beneath him to make" can be considered unworthy of a writer's attention, he is using almost exactly the same language that William Dean Howells was to use. Lowell found the kind of realism he believed in in Howells,[15] but not only there. He found it also in James, Fredrika Bremer, Hawthorne, Sylvester Judd, even J. G. Holland, but for his supreme examples of it, he, not unsurprisingly, went to Shakespeare and Cervantes:

Give me the writers who take me for a while out of myself and . . . away from my neighbors! I do not ask that characters should be real; I need but go into the street to find such abundance. I ask only that they should be possible, that they should be typical, because these I find in myself, and with these I can sympathize. Hector and Achilles, Clytemnestra and Antigone, Roland and Oliver, Macbeth and Lear, move about, if not in worlds not realized, at least in worlds not realized to any eye but that of the imagination. . . . Don Quixote and his Squire are inhabitants of this world, in spite of the prosaic and often vulgar stage on which their tragi-comedy is acted, because they are symbolical, because they represent the two great factors of human character and springs of human action—the Imagination and the Understanding.

The writer must use the materials which lie ready to his hand, but he must treat them so as to bring out their universal qualities. "The true ideal is not opposed to the real, nor is it any artificial heightening thereof, but lies in it, and blessed are the eyes that find it!" Not "something out of and beyond Nature," it is rather "Nature as seen through the eye of the Artist," but its visibility depends upon the presence of that eye.

IV

Though Lowell may sometimes have indulged in direct moralizing in literature, he did not approve of it, any more than Howells did. Indeed he praised Howells's *Hazard of New Fortunes* precisely because Howells had avoided it. He urged Mrs. Stowe to deal with theology in her New England fictions only where it came naturally to the surface in the life she described, and he warned himself that, having grown up in a New England that was "all meeting-house," he would never be a real poet until he got out of the pulpit.

The relationship between the quality of a work of art and the character of the man that produced it gave him considerable difficulty. He was unwilling to claim any immunities for poets, and he found it hard to believe that a man could create anything greater than his own soul. But he knew too that aesthetic creativity was more complicated than human logic, perhaps even more complicated than man's moral codes. So he calls Rousseau "a quack of genius" and declares that "whatever he was or did, somehow or other God let him be worthy to write *this*, and that is enough for us." He is not entirely consistent in these matters; he shows Rousseau much more charity than is accorded either Petrarch or Victor Hugo. He believed that if the moral sense predominated in a man over the aesthetic, he became a reformer or a fanatic rather than an artist, and his imagination expressed itself in his life (Bunyan would never have written *The Pilgrim's Progress* without being shut up in jail and cut off from his usual activities). Yet, even though it was the writer's function to stimulate thinking in his readers rather than to do their thinking for them, creativity itself withered without faith, moral and aesthetic faults and virtues were much more closely associated than most people realized, and if an ideal world did not exist, then all the greater was the need that the poet should create one. Nevertheless, beauty involves and embraces its moral; it does not need to be "stuck on," and "poetry is a criticism of life only in the sense that it furnishes us with the standard of a more ideal felicity, of calmer Beauty." "No verse, the chief end of which is not the representation of the beautiful, and whose moral is not included in that, can be called poetry in the true sense of the word."

At times, in fact, Lowell seems willing to accept only the Shakespearean type of imagination, which he makes almost mediumistic. Shakespeare is only a voice, and "we seek in vain in his plays for any traces of his personal character or history." He is not expressing himself but rather giving voice "to the myriad forms of nature, which, wanting him, were dumb."

In proportion as the poetical sense is abundant in a man or in other words in proportion as it is the law of his nature to surrender himself to the possession of his sensuous impressions—will he be without what we call *character*. The more poet, the less character. I cannot find that Shakespeare had any at all.[16]

At least, the artist must have the privilege of treating both good and evil—

> Yet let us think, that, as there's naught above
>   The all-embracing atmosphere of Art,
> So also there is naught that falls below
> Her generous reach, though grimed with guilt and woe—[17]

and sometimes, again with such dazzling talents as Shakespeare's, the two may almost be said, aesthetically speaking, to have coalesced:

Only Shakespeare had that true sense of humor which, like the universal solvent sought by the alchemists, so fuses together all the elements of a character (as in Falstaff), that any question of good or evil, of dignified or ridiculous, is silenced by the apprehension of its thorough humanity.

V

I know of no other writer of comparable fame who is quite so modest about his achievements as Lowell. He claimed that he always lost interest in a book as soon as it was published. When his 1848 collection appeared, he forgot to possess himself of a copy of it, and in 1885 he told Curtis Guild he could not answer any questions concerning the publishers of his early books as he had no copies on hand. The modest dedication of *Conversations* to his father[18] is charming, but he is nearly as diffident about *My Study Windows* many years later.[19]

He had a worse opinion of himself than of most authors, considering himself a third-rater compared with the masters. He "hated" his books and would rather be valued for his personal qualities than for them,[20] yet he declared inconsistently that the best of himself went into his books. He often lamented that he had done so little and wasted so much, and once, when a young

Englishman was gauche enough to tell him that he had read none of his writings, he replied that he did not regard them as necessary to a liberal education.[21] He did not think he would have cared much for his poems if they had been written by somebody else, and he told Fields he could be mistaken for a lion only by persons not well acquainted with that animal. Making his selections for *Under the Willows* he thought what he had to choose from on a level with ordinary newspaper verse. After expression for expression's sake had lost its appeal for him, he had more faith in his insight than his expression. Once he said he thought he had "too many thoughts and too little thought." In later years, when authors' readings came into vogue, his natural dislike of public speaking was reinforced by the fact that he could never find a poem he thought worth reading.

But why, then, did he write at all? Obviously, because he had to and wanted to. In the beginning he desired fame ("it's *in* me and it shall come out!")—

> I too am a Maker and Poet;
> Through my whole soul I feel it and know it!
> My veins are fired with ecstasy!
>   All-mother Earth
>   Did ne'er give birth
> To one who shall be matched with me;
> The lustre of my coronal
> Shall cast a dimness over all.

But even then the reaction was swift:

> Alas! alas! what have I spoken?
> My strong, my eagle wings are broken,
> And back again to earth I fall! [22]

Perhaps he continued to desire fame, but the number of now meaningless names in Allibone's *Dictionary of Authors* reminded him how heavy the odds were against any particular man's being remembered. "Formerly, a man who wished to withdraw himself from the notice of the world retired into a convent. The simpler modern method is, to publish a volume of poems." And when Beatrice Müller asked him for an autograph, he wrote in her album—

> O'er the wet sands an insect crept
> Ages ere man on earth was known—
> And patient Time, while Nature slept,
> The slender tracing turned to stone.
> 'Twas the first autograph: and ours?
> Prithee, how much of prose or song,
> In league with the Creative powers,
> Shall 'scape Oblivion's broom so long? [23]

By this time, fame had become less a motive than the mere desire to do good work, but alas! this was the most difficult thing of all. How close exaltation lay to discouragement in his mind may be gauged by what he wrote Sydney Gay about the *Fable*. In a single paragraph he declared both that "there are not above half a dozen persons who know how good it is" and that "it seems bald and poor enough now, the Lord knows."

The thing to do, he knew, was to strive for a sane, balanced, and objective view of one's own work and one's relationship to it, avoiding the melodramatism of both self-vaunting and self-abasement. You could value your natural gifts even while you disparaged your performance, knowing that you were "better at a *spurt* than a steady pull," and that you had fought as good a fight as many who had claimed more. You could know that you had achieved a great strain now and then, that you were "the first poet who has endeavored to express the American Idea," and that sooner or later this must be recognized, even though you might have to die first. You could be sure that *Biglow* II was better than *Biglow* I, though it lacked something of the verve of its predecessor, because it was less the work of an improviser and more that of an artist, and when you sent "Launfal" to Briggs, you could rather "guess" it was good, though you still planned to write something "gooder and newer." At times you could even stubbornly continue to believe in work of such inferior quality as "Our Own." You could, on occasion, deny yourself genius, yet somehow manage to make a merit of the lack. ("A genius has the gift of falling in love with the side-face of truth, going mad for it, sacrificing all for it. But I must see the full face, and then the two sides have such different expressions that I begin to doubt which is the sincere and cannot surrender myself.") In later years, Lowell was capable, in the course of a single letter of giving himself a vote of no confidence as a poet and at the same time half resolving to relinquish all his other activities on the ground that this might help him to become a better poet. But even when he was an old man, he could keep his hopes pinned to the future, always being conscious of greater power than he had yet shown.

Lowell professed to believe that "criticism can at best teach writers without genius what is to be avoided or imitated." Moreover, genius or not, "one can't do his best for a theater that has more than one person in it, and that one himself." Claiming "a self-sustaining nature," he did not need encouragement from others. "I am *teres atque rotundus*, a microcosm in myself, my own author, public, critic, and posterity, and care for no other." Praise might make him doubt himself, but in the long run praise and blame were equally immaterial, since no matter what critics said, a writer of quality must ultimately find his proper place.

Even if you are prepared to grant these premises, however, they will not get you far, for the question still remains: When you *cannot* secure your own approval, what do you do then? And this, as we have seen, was Lowell's condition an uncomfort-

ably large number of times. But he himself made the perfect
comment on his own declaration of independence when he
wrote, "I never saw a man who did not think himself indifferent
to praise, nor one who did not like it."

Actually, his own self-doubts made him more dependent upon
the praise of others than he would otherwise have been. Howells
sensed that any criticism hurt him, especially from those whose
opinions he valued, though he never knew him to alter anything
he had written merely because of disapproval expressed, and
Mrs. Fields records several instances of his sensitiveness. When
Emerson once remarked that his humorous poetry was best, he
muttered "The Washers of the Shroud" and walked away.

When E. P. Whipple, editing the Boston *Notion*, praised him
in 1841, Lowell wrote him warmly, not even knowing his name:

It was very grateful to me as I took up your paper in a public room,
where there was but one face among many that I knew, and saw
some kind words about myself, to think that, perchance, the writer
was now in the room and that among these strangers I had yet a
friend.[24]

The friendship which developed between Lowell and Mrs. S. B.
Herrick of Baltimore grew out of a "fan letter" she had written
him, and he told Charles Eliot Norton that "what I have done
has been due to your partiality more than anything else, for you
have given me a kind of faith in it." Sometimes he was even
willing to reconsider the claims of a poem he had disparaged
because somebody else had liked it. "I need every sort of petting
on the back," he told Mrs. Wirt Dexter, "for I myself am never
pleased with what I do."

This much remained, however, of his professed indifference to
criticism—that he would never argue about anything that mat-
tered to him or about which he had made up his mind. Nothing,
I am sure, could have bored him more than what are now called

"panel discussions." "I seldom care to discuss anything." He was "contemptuously indifferent about arguing matters that had once become convictions." "A man who is in the right can never reason. He can only affirm." "It fags me to deal with particulars." And again:

I don't very often look into my books but when I do I seem to find a certain vivacity and suggestiveness that are worth something. My impatience of mind is my bane as a critical essayist. I expect everybody to understand *à demi mot*. Perhaps an enemy would call it indolence and perhaps he would be right.

Different as he was from Emerson in many respects, Lowell resembled him in that both possessed essentially deductive minds. They *perceived* truth, made a priori assumptions, and, like the prophets of Israel, *proclaimed* the will of the Lord. A more prosaic or inductive type of mind feels this tendency as working for weakness in his critical essays, and Lowell himself was very well aware of this reaction.[25] But he knew too that both he and Emerson were essentially poets, almost as much so when they wrote prose as when they were writing verse. "What a true poet says always *proves itself* to our minds, and we cannot dodge it or get away from it."

VI

Obviously all this must be taken into account and allowed for by anyone who would understand the poet Lowell. But though Lowell may have been essentially a poet, he was not all poet. He was a man, with a man's emotional needs and hungers. He lived in a community and in the larger community which is the world, coming in contact with his fellows in many different ways, and affecting and being affected by them even when there were no personal ties. Finally, he was a human soul, living, as we all do, under the necessity of achieving, or failing to achieve, harmony with the universe itself. All these aspects of this experience must be explored before we can take our leave of him, and these quests will fill up the rest of this book.

CHAPTER FIVE

LOWELL THE LOVER

Character is continuous, it is cumulative, whether for good or ill; the general tenor of the life is a logical sequence from it, and a man can always explain himself to himself, if not to others, as a coherent whole, because he always knows, or thinks he knows, the value of x in the personal equation. . . . It is with the means of finding out this unknown quantity—in other words, of penetrating to the man's motives or his understanding of them—that the biographer undertakes to supply us. . . .

JRL, 1876

I

A critic who wished to write Lowell down a prude would have no difficulty finding material to support the charge. He objects to Wordsworth's finding the first verse of Keats's "Ode on a Grecian Urn" indecent, but he nearly equals him when he finds "fleshliness" in some early lines of Wordsworth's own.[1] He found "something very like obscenity" in what Dryden gave Eve to say in *The State of Innocence*, and apparently Milton himself shocked him in the divorce pamphlets. He recommended *Eugénie Grandet* to Lady Camilla Gurdon as a book which would give her some idea of Balzac's power without shocking her,[2] but he thought Swinburne and Zola quite beyond the pale. He sometimes objected to particular passages even in writers whom he admired, and he told Mary Anderson that so long as Sarah Bernhardt appeared in such plays as *La Tosca*, he would

127

not go to see her, since he did not care to have his mind dragged through the gutter.[3]

Lowell carefully explains his standards in these matters in a letter to an 1874 correspondent:

As for the aphrodisiac or cantharides style of verses, I do not believe that the sexual impulses need any spurring, nor, if they did, that the rowel would be forged of that most precious metal of poesy whereof the Shield of Achilles or the Grecian Urn could be hammered. The line between the sensuous and the sensual is that between sentiment and sentimentalism, between passion and brutish impulse, between love and appetite, between Vittoria Colonna and Madame Bovary. Cleopatra, one may suspect, was much rather a harlot of the brain (that is, from political motives) than of the senses, though Shakespeare, and even Dryden, have idealized her in the only possible way by throwing around her the lurid light of a sublime passion, and even then there is the inevitable aspic at the end of the rose-strewn path of dalliance. To show her disidealized into a mere lustful animal, is to degrade her to a Catherine II., and thrust her beyond the pale of poesy. Shelley almost alone (take his "Stanzas to an Indian Air," for example) has trodden with an unfaltering foot the scimitar-edged bridge which leads from physical sensation to the heaven of song. No, I certainly do *not* believe in the value of any literature that renders the relation between the sexes any more ticklish than nature has already made it, or which paints self-indulgence as nobler than self-restraint. That is to unsettle the only moral centre of gravity we have.

This does not sound either Miss Nancyish or holier-than-thou. It is the utterance of a man who wishes to lead a decent life but who recognizes his weaknesses and does not intend to use his books as panders. And this, I think, is just what anybody who knows Lowell would expect from him. When it was remarked concerning Hazlitt that it was hard to believe a man of such attainments could behave as he speaks of having behaved in *Liber Amoris,* Lowell spoke frankly of his own "animal passions" and declared that "there is no telling what any one of us may yet become through a woman." In one of his lectures he said, "I think that every man is conscious at times that it is only his borders, his seaboard, that is civilized and subdued. Behind that narrow strip stretches the untamed domain, shaggy, unexplored, and the natural instincts."

The truth of the matter is that in sexual matters Lowell was less Puritan than Platonist, taking Puritan in the modern cant sense, that is, and forgetting for the moment that the Puritan moralists were themselves profoundly anti-ascetic.[4] In the autobiography he contributed to the Harvard 1838 Class Book, Lowell disdained greed for wealth but desired

> a wife o' my ain
> There, thanks to naebody
> I'll gie cuckold to nane
> I'll take cuckold frae naebody!

In literature, in art, and in life, he tried to distinguish between sensuous and sensual, finding his ideal in Spenser[5] and the best of the Greeks—"a kind of rosy nakedness of . . . freedom which yet has no touch of immodesty in it."

To be a sensualist in a certain kind and to a certain degree is the mark of a pure and youthful heart. It shows that our animal nature is fresh and incorrupt. . . . To a soul which is king of itself and not a prisoner in its delicate palace, all things beautiful minister not *to* sense, but *through* it. Our bodies were given us only to make our souls invisible, it is only our own sin which makes them a cloud rendering their heavenly inmate *in*visible.

He believed that the kind of false delicacy which makes ladies and gentlemen ashamed to remember that they were ever suckled at their mothers' breasts is as much a handicap in the way of achieving this ideal as libertinism itself, and that God did not give us our "fine senses as so many posterns to the heart for the Devil to enter at."

In *Conversations* Philip praises the beauty of the human body. In 1856, when W. W. Story was considering the Pied Piper as a subject, Lowell wrote him that "you will be able to have the nakedness and drapery too—that is the half and halfness which suits us." But there was no half and halfness about William Page's Venus, which had been turned down by the Paris Exhibition, but which Lowell helped buy for the Boston Athenaeum in 1856: "But think of sending such a stark nakedness to proper Boston! We have some doubts the Athenaeum may decline it." [6]

Good examples of Lowell's use of the "sensuous" in poetry will be found in "A Mystical Ballad"—

> Unbound, her heavy golden hair
> Ripples across her bosom bare,
> Which gleamed with thrilling snowy white;
> Far through the magical moonlight;

in "Rhoecus"—

> All naked like a goddess stood she there,
> And like a goddess all too beautiful
> To feel the guilt-born earthliness of shame;

and in "The Parting of the Ways"—

> Then glowed to me a maiden from the left,
> With bosom half disclosed, and naked arms
> More white and undulant than necks of swans.

Occasionally he uses sexual imagery even when discussing subjects that have nothing to do with sex.[7] And though he knew that "the intellect is easily bribed to play the bawd to the passions," his judgment of literature was not wholly prudish.

He found the *Decameron* full of charm, humor, "singular sweetness, ease, and grace," with "no great mischief" in its "dirt," and he once inspired Longfellow to call him a "New Adam" by finding Donne's "Going to Bed" a pure poem because the writer was pure. Of *Aucassin and Nicolette* he once wrote:

> Here lips their roses keep and locks their gold;
> Here Love in pristine innocency bold
> Speaks what our grosser conscience makes a crime.[8]

And I confess I am surprised to find him summing up the faults and virtues of Samuel Pepys with no mention of his wenching.

Despite all his idealization of women, Lowell sympathized with wayward girls, as such poems as "The Forlorn," "A Legend of Brittany," and "The Ghost-Seer" show, as well as the reference to "vice's nursling adrift on Broadway" in *A Fable for Critics*. "It has been remarked," he says, "that *demireps* are always loudest in expressing their indignation, and always readiest to cast the first stone at any sister detected in frailty." Surely he was right, and if rakes do not express indignation, they do characteristically feel contempt. Lowell was very charitable too in his judgment of William Page's wife, Sarah.[9]

His own reverence for women was steady and constant.

> Thou art a woman, and therein thou art
> Fit theme for poet's songful reverence.

Lowell thought nature made Hawthorne a perfect man by filling out her model "from some finer-grained stuff for a woman prepared." He criticized Beaumont and Fletcher when they slandered women, and he refused to excuse Pope's characters of women even upon the hypothesis that women in his time were as bad as they could be, for "if God made poets for anything, it was to keep alive the traditions of the pure, the holy, and the beautiful." The origin of love is divine; it elevates everything that is human; it is humble, unmindful of faults, and can dispense with beauty. The sight of lovers restores Arcadia even to those who have lost it.

Since Lowell was not a writer of fiction, it did not fall to him, as a writer, to create many female characters. The "Widder Shennon" in *The Biglow Papers* is a wealthy termagant, but the animus in this portrait is directed against the South, not against women. Theoretically he was willing to grant the complexity of women, but in actual practice he seems to have accepted many simplified stereotyped notions regarding them. They shared the spiritual quality of children. It was impossible to argue with them. They were not logical and therefore could not be Calvinists. They understood human nature in general much less than men did, but they had a much firmer grasp upon such individual specimens of it as came their way. He did not believe that they saw men clearly, but he considered it fortunate for men that this was the case, as it gave women a chance to fall in love with what they imagined men to be. "When I consider the average dullness of our own sex, I am delighted with that economy of nature which makes it perennially interesting to the other." As for the men, they were so self-denying that they could always bear "to let a dozen women be sacrificed to them."

In his reactionary Class Poem, Lowell was against the emancipation of women and all other liberal causes; later he changed his mind about many of these things. Once he goes so far as to plump for Bloomers! In *Conversations* John argues that the platform should be opened to women on the ground that speakers have the same right to appear there as singers, but his quotation from Coleridge is vulgar and insulting to singers:

> Heaves the proud harlot her distended breast
> In intricacies of laborious song.

Though Lowell once told Norton his opposition to woman suffrage was only a sentiment, he admitted being "joined to my idols" as late as 1867;[10] he even gagged a little over Higginson's article, "Ought Women to Learn the Alphabet?" Once he felt that "the number of women in the Slave States is an encourage-ment . . . to hope for Antislavery"; later he was not so sure enfranchised woman could be counted upon to be on the right side. An unfinished essay on "Men and Women"[11] opens with an indictment of man's brutality in making woman a plaything, but goes on to affirm the ineradicable differences between the sexes:

It may fairly be questioned whether women in their corporate capacity will be very effective peacemakers (as has lately been assumed) so long as individual women continue to rate personal courage so highly as they do in their estimate of men. The fear of women has made many an unwilling soldier, and the desire to satisfy this craving of hers has been the mother of many a daring feat.

II

Though Howells thought Lowell "diffident" with women, he himself tells us that he was desperately in love before he was ten and frequently thereafter. The sonnet to "my ever-lightsome, ever-laughing Rose" in *A Year's Life* records that

> Thy name reminds me of old romping days,
> Of kisses stolen in dark passage ways,
> Or in the parlour, if the mother-nose
> Gave sign of drowsy watch.

But whether this was memory or imagination, who can say?

When Lowell was rusticated to Concord in 1838, Frost and his wife apparently trusted him enough to leave him alone in the house with "the buxom serving wench" while they went to

Boston. "I hope she'll not be frightened in the night and come
to me for protection—'twould be an alarming case truly and one
that would require deliberation." But the buxom one seems to
have attracted him less than Mrs. Frost herself, whom he greatly
admired, though apparently most of all for her kindness toward
and diligence in taking care of him. "If she were not married
and not old enough to be my mother—no, my eldest sister—I'd
marry her myself—as a reward for so much virtue." But he was
more seriously attracted in Concord to Caroline Brooks, whom
he thought he could have fallen in love with if she had not been
engaged to E. R. Hoar.[12] "I don't know what to do with Miss B.
She runs in my head more than she has any right to." Next
spring, at an art exhibition, he saw a Jewish-looking girl who
drove him "almost crazy with delight" and struck him as "the
most beautiful creature I ever set these eyes upon." He disclaims
falling in love with her in precisely the manner Keats first denied
he was in love with Fanny Brawne, but he admits that "she gave
me more poetry than everything I have seen or thought this
year."

Actually it seems odd that Lowell should have had eyes for
either Caroline Brooks or the beautiful unknown Jewess if he
was at this time so much enthralled by Hannah Jackson as we
have every reason to suppose him to have been. She was the
sister of his brother Charles's wife, he met her in the summer of
1837, and their relations were broken off, apparently upon her
insistence, in the spring of 1839. This was Lowell's only serious
affair of the heart before Maria White, and it was a bitter experience altogether. Though he was afterwards fond of distinguish-
ing in kind between what he had felt for Hannah and what he
afterwards felt for Maria, there is no reason to suppose that the
girl herself was in any way unworthy. "I have been climbing
down these three years after the little Sodom fruit of love that
dangled on the tree above me," he wrote Loring in June 1839,

"and if I have not bitten and found the bitter ashes at the core, it was because the limb broke and got a fall ere I could reach the fruit." His arithmetic was a little shaky here, but he was right about missing the fruit. "Sodom" we may forget, and the "lurid and sulphurous glow" and the "fierce" and "savage" love he speaks of elsewhere, and the poem of 1842 in which

> A cold snake gnaws my heart
> And crushes round my brain,[13]

which seems pretty late to refer to Hannah. When he read Goethe's correspondence with Bettina Brentano in 1840, Lowell was greatly taken with "the most loving heart that ever came directly from God and *forgot not whence it came*" but lamented that such devotion should have been wasted on "the cold, hard Goethe."

I wanted such a soul for myself. M.W.'s is nearer to it than any I have ever seen. But I should have seen her three years ago. If that other love could raise such a tempest in my soul as to fling up the foul and slimy weeds from the bottom and make it for so long sluggish and muddy—a disappointment from her would I think have broken my heart.

Perhaps he himself had loved unworthily. Perhaps the only difficulty was that he and Hannah never came to see things eye to eye. The one word we have from her concerning her lover seems to indicate a certain disapproval or mistrust of him.[14]

Lowell met Maria White late in 1839 through her brother William, who was one of his Harvard classmates. She had been a pupil at the Ursuline convent in Charlestown when it was burned by a mob, and she was a member of Margaret Fuller's first class at Elizabeth Peabody's room in West Street. A descendant of Anne Hutchinson, she might be said to have come

by her "advanced" ideas honestly. She was a Unitarian, and she
admired Emerson extravagantly. She had a delicate face with
enormous soulful eyes, and Lowell seems first to have been
attracted by her knowledge of poetry, though he somewhat
superciliously notes that she was more familiar with modern
poets "than with the pure wellsprings of English poetry." In the
circle in which she moved she was noted for her recitation of
ballads. Naturally she encouraged her lover in his literary ambitions, and she had a part in persuading John Owen to publish
the *Conversations*. After they became engaged, she and Lowell
were regarded as "King" and "Queen" of "The Band." Higginson says, somewhat pretentiously, that they were "a modernized
Petrarch and Laura, or even Dante and Beatrice." We are also
told that their love letters were passed about and read, which
does not sound much like reserved New England. But though
Lowell was immediately attracted (Maria was "a glorious girl,"
a "pure woman" of "Heavenly influence," and "the greatest
woman I ever saw"), he was comparatively slow to give himself
up to the attraction. The burned child dreads the fire, and,
strange as it seems, there was apparently some lingering vestige
of loyalty to Hannah Jackson. Once, even before the engagement, he had a strange and prescient dream of loving Maria and
losing her "down the happy road." Greenslet says they became
engaged in August 1840, but on the last day of that month,
Lowell was still writing Loring that if he had known Maria
three years ago, things might have been different. He added that
he "would not give up the bitter knowledge I gained last summer for much—very much." Once the engagement had been
achieved, his poverty stood in their way, and they were not
married (even then, apparently, quite without her wealthy
father's enthusiasm), until December 26, 1844.

Having won her, he knew "the perfect joy of loving and being loved." Her "blessed eyes" circled and fenced him in from

every ill; he had "passed thro' the furnace seven times heated" and become a man. Apparently he never ceased to feel this sacred, purifying quality in her. When, in his Lowell lecture on the metrical romances, he wished to refer to Joan of Arc as the flower of chivalry, he quoted two verses from Maria's poem about the Maid, though without identifying it.

Love changed the whole world for him—and, we may assume, for her, though she had no need of redemption, being, apparently, one of those fortunate people who somehow escape the primal curse and are born "saved." It was entirely suitable that she should experience no pain when her first child was born. Theirs was a transcendental kind of love.

If we love one only [wrote Lowell] we may be sure that our love is imperfect. The very overflowings of the heaping cup of the heart, when we love one truly, demand other objects besides that which so luminously enfloods the heart.

Even the physical side was glorified by this idealism:

Men make prostitutes of their wives and then pass laws for the suppression of licentiousness—the seeds of which they have sown in their children. Though Maria bears such a blessed burthen close under her dear heart there, yet I love to call her (as she is) a virgin still. . . . If men were chaste toward their wives they would never feel a movement of unchastity toward other women. I thank God that I never go to our bed with less reverence or less joy than to our bridal bed and I believe it will be so to the end of my days. When men have besmeared their wives all over with the slime of their lust, what wonder if they appear unsightly or undesirable? [15]

Aside from her delicate health, however, Maria was in no sense too fragile for this life; neither are we to assume that she and her husband lived in a child's story book world without ever needing to assert themselves against it, or even against each other. We have already seen that she had "views" and took stands on the issues of the time. Many of Lowell's early poems to her combine his recognition of her idealism with his appreciation of her practical capacity. When a poem fell below what she considered his standard, she did not hesitate to tell him so, and she recognized that he could fail in more personal aspects too, as in placing too much relative emphasis upon self-culture. When, in 1853, Mabel developed notions about various parts of her body being incapacitated, Maria told her husband: "Remember, darling, it comes from *thy* side of the house. Mr. John Lowell fancied himself dead once. I know of no such fancies in *our* family." A husband brooded over with the horror of his mother's and sister's derangement can hardly have enjoyed hearing this. Perhaps this was what he was thinking of when he remarked that there was "no such conductor of feminine electricity as a husband," and that the female mind contained two quarters "in which thunder and lightning are brewed. The Western of positive storm and the Southern of meekness." In her poem, "The Slave-Mother," Maria faced miscegenation and all the other problems involved in slavery as bravely as Harriet Beecher Stowe did. Foster Damon called "Africa" the only abolitionist poem "which rises above oratory and propaganda to pure literature," and Amy Lowell was greatly impressed by "An Opium Fantasy," which deals with the unhealthy subject of invalidism, and especially by the verses:

> The graceful play, a moment stopped,
> Distance again unrolls,
> Like silver veils, that softly dropped
> Ring into golden bowls.

Maria said of Hiram Powers's statue of the Greek Slave that "it was such a vision of beauty that one must always look back to the first time of seeing it as an era," and her comment on *The*

Chimes shows a more sophisticated critical capacity than some of
Dickens's latter-day critics have exhibited:

How very touching it is, sadder than the Christmas carol and therefore truer I suppose. To me the dream does not cease to be a reality
though Trotty wakes to find it all turns out so well. . . . The last
happy chapter seems only added to satisfy the tender-hearted of
which number Dickens himself is one, but the last happy chapter I
suspect is the least natural and probable part.

She loved, she went to Philadelphia and to Europe with her
husband, she bore four children and buried three of them, and
she died of tuberculosis in 1853. Despite all the superstitious
fears of her possible death that he had experienced, Lowell seems
not really to have expected the end until it came. At the burial
in Mount Auburn, under a "western sky all red with sunset, the
leafless trees, the silent street of water, the rustling leaves under
our feet," the Longfellows were shocked to see the coffin opened
that Mabel might look again upon her mother's face. Lowell himself "leaned for a long while against a tree weeping." It has been
said that he never spoke of his loss, but this is not accurate. He
said that Elmwood died with his wife, and that it was better to
have loved and lost her than "to have had and kept" any other
woman, and when he saw Winifred Howells, he wrote that
"her eyes recalled to me with exquisite pathos other eyes known
and loved so long ago."
His sufferings were terrible and protracted. "I understand
now what is meant by 'the waters have gone over me.' Such a
sorrow opens a door clear down into one's deepest nature that
he had never suspected before." He cherished her promise to be
with him, and he knew that "the little transparent film" over
his eyes was the only wall between her world and his, but it
was a wall for all that, and he was on the wrong side of it.
"I cannot see her, I cannot feel when I come home that she comes

to the door to welcome me as she always did." He learned to pray, he says, but he also tortured himself with the thought that he had sometimes troubled her when she was here; he must make up for this by being completely "faithful" to her and keeping himself wholly "pure" for her sake. But because he knew that his temperament was "naturally joyous," he feared "the world and its temptations"; therefore even the thought that time might bring healing was an added torture, not the alleviation to which he was entitled. For the most part, he kept to himself, staring at his wedding ring or scrawling her initials across the pages of his journal, but when he did go into society, he controlled his sorrow, thus occasioning cruel misunderstandings in the minds of those who did not know him well. And so the weary months dragged on.

III

In 1857 Lowell wrote Charles Eliot Norton:

I have told you once or twice that I should not be married again if I could help it. The time has come when I cannot. . . . I rejoice in it for I feel already stronger and better with an equability of mind that I have not felt for years.

It was harder to tell Maria's sister, Lois Howe, but he did it, explaining that he needed marriage, and that he had found in Frances Dunlap "a person of very remarkable strength and depth of character and of corresponding gentleness—who liked me and who would stand by Mabel in case I died." [16] Nobody has ever claimed that Frances Dunlap was, like Maria White, an instrument for the gods to play on, but she had a very important place in her husband's life. When Lowell announced his intended marriage to Mrs. Sydney Gay, he said Frances had "one of those characteristic faces which some people think plain and some beautiful" and that she was "as good as she can be—upright, brave, and gentle, and in short worth six of me." Mrs. Longfellow first thought her very "sweet looking," but she soon decided that she was "neither pretty nor attractive." Mrs. Longfellow was prejudiced, however, for she had wanted Lowell to marry Jane Norton.[17] Mrs. Fields admired Frances Dunlap and resented all disparagement of her. Howells called her "a woman perfectly of the New England type and tradition; almost repellently shy at first, and almost glacially cold with new acquaintance, but afterwards very sweet and cordial," and Henry James seems to have shared this impression, for he found that she "improved" upon acquaintance, until at last he called her "a very sweet and excellent woman." Perhaps her warmest admirer was William J. Stillman, who calls her "one of the rarest and most sympathetic creatures I have ever known," and who paints an attractive picture of her,

lying in a long chair under the trees . . . and laughing with her low musical laugh at a contest in punning between Lowell and myself . . . her almost Oriental eyes twinkling with fun, half closed and flashing from one to the other of us; her low, sweet forehead, wide between the temples; mouth wreathing with humor; and the whole frame, lithe and fragile, laughing with her eyes at his extravagant and rollicking word-play.

She managed all Lowell's practical affairs, and she seems never to have given him a pang, except for her childlessness (she had one miscarriage) and the terrible sorrow of the harrowing and protracted illness with which her life ended. Her only fault was that she did not like his humorous poetry, and he never complains about that. Certainly he loved her; he signs one letter, "Your loving and grateful husband," and he states categorically that in twenty-two years there had never been a cloud between them. He thought her nature "shy and beautiful" and so cheerful that he could not have been depressed in her society if he had tried. Stately as she was, she knew how to play too. He speaks of kissing her when her face is swollen and keeping her pretty jolly, and when he met Lydia Blood in *The Lady of the Arroostook,* he told Howells that "whenever I come across an imaginary woman that charms me I feel new life stirring in the roots of my love for the best of women—whom (I say it in confidence) I kiss with especial fervor the first time I catch her." And in 1878 he wrote Mabel from Spain that he and his wife often played "grandmamma and grandson together and I find it very nice to be petted." In 1858 he had told Sydney Gay:

My second marriage was the wisest act of my life, and as long as *I* am sure of it, I can afford to wait till my friends agree with me. . . . I have known her intimately for five years and love and honor her more than I can say. She has a genius for womanhood—a very rare gift in women. . . . I would lay my life under her feet if it would soften the paths of life to her and that is mere chaff to what I owe her.

Nor was he ever to change his mind about this.

Her illness, which began in Spain, during his ambassadorship there, and ended in England, where she died, was a dreadful one because much of the time she was out of her mind. Her wildest delusion was that her leg had been unscrewed and that of a certain Mrs. Turner substituted for it. He gave her the tenderest care, cherishing every lucid interval, but there were times when, in her insanity, he had to leave her, for she turned against him with wild accusations; "we ground into each other," he says. The cause of the difficulty was at first supposed to be typhus; later a brain ailment was suspected.[18] After all this, death might well have been welcomed as a relief, yet Lowell's loneliness was almost unbearable at first, and he wrote Child that he now looked forward to nothing.

> I am getting on as one does [he wrote Mrs. W. K. Clifford]—gradually getting my wits together, like a man who has been knocked by a cab in the street. I had always reckoned on going first and cannot get over the irreparable loss to my daughter and her children. She was a very noble and wise woman—the most perfectly unselfish I have ever known.

Lowell's closest friendships with other women came late in his life, involving Señora Emilia de Riaño in Spain and Lady Sybilla Lyttleton and Phoebe Smalley, wife of an American journalist, in England. He did not, generally speaking, think Spanish women beautiful, but Señora de Riaño was half English. On a poem Lowell wrote to her, Duberman comments amusingly: "In case the reader may be in doubt, there is no evidence that Lowell's relationship with Señora de Riaño was anything but platonic." He is certainly right, though Lowell's poems to the lady do show a very warm feeling on his part.

> If your youth call the ghost of mine
> Back out of the twilight glooming,
> I thrill as the prisoned wine
> Once more feels the ferment divine
> In May when the vines are blooming.[19]

Once a Boston newspaper made a quite unauthorized announcement of his engagement to Lady Lyttleton, and the report had to be formally denied, which was an embarrassing business. Mrs. Smalley, however, was gossiped about in a more malicious way. Lowell had never made any secret of his friendship with her. "I have enjoyed as always the society of our dear and charming friend Mrs. Smalley," he wrote Henry James from Whitby, "who has been as kind as only she has the art of being." And in a letter to G. W. Smalley himself he writes, "Tell Mrs. Smalley that if I don't find a letter from her waiting for me at South-borough, I shall write to her! If this threat doesn't scare her, I know not what will." The gossip was obviously baseless as well as base; the tone of the lady's husband, both in what he published about Lowell and in his private letters, is quite conclusive.[20]

Since Lowell was a family man, children and grandchildren naturally absorbed much of his love feeling. I don't know how seriously to take his statements that he has no faith in "what are called natural affection," and that he lacks "that natural fondness for children which some people have, who also, I have observed, like puppies in the same indiscriminate way." He admired Burne-Jones's goodness toward children, adding that he lacked it himself. But Sir Leslie Stephen says he was excellent with them (he was godfather to Stephen's daughter, who became Virginia Woolf),[21] and there are many expressions of his fond-ness for his children, nephews,[22] and grandchildren in letters to them and to others.

When the first baby came, Lowell tended her, relieving her mother of much of her care. "I belong to a class of philosophers . . . who do not believe that children are born into the world to subject their mothers to a diaper despotism, and to be brought down to their fathers after dinner, as an additional digestive to the nuts and raisins, to be bundled up and hurried away at the least symptom of disaffection or disturbed digestion." Nor did he find this an onerous task. "Our little Blanche is everything to me. She almost hinders me from doing anything but tend her and look at her." When she died, he hung up her baby shoes in his study, where they stayed as long as he lived.

Mabel, too, was an "unlimited darling," though he did not think she had "those spiritual characteristics which distin-guished her Divine little sister. . . . She is certainly not so beau-tiful as Blanche. Yet I love her, if possible more."

Massachusetts (you will admit) is the first state in the Union, Middlesex County (you can't deny) the first in the State, and Mabel is the prize baby of Middlesex. That settles it.

But when Rose came, she was "in some respects the finest of our three daughters," and he decided to reduce Mabel to a boy. As late as 1888 he was sending kisses to Mabel and her children, as he had used to send them to her when she was a child, and when she said he was very kind to her, he replied:

And so I am kind to you, quotha? To whom else should I be kind? I think you are gradually getting fond of me which I find not at all unbearable. Make the most of me while I last for you won't get another.

When he had no boy, boys were much less desirable than girls. "When are you coming to see us?" he asks Sydney Gay in 1849. "It will be worse and worse for you the longer you wait, for if we should have another girl, you would be ashamed to bring a great, lumbering boy among 'em." After Walter came— and went—this was different. He made poetry of it in "Threnodia," and many years later he wrote Norton, "If you only knew how much I wish *I* had a son, and how fresh after so many years the life of our little Walter is to me, you would understand how fully I sympathize with you."

The loss of all three of the children who died was very bitter to the Lowells. "It is a terrible thing to have only one child. It seems as if the air were full of deadly, invisible bullets flying in every direction, so that not a step can be taken in safety." When Rose was taken sick with the same complaint that had killed Blanche, he gave up hope from the first. And when Mabel, in what turned out not to be a serious childish ailment, put her head on his shoulder and her arms around his neck, it nearly killed him. She was so confident and he "so helpless and so in the dark!" [23]

Grandparents are proverbially more indulgent than parents, but I am not sure this was true of Lowell. To be sure, he finds it wonderful to be a grandfather, hopes to live to see his grandchildren grow up, and works hard in the hope of leaving them a competence. Yet he still preserves something of his old detachment. He is not sure he has enough grandfather in him to divide among five, nor does he think any of the children very clever, "but they make it up in being fairly good, as the child world goes." Above all, however, they must be kept up to the mark in speech, grammar, and intonation, as his mother had kept him and he their mother before them. One of his granddaughters, Esther Lowell Cunningham, paints a rather austere picture of him when they lived together.

We children had to be on our best behavior, and we were very much interested that he had breakfast very late in the morning. He used to come down to the dining room and we were allowed to sit with him occasionally. He had the cook make him some little oaten cakes of Scotch oatmeal, and they were very delicious. . . . Occasionally he gave one to each of us.[24]

This is from a young child's point of view and may not be wholly fair. When Mrs. Cunningham wrote that her grandfather "wasn't used to young children," she ignored much of the record that has been cited here. Enough remains, however, to show that his relations with his grandchildren, at the period indicated, must have been on a fairly formal and limited basis.

CHAPTER SIX

THE WORLD AND THE PARISH

The main ingredient a biographer should contribute is sympathy (which includes insight). Truth is not enough, for in biography, as in law, the greater the truth sometimes the greater the libel.

JRL to Charles Eliot Norton, 1886

I

If one were to take Lowell literally in what he says about himself, one would be obliged to conclude that he had the temperament of a hermit. He was the baby who won't go to strangers, and though he was always glad to learn to like people, it was slow work in most cases. "Not the stuff of which lions are made," he was easily bored and often had to struggle against suspicion even of those he liked. Not only could he seldom "companion" comfortably with more than one person in a day, but he seldom dreamed of more than one person in a single night! "I never can know people somehow till I have known them a good while and by accident as it were," and he could about as well have commanded the Channel fleet as headed a committee.

This is far from being the whole truth about Lowell, but there is truth in it. Minot J. Savage says he was not so "easily accessible" as Longfellow, and even Howells admits that Lowell "could snub, and pitilessly, when he thought there was presumption and apparently sometimes merely because he was in the mood." Higginson thought him cold and self-centered.[1] Both

E. S. Nadal and Nathaniel S. Shaler[2] found him intolerably affected, and Moncure D. Conway found "a certain provincialism" in him in the 'fifties, though he admits that it may have been his own "Southern provincialism" and "lingering Methodism and heretical enthusiasm" that were offended by it.[3] To the contrary, Bronson Alcott, meeting him about 1850, found him "about the heartiest and best-natured person I have met with lately. His ruddy health and flowing spirits render him the best of company; and one asks how he came by these qualities, so rare to be met with here amongst the severe and staid Puritan people." [4]

Howells too invokes Lowell's Puritan background in explaining his social reticence:

At the first encounter with people he was always apt to have a certain frosty shyness, a smiling cold, as from the long, high-sunned winters of his Puritan race; he was not quite himself till he had made you aware of his quality: then no one could be sweeter, tenderer, warmer than he; then he made you free of his whole heart; but you must be his captive before he could do that.

Possibly Henry James had the same thing in mind when he complained of the older man's indisposition "to make any of the Parisian acquaintances which his 'eminence' would give him admission to" when he and James were in the French capital together. But if Lowell's Puritanism was a factor here, the "Brahminism" some people are fond of talking about was not, or if it was, then it operated in a curiously perverted way.[5] It is true that Lowell sometimes calls himself a Brahmin; he thought it the tendency of a house like Elmwood to make tories of those who lived in it, and he deplored his own commitment to familiar and established ways. He "always maintained that the upper classes were quite as liable to be influenced by stupidity, selfishness and passion as the lower," and from boyhood on he never had any difficulty in meeting "common" people on their own ground.[6] "A consciousness of external superiority to other men" was the one thing he could not cope with comfortably; it made him nervous and uneasy.

I could never ride in a two-horse coach with any comfort. I am afraid to meet the eyes of passers-by. I know they detect me as an impostor at once. On the other hand I drive my father's venerable "September" (my senior by several years) with entire satisfaction. I am certain to be rather pitied than envied by the shabbiest pedestrian.

There is shyness here, self-centeredness certainly, lack of confidence, but surely there is no upper-class arrogance. He lamented the shyness to Grace Norton as late as 1878:

With my manly beard and masculine visage I contrive to put a good face on it, I believe, but the misery I have gone through all my life from this cause (the result in part, I fancy, of my solitude when a boy) will I trust be counted to me hereafter.

And Frank Stearns says that though he could be sociable if encountered in a fairly empty public vehicle, he would grow silent just as soon as it filled up.

Obviously our relations with others must be importantly influenced by our attitude toward ourselves. Lowell's modest attitude toward himself as a writer has already been considered, and he was not much better satisfied with himself as a man. His feeling that it was unwise for people to write about themselves, "for there is nobody of whom they know so little," and that the value of memoirs depends upon the amount of space they devote to other people, may have been determined by his dislike of the book he happened to be reviewing when he expressed it[7] —it certainly suggests a curious criterion for the evaluation of autobiographical writing—but I have found no evidence that he thought of himself more highly than he ought to have thought. That he was careful of what is now called his "image" is quite true. Once a lady sent him a photograph of himself which he did not like, with a request for an autograph; he neither signed it nor returned it but supplied her with another which he liked better. When he was sent to Concord, he disliked the Reverend Barzillai Frost for what he considered his egotism ("He loves the sound of his own voice—So do I—ergo, I hate *his*"). But real egotists do not see themselves as clearly as this. Lowell relished the idea of being an ambassador for the sake of his grandchildren (which in itself involved a modest estimate of his achievements as a writer), and when he insisted upon protocol, it was because he was jealous of the dignity of the United States rather than his own. He may or may not have had himself in mind when he made the speaker in "Sunthin' in the Pastoral Line" refer to "the crook'dest stick in all the heap,—Myself," but he did see himself "made up, in part, of shreds and leavings of the past, in part of the interpolations of other people," and he was so certain that every man who is not a complete fool must know his own faults better than anybody else can know them that it was hard for him to feel personally puffed up, though he did learn how to accept himself and the circumstances in which his lot was cast.[8] When, in England, he saw a picture of Saint Paul which everybody said resembled him, "it gave me a very odd feeling, raising vague doubts as to my personal identity." But his feelings when he himself noticed a resemblance to himself in his infant daughter Rose were much more complicated:

I cannot tell what the feeling is—it is certainly of no kin either to vanity or selfishness—at seeing one's own spirit, as it were, building another tabernacle. It is rather a sad feeling, for we are all more conscious of our weakness than of our strengths, and we know not which of these will be reproduced and dwell in this new tent after we have struck ours and gone in search of other cases.

And when he encountered a man he really revered, like Francis James Child, he could exclaim, "*How* good he is! I smell sulphur about myself when I am with him."

II

General sociality, however, is not at all the same thing as either a warm affection for individuals or a sympathetic attitude toward humanity in general, and Lowell was well aware of these differences. It was his own view that he "had a really friendly feeling for everything human"; this of course was one of the aspects of his nature that drew him so strongly toward Chaucer. More than once he said he would rather be loved than anything else in the world. He frankly acknowledged his dependence upon affection and boasted that he had never lost a friend. "It is better to be a good fellow than a good poet." And he told Norton that all he wanted on his gravestone was "He had good friends, whom he loved."

In the early days his emotionalism was so strong that many would call it maudlin: "I go out sometimes with my heart so full of yearning toward my fellows that the indifferent look with which even entire strangers pass brings tears into my eyes." And, more individually, "Your letter, Shack, was a delight to me (though I am not ashamed to confess that it [made] me cry)." As he grew older, he learned how to control himself, but he never really changed. "I don't readily forget old friends, nor easily stop loving anybody I have ever loved." He knew that the impulse to tell people how much he liked them might be a weakness, but he could not resist it, and he would have thought himself a beggar indeed if he had not had even sympathy to give away. When he first wrote Sir Leslie Stephen of the affection he felt for him, he was embarrassed afterwards, but Stephen's reply reassured him "that you did not feel as if you had been *pawed.*" He met both English and Spanish royalty on the ground of the humanity they shared with him. It is said that some of Queen Victoria's admirers were somewhat taken back by this, but it did not offend that lady who differed so strikingly from the curious "Victorian" stereotype that has been tagged with her name.[9]

To be sure, Lowell was not completely consistent about all these things. He once wrote the Sydney Gays that most men and women were indifferent to him, they being among the exceptions. He frequently complains that he is too shy or too awkward to express the affection he feels, though anybody who has read as many of his letters as I have must, I think, feel that nobody ever expressed it more. He also had the idea that he took more from his friends than he gave. "I can't be as good a friend to you as you have been to me," he writes Norton. "My temperament is against it. I am faithful enough, but you *do* while I meditate what 'twere good to do." In this there is, perhaps, some truth, but Norton pitied Lowell because he could never receive from anybody anything like such good letters as he himself sent off ("you will always lack one of the pleasantest experiences in life"), and after the poet died, F. J. Child wrote, "I am going on with my work in an easy way. I can't say that I care so much about it without J.R.L., who has done much for me." [10]

Insofar as Lowell's personal benevolence took the form of giving money, it has been considered elsewhere in these pages. But many letters remain to testify to the pains he took in performing services of many kinds for a wide variety of people. His kindliness toward young authors is best exemplified by the way he took Howells under his wing, but the people he tried to help were not all Howellses. In 1849 he conspired with T. W. Parsons to prevent Elizabeth Peabody's *Aesthetic Papers* from getting a rough review in the Boston *Courier*, and in 1868 he doctored some verses sent to him by a poor woman and sent them to Fields, hoping he would take them (he didn't) for either the *Atlantic* or *Our Young Folks* and pay her $20 for them.[11] After the artist Charles Akers had been burned out in Portland, Lowell invited him to stay at Elmwood and gave him introductions which led to his modeling a number of distinguished men in the Boston area and inaugurated a new phase of his career.[12] When G. W. Smalley once rebuked Lowell for encouraging bores, he replied, "Poor things! they have nobody else to encourage them." But he did not stop with bores. He placed the giving of aid on a simple basis of human need, not merit. Sending Horatio Woodman ten dollars for a feckless pensioner of his, he added, "If you think it will give the poor fellow any pleasure to swallow it dissolved in drink, why, just send it to him. But if there be a better way, I am sure you will be kind enough to give it so." He once refused to discharge a dishonest servant on the ground that if he discharged him, he could not give him a character, "and he must live somehow." His sympathy for outcasts sometimes equalled or surpassed the more vociferous and flamboyant emotionalism of Whitman. He thought sin "sometimes but a thwarted and misdirected virtue," and though he never palliated or excused moral weakness, he had no sympathy with those who exploited or made capital of such things in others or took up a Pharisaic attitude toward them.

Since Lowell was a man and not a god, his charity was not, of course, all embracing, as his attitude toward Whitman and Thoreau, to go no further, shows.[13] But it obviously hurt him to be forced to think ill of anybody, since he told Barrett Wendell that the comfort of death was that "then, at last, we can begin, with certainty of no awaking disenchantment, to idealize those we love." When he engaged Poe to write for *The Pioneer*, he gave him a free hand, except that "I do not wish an article like that of yours on Dawes, who, although I think with you that he is a bad poet, has yet I doubt not tender feelings as a man which I should be chary of wounding." [14] When Leslie Stephen went over his collection of Lowell letters to send them to Norton for his edition of the correspondence, he found not "a single unkind phrase about anybody. The absence of even an occasional sarcasm struck me as remarkable." E. S. Nadal testifies that he was the kindest chief possible to his ambassadorial subordinates and adds that the only person of whom he ever heard him speak severely was Henry Ward Beecher. "Not only did he not speak ill of people, but he would be silent and look rather uncomfortable, when unkind things were said about people in his presence." Nor was he intolerant about differences of opinion. In early life he loved the brilliant Southerner, John Francis Heath, despite their differences about slavery; later he was well aware that he and Howells differed on many social issues, but he never challenged the younger man's right to dissent. "In the whimsicalities of others he delighted as much as in his own and would frankly own up to inconsistency." Their sharpest division came on the Chicago anarchists in the late 'eighties, and one need not "agree" with Lowell's view of the case to admire him when he writes the novelist, who had imperiled his position as a writer to assail what he regarded as inhumanity and legal injustice:

You know I don't share some of your opinions or sympathize with some of your judgments, but I am not such an ass as not to think better of a man for saying what he thinks and not what I think. Though I thought those Chicago ruffians well hanged, I specially honored your courage in saying what you did about them. You can't make me fonder of you, but I am sure you will make me prouder of you.

Nearly everybody admits Lowell's brilliance as a conversationalist and his great social charm—at least when he chose to exercise it. There is an amusing letter to George Loring, written at the age of eighteen, in which he rhapsodizes in a rather mocking style about his first "Grown-up Ball!" "Imagine . . . me prancing along the floor, chalked neatly for the occasion, in a pair of new pumps, with a partner I never saw in my life before." His brother had given him five dollars to cover the cost of pumps, stock, and white kid gloves; but after he had bought them he had one dollar left; hence he made money on the ball. It was only from the financial point of view that it was a success, however. As he reports to the same correspondent the next day, when he got there he refused to dance because the girl he wanted to dance with had not come, and the horrible silliness of those who were there nauseated him. Not one knew Mrs. Nature or Miss Simplicity by sight, and the only thing they did naturally was to eat.

This was not a very auspicious beginning, and it was a long time before it was brilliantly followed up. During his active abolitionist years, Lowell was not welcome in some areas of "good society," and he cannot be said ever to have led an active social life in Cambridge. As late as the time of his Spanish ambassadorship, he hated his social duties. His late social blooming came in England, where he ultimately came to dine out seven days a week. Even here, however, he entered one hostess in his engagement book as the Witch of Endor.

George Smalley goes so far as to say that in this matter Lowell's character changed after he came to England and that it was then that he first became a man of the world. This would indicate a very late development (or capacity for development) in him, not out of line with either his perpetual youthfulness of spirit or his remarkable sensitiveness to stimuli. Theoretically, however, Lowell had always been convinced of the value and importance of society; his prejudice against Thoreau was largely determined by what he regarded as his confirmed solitariness, and

he felt the same shortcoming in Wordsworth. Even for scholarship society was important. "I have often been struck with the
many-sided versatility of the Fellows of English colleges who
have kept their wits in training by continual fence one with
another."

He could have held his own with them, as he did with (or
against) Holmes and Motley at the Saturday Club. Greenslet says
he never visited his publishers upon even a trivial errand without
dropping some word that was passed about among them for days
thereafter.

Other men may have been as witty [says Underwood], though we
recall but three or four in our day; some may have had a similar
fund of wisdom mellowed with humor; others have talked the
staple of idyls, and let off metaphors like soap-bubbles; but Lowell
combined in conversation the varied powers of all.

The only question would be as to his manners as a conversationalist. Higginson says he and Holmes virtually monopolized
the conversation at the *Atlantic* dinners. Alexander Ireland denies
this, insisting that conversation with Lowell was just that, and
that, when speaking, "he looked straight at you, with his res-
olute, searching, honest eyes, lit up with humor and kindliness."
Moreover, "he frequently endeavored to withdraw attention
from himself by gracefully making openings for them in a very
delicate and skilful way." [15] In between the two falls the author
of "Conversations with Mr. Lowell," [16] who says that Lowell
"could listen, he wanted to hear what you had to say, but he
could not help interrupting you, for he always had something
to say." E. S. Nadal brings up an interesting special point when
he says that Lowell was always modest and cautious when speaking on a subject upon which he was well informed but inclined to
bluff when he had little information in hand.

Of Lowell's social charm, F. J. Child once remarked that his "good looks and insinuating ways carry off the palm entirely from my genius and learning, but then I am as much fascinated as anybody, and don't mind." Though this is whimsically expressed, there can be no doubt that Lowell had the kind of charm Child here attributes to him. Only, one feels that he must have needed it to overcome the social handicap of the combative tendencies which seem to have embarrassed so many English hostesses. To be sure, he was more touchy for his country than he was for himself, or as one Englishwoman puts it, "Hawthorne insulted us all by saying that English women were fat, but I dare not say in Mr. Lowell's presence that an American woman is thin." But this does not wholly cover the case. Socially Lowell seems to have been an incorrigible schoolmaster; if anything was said in his presence which seemed to require correction in any aspect, he was sure to enter it. No doubt he was often right, as he was with the bad-mannered Scot who was so amazed that an American should speak English correctly that he asked Lowell where he had learned it, only to be crushed by a quotation from a Scottish ballad—

> "I got it in my mither's wame,
>   Whaur ye'll get never the like!"

He could manifest angelic patience upon occasion, as when Dion Boucicault declared that no Englishman had ever written a good play, and he merely inquired, "Not even Shakespeare?" and, the exception not being granted, only subsided into disgusted silence. Yet he rebuked both Longfellow and Emerson at the Saturday Club, and he once called Lee a traitor in the presence of Southern friends.[17] Norton admits that Lowell's "want of ease sometimes resulted in a lack of amenity and in a display of the brilliant rather than the genial side of his nature," while Leslie Stephen found him "apt to be a little perverse in the views he takes of things just out of perversity." Henry James, as was his wont, attempted a more subtle explanation. Nobody, he thought, "was ever more in love with the idea of being right and of keeping others from being wrong. The famous Puritan conscience, which was a persistent part of his heredity, operated in him perhaps most strongly on the scholarly side."

Lowell's criticism of what his friends wrote was equally frank, though certainly in a much less gauche way. He once told Howells that he would not flatter Neptune for his trident, and he criticized *The Newcomes* to Thackeray's face. He remarked that the Adamses had a genius for saying even gracious things in an ungracious way, and Charles Francis Adams found this so "keen and true" that he thanked Norton for not having edited it out of Lowell's letters.[18] Lowell himself believed that his sympathy with his friends handicapped him as a critic—or else made him a very good one—but he also said that he was "apt to criticize most severely the works of those in whom I am personally interested." Whether he dealt with friend or with foe, he was never a pernickety critic like Poe, but he did not pull his punches, either privately or publicly. Stephen's agnosticism takes him further than Lowell is willing to go. Stedman improvises too much. He enjoys Lilla Cabot Perry's verses, but "there was a crudity here and there that might have easily ripened into better form." Where W. W. Story

narrates or describes he is always lively and interesting; where he dissects or grows learned, he gives up his vantage-ground, and must consent to be dull like everybody else. . . .[19]

In his memorial tribute to John Pendleton Kennedy before the Massachusetts Historical Society, Lowell denied that Kennedy could "be called a man of genius in the creative sense of that somewhat elastic word," but concluded that he was "something

better than his books." "Perhaps we overestimate the worth of
mere literary ability." [20] Discriminating as this is, it does not
represent the usual tone of memorial tributes.

One specialized form of communication with his fellows—
public speaking—Lowell always disliked, but, though some
thought him stiff on public occasions, he seems to have conducted himself to the satisfaction of everybody except himself,
and in later years, in England especially, he became a famous
after-dinner speaker. "His voice," wrote George W. Smalley,
"was deep and full, with vibrating tones. He understood . . .
how to take and sustain a note and not let it go." He gesticulated
little and avoided all manner of theatrical climaxes. Henry Cabot
Lodge always heard him with "envious delight."

Yet when Lowell sent Horatio Woodman a ticket for his
Lowell lectures, he called it "a ticket to the jail-yard." "You will
have a fine view of the adjustment of the rope, and the swinging
off. I feel already the cap over my eyes, but try to be a Barnard-
ine." In 1868 he wrote James T. Fields that he was always as
"nervous as a terrier" on lecture day and worried himself for
lack "of anything better to worry." When he toured the Middle
West, he was so miserable that he tried vainly to cancel part of
the series, though he admitted that "one or two" of his lectures
had been "pretty good," and that they had succeeded "quite
beyond my expectation." And at the very end of his life he
begged off from an engagement in Philadelphia: "It is absurd,
but I was made so. I won't torment myself by speaking in public
any more."

He admitted that as ambassador he became "the greatest orator
in England (next to Mr. Gladstone) and might speak almost
every day in the week if I were fool enough." Yet he insisted
that his speeches always seemed dreadful to him after they got
cold, "as the dead body used to be to the murderer," and that
the only good ones were those he made to himself on the way

home in the cab. He must have gained power with practice, and he must have enjoyed himself in a measure (otherwise he surely would not have continued as long as he did), but if you will listen to him, worse terrors were added with years and practice, for words became less obedient as he grew older, and he had spoken so much that he was now desperately afraid of repeating himself.

There was a time when, after thinking over a subject rapidly, I could speak my ten minutes upon it umprompted by notes, with assurance . . . that the right word would sometimes come at the right time. Now I must write down beforehand what I have to say and a speech loses half its effectiveness if it hobble along with the staff of manuscript.[21]

III

But a man's relations with his fellowmen involves much more than generally comes under such headings as general sociality or personal friendship; it concerns such vast areas as his political consciousness and social awareness. What it was once the fashion to call Lowell's "Americanism" stands in no need of demonstration: of all the New England poets he is the most "public." Except for Longfellow's "The Building of the Ship" and Moody's "An Ode in Time of Hesitation," the Commemoration Ode has no rivals in American poetry of its kind, and the "Three Memorial Poems" are not far behind it in fame. In prose the same kind of testimony is borne by "Cambridge Thirty Years Ago," "New England Two Centuries Ago," and "On a Certain Condescension in Foreigners." The "New England" piece begins uncompromisingly: The history of New England is written imperishably on the face of a continent, and in characters as beneficent as they are enduring," and before the reader has had a fair chance to digest this, Lowell flings another tremendous proposition at him: "Next to the fugitives whom Moses led out of Egypt, the little shipload of outcasts who landed at Plymouth two centuries and a half ago are destined to influence the future of the world." His early contacts with Europe only increased his devotion to America. He wrote his daughter from Paris that "we are the happiest and most civilized people on the face of the earth" and he thought the best society in the world was in Cambridge and the best English spoken there, all of which may perhaps profitably remind us that the time came, after World War I, when one of his admirers, Agnes Repplier, should find it necessary to show us the other side of one of his coins in an equally trenchant essay, "On a Certain Condescension in Americans." [22]

Lowell's America then, was largely New England and his New England centered in Cambridge. Howells, to be sure, says that unlike many New Englanders, Lowell was never condescending toward the West, yet as late as 1887 he had no idea how long it was going to take him to get from Boston to Chicago,[23] and Poe's complaint that Southern writers were ignored in *A Fable for Critics* was just, whatever may be said of some of his other criticisms.

Lowell prized New England because it had been founded by those who sought God, not gold, and he resented the insinuation that New Englanders came of inferior stock to Southerners. I think one must admit that there was a certain amount of what we would call snobbery about this. He did not care for a biography but he did want a memorial in College Hall, and he craved seeing his name in capitals in the Harvard triennial catalogue. Yet there is at least one passage in which Harvard herself seems most prized because she is in Cambridge.[24] As has already been observed, Cambridge and New England aristocracy was a homely kind of aristocracy, and there is evidence to show that Lowell both understood and relished the countryman (see, for example, the praise of homely New England names in "Pictures from Appledore"), but this does not quite cancel out either the snobbery or the provincialism. "Condescension" itself opens with an unabashed reference to "the good old days, when almost every dweller in the town had been born in it," and the paper on "The Rebellion: Its Causes and Consequences" actually finds the seeds of our downfall in the sending to Congress of "men without the responsibility or the independence which only established reputation, *social position*, long converse with great questions, or native strength of character can give." [25]

Being both an artist and an idealist, Lowell understood both the strength and the weakness of New England Puritanism. He believed that "our Puritan ancestors have been misrepresented and maligned by persons without imagination enough to make themselves contemporary with, and therefore able to understand, the men whose memories they strive to blacken," but he also admitted a hard, narrow formalism, especially in the second generation. "The Puritans divorced the Church from Art . . . crushed the poetical element out of religion," and preserved only the darker side of folklore. Their religion centered on fear rather than love, and "the nearness of God was oftener a terror than a comfort to them." The New England air was "parsimonious" therefore, its dogmas "drear," its faith "austere," and its "practical horizon grimly pent," while its hazeless atmosphere forced "hard outlines mercilessly close." Yet he could never forget the something "sensitive and fine" beneath the "drift of puritanic snow," and, despite all his aestheticism, he is boasting, as well as acknowledging a limitation, when he says, "We value character more than any amount of talent."

In his heart he knew that New England—and America—remained provincial, though sometimes he fought against accepting this. "Literature thrives in an air laden with tradition, in a soil ripe with immemorial culture, in the temperature, steady and stimulating, of historic associations." American history had been too brief to be very interesting, even to Americans, and the early settlers had "felt the bleakness at their backs" so desperately that they accepted even Indian legend when they could find nothing better "to get up a screen of legend and tradition behind them." [26] What had followed since then was "a record of advances in material prosperity and scarce anything more." Europe might be the past and America the future, but America still needed European criticism if it was to make anything of itself. We had not even a cultural center. Boston at her best had come closest, but she had now passed her crest. Lowell had ambitious plans for a "Foreign Literary Intelligence" section in *The Pioneer,* and it was not his fault that this did not work out successfully.

Of course Lowell knew the values as well as the limitations of nationalism in literature. He agreed with Noah Webster that in this country as everywhere else, language must enjoy the privilege of living and growing, but as late as 1860 he thought the title *An American Dictionary of the English Language* absurd. He was not completely consistent; neither was he incapable of changing his mind with the changing times. In 1845 a poet's inspiration had "no more intimate connection with the country in which he chances to be born, than with the village or garret in which he may dwell." [27] But the introduction to *Biglow* II is much more nationally minded than this. Here a national literature reflects, as it should, the character of the people that produced it.

Lowell was very frank in indicating both the faults and the virtues of the various foreign peoples with whom he came into contact, but his criticisms of England are often unbalanced and intemperate. The most extreme statement is in a poem called "Merry England," published in *Graham's Magazine* in 1841. Here he contrasts the Merry England of days gone by with her melancholy state now,

> With sweat of agonizing years
>   Upon thy harlot brow,
> Grimed with the smoke of furnaces
>   That forge with damned art
> The bars of darkness that shut in
>   The poor man's starving heart.

She ships poison

> Wrung from lean Hindu slaves,
> To fill all China with dead souls
> That rot in living graves.

At St. Jean d'Acre she sent 3000 Turks to heaven to prove her faith not "barren of goodly works." And since Parliament can always talk, it is not necessary to be concerned about

> Ye factory children thin,
> Upon whose little hearts the sun
> Hath never once looked in.

He also hits Irish oppression and the domination of the Church of England and denounces a people willing to tolerate outrages

> That one weak Guelphic girl may wear
> Her plaything of a crown.[28]

Other utterances, though less extreme, are hardly in fundamental disagreement with this. Revolutionary and War of 1812 animosities were partly responsible and of course during the Civil War, Lowell was afraid England might be getting ready to recognize the Confederacy. But he always inclined to believe that the best of England had come to America and that the old English virtues had been best preserved here. Like Hawthorne, he considered Americans quicker and more sensitive than Eng-

lishmen. When the Earl of Derby translated the *Iliad* he remarked rudely that "for the first Earl in England to know *anything* . . . is a concession to popular prejudice as unusual as it
is gratifying,"²⁹ and in 1858 he was determined to reject "at the
risk of war" any attempt English writers might make to get
their "milk and water" into the *Atlantic*. Naturally, then, the
condescension which many Englishmen showed toward Americans, American culture, and American literature could only
infuriate Lowell.³⁰

As early as 1849, Lowell thought about the possible separation
of Canada from the mother country and her annexation to the
United States. On April 20, 1863, he sounded out Richard Henry
Dana on the possibility of his saying something on the importance
of avoiding an English-American break,³¹ but in 1865 he told
Norton both that he did not think peace with England "the
summum bonum" and that he feared we might have to fight her
some day. After the Civil War began, he himself did not write a
single letter to an English friend until 1866. By 1869, however,
war with England would be "the greatest wrong and calamity
to civilization in all history" and those who talked about it were
fools, but ten years later England is again "the incarnation of
the Kingdom of this World," apparently because she has criticized America.³²

Yet during the last years of his life, even after his ambassadorship had ended, this man elected to spend much of his time in
England. Had he, then, changed his mind about her? The answer
is both yes and no.

Traveling in Europe as late as 1873, Lowell would rather be
at home, and can't work anywhere except at home, but when
he went to London as ambassador, he found the climate better
than any other he had ever lived in, "and as for the inward
weather, I have never seen civilization at so high a level in some
respects as here." As late as the last year he lived, he is capable of

calling London "the best place for dwelling in the world except the house where I was born," but the qualification is not always there, and one wonders how much it meant. The rattle of a London hansom shook new life into his old bones, and even the fog enlivened him. It smelled better than truffles, had a wonderful "knack of transfiguring things," and flattered one's self-esteem by creating a cloak of golden seclusion. In 1886 he told his daughter that he liked London better than any other place and that England was so beautiful that he wondered how the founding father of the Lowell family in America was ever able to leave it. And two years later he wrote his sister unequivocally that "Boston is very nice in its own way though it has not the charm for me that London has. I am grown civic in my old age—I couldn't have believed it thirty or even twenty years ago."

There were those who still found it hard to believe, for he was still very much on the defensive about America and Americans. He still felt that the English mind was dull and English nerves so deeply embedded in fat and muscle that it took a pitchfork to get at them; it was never safe for an American to let his mind "gambol" among Englishmen. Henry James, he says, agreed with him about this, and was impressed by it anew whenever he returned to England from the continent.

In his speeches Lowell told English audiences that Americans had not only inherited English civilization but developed it, and that they served England as a kind of posterity by sometimes recognizing their great writers before they had been recognized at home; that England had been wrong in both her wars with America, and that America was a living demonstration of what other English colonies might come to if they were not wisely handled; that though the War of 1812 had been creditable to neither party, it had been just and necessary and had contributed helpfully to the development of international law; and even that, though international copyright was necessary and desirable,

America did not deserve to be charged with moral degradation for her failure hitherto to achieve it.

In 1871 Lowell called Rome and Dresden the continental cities he knew best; Dublin interested him because it was "Hogarthian," but in 1890 Venice was the only city outside London he ever cared to see again. Though he regarded Paris as the handsomest city in the world, he does not seem to have been greatly taken with it, and once at least he called Parisians provincial in a small-townish way.

His two ambassadorships stand somewhat apart from the rest of his activities and, for that matter, judgments. By modern standards, no problems of earth-shaking importance came before him in either Spain or England, but no doubt his problems looked bigger at the time than they do in retrospect, and when we consider his lack of training and interest in most of the areas with which he had to deal, combined with his impatience of protocol and dislike of routine, he must be judged to have been not only successful but splendidly successful. As he himself wrote Richard Henry Dana from Spain, "I have not done badly, I think, but as one of 'them littery fellers' (who are supposed not to understand business) I am sensitive." Certainly his conception of the basic function of ambassadors as "the buffers of society, preventing the too violent collision of men and nations" was right, and he lived up to it nobly. "Without them the world would soon fall back to the primitive system of *faustrecht,* and we should have private or public war on our hands all the time." [33]

Charles Sumner tried to get a diplomatic appointment for Lowell as far back as Lincoln's time, but was not successful. In 1874 Senators Hoar and Fish got Grant to offer him Russia, but he declined.[34] After Hayes had been elected in 1876, the President's kinsman, W. D. Howells, brought up the matter again. Lowell once more declined St. Petersburg and Vienna too, but, perhaps injudiciously, remarked to Howells that he would rather like going to Spain, so that he might see a play by Calderón. "Upon this hint," Howells, like Othello, "spake," and the appointment was arranged.[35]

Lowell rode the wave of the future most successfully when, during his English ambassadorship, he was called upon to consider the alleged importation of diseased cattle into England, and, as Beatty points out, made recommendations which antedated by a quarter of a century some of the requirements of the Pure Food and Drug Act, which the United States did not acquire until Theodore Roosevelt was president. But the thing that gave him most trouble was the Irish question, and his handling of it was so unsatisfactory to extremists that his recall was angrily demanded both in public meetings and in Congress. Lowell believed that English and Irish interests were too closely related ever to permit a complete separation between the two countries, but his sympathies were all with the Irish. About Gladstone he had a somewhat divided mind.

> His greatness not so much in genius lies
> As in adroitness, when occasions rise,
> Lifelong convictions to extemporize.

He disapproved of English intervention in Egypt; as to Ireland, he approved of Gladstone's policy as far as it went (William Roscoe Thayer says he believed himself to have influenced it), but he would have gone further.

IV

Lowell, however, was much more interested in reform in his own country than he was in reform abroad. In 1844 the Boston *Transcript* thought him "determined to bring down with a mighty crash the whole social system." This was an absurd judgment at this or at any period of his life, but there was more show of justification for it in the 'forties than there was ever to be again. On January 25, 1845, he published in the *Broadway Journal:*

AN EPIGRAM ON CERTAIN CONSERVATIVES

In olden days men's ears were docked
For thinking, and for other crimes;
And now, some worthies overstocked
With these commodities are shocked
At the false mercy of the times,
Which spoils their chance of being shortened
In their own feature most important.

Like other undergraduates, Lowell had conformed to the currently fashionable Harvard indifference to public concerns, but there was no lack of interest in social wrongs in his background. As we have seen, his father wore himself out trying to help poor slum-dwellers near the West Church, and John Lowell the Rebel gave up a $9000-a-year law practice over his disgust at what seemed to him the judicial murder of a client, Jason Fairbanks.[36]

Lowell was not a political philosopher, and his value does not lie in any formulation which he may have made or suggested along this line.[37] Here, even more than in the aesthetic sphere, his value lies in his perceptions and intuitions. He had no delusions about the alleged democracy of the Founding Fathers, and the best he could say of Puritanism was that "believing itself quick with the seed of religious liberty," it "laid, without knowing it, the seed of democracy." Even the Puritan's devotion to the liberty he understood, and demanded for himself, was limited, and Lowell praised Cromwell for knowing that though enthusiasm can overthrow a government, it cannot administer one, and the Pilgrims for being ready to give up all for a principle but also for being too sensible "to sacrifice their principles to the fantasy of every wandering Adoniram or Shear-Jashub who mistook himself for Providence as naturally and as obstinately as some lunatics suppose themselves to be tea-pots." His utterances on the subject of democracy are not completely consistent. He ties it up with Christianity—Christ was "the first true democrat that ever breathed"—and thinks that in the long run the majority always comes round to the right side, but when he is opposing Johnson, "the true many-hearted tyrant" that the President is courting becomes "the Mob." There were times, too, when he doubted whether the democratic system could be made to work for foreigners, even in America. Certainly he never thought the American government perfect—or even consistently admirable—in its working. In the early days the Constitution was a "Sacred Parasol" to keep out light. He later changed his mind about this, but I am not sure he ever ceased to feel that we elected a dictator every four years, who never became more than a prospective president during his first term because he spent all his time laying plans for his re-election. "Mr. Everett long ago pointed out the advantage we should gain by having a responsible ministry. As it is, the representative branch of our government is practically a nullity." [38]

But his feelings *were* democratic. He may have been a "natural Tory," as he called himself, and it may be that he never remembered Fields's office boy, but there was no class feeling about this. In 1849 his daughter Mabel seems to have thought it advisable to ask him whether he objected to her husband's name going up on a tradesman's sign. He replied that he had not the slightest. "The only shame would be to sell dishonest goods, and that I am sure he never will." The Messiah came of common stock, and he rejoiced that Lincoln, too, had come thus. No man was free until all men were free; exploitation of labor in the North was the other face of slavery in the South; "good" families were involved in the degradation of the outcast; even poetry was impossible without social justice. God has not willed existing conditions, and if we will not change them voluntarily, force will step in and change them for us, for "want, and not wish, is at the bottom of armed insurrections." Conservation takes care of itself with healthy organisms, but legitimate complaints unheard find dangerous outlets. Men throw off all reverence when you ask them to revere falsehoods, and "where there is no freedom . . . anarchy is to be dreaded; even the excesses of the French Revolution of 1848 were caused by iniquitous conditions and not by the revolutionaries. Moderation is an agreeable opiate, but it stupefies the conscience, and though narrowness may involve bigotry, it sometimes only implies concentration. Trade itself is encrusted with blood and guilt. "Poets prophesy what is right, philosophers see it, fanatics accomplish it."

Only one reservation needs to be entered to all this. As Lowell grew older, he realized increasingly that one could not seek the source of *all* evil in either corrupt institutions or the misadministration of good ones. Create an ideal environment for man to live in, and his problems will *not* all be solved, for he will still be himself, and part of the trouble is in him. Early in life, Lowell blasted Wordsworth for his defense of capital punishment, but in 1844 he praised him for having "been convinced, perhaps against his will, that a great part of human suffering has its root in the nature of man, and not in that of his institutions." Yet it is easily possible to exaggerate the difference between the early and the late Lowell in this matter, for it was in the very first volume of the *Atlantic* that he wrote that "the only responsibility which is of saving efficacy in a Democracy is that of every individual man in it to his conscience and his God." [39] Has anybody of Puritan stock ever believed anything else?

V

Lowell's reformism first expressed itself clearly in connection with abolitionism.[40] His biographers have differed as to when he became an abolitionist. Greenslet said 1840, which was the year he wrote his recantation on the cover of his Class Poem—

> Behold the baby-arrows of that wit
> Wherewith I dared assail the woundless Truth:
> Love has refilled the quiver and with it
> The man may win forgiveness for the youth:—
> And yet from whom? for well ere this, I know
> That Truth hath no resentments: she returns
> A kiss in full atonement for the blow:
> Let who hath felt it say how deep it burns.

Leon Howard seems to place it in 1842 or 1843. Duberman says 1839, and in 1885 Lowell himself encountered a letter of 1838 which seemed to him to make him an abolitionist two years earlier than he had supposed,[41] which would tend to minimize the importance of Maria White's influence in bringing about the change. To be sure, Harry Hayden Clark has now shown that Lowell's Class Poem was less an out-and-out attack upon abolitionism per se than a denunciation of abolitionist fanatics,[42] but it is still difficult to believe that anyone committed to abolitionism could have written it.

Once he had been converted, he spoke out even in *The Pioneer* (though it was customary for editors of literary magazines to hold their fire), for

> the slave's stifled moaning broke my sleep,
> Heard 'gainst my will in that seclusion deep.

Writing for the anti-slavery papers, he was eager that his name should appear,

because I scorned to be indebted for any share of my modicum of popularity to my abolitionism, without incurring at the same time whatever odium might be attached to a complete identification with a body of heroic men and women, whom not to love and admire would prove me unworthy of either of those sentiments, and whose superiors in all that constitutes true manhood and womanhood I believe never existed.

He named names and hit hard. To J. G. Palfrey he wrote in 1846 that New England could not claim even deference to external morality "while she allows herself to be represented by Webster, and claims the first place in voting for Clay—two men notoriously debauched—the one of them a slaveholder and the other a slave." If he had attended the Pilgrim dinner, he would have been tempted to offer the toast: "The good old red heart of Massachusetts, may it one day be disenthralled of its deadening wrappings of *cotton* that its beat may be again heard as of yore—the drumbeat of the forlorn hope of Man!" He did not attend the dinner, but both his poems and his editorials in *The National Anti-Slavery Standard* made his position abundantly clear. Webster was a coward, of bad reputation, sophomoric and shallow, who had stood for nothing, "the most meanly and foolishly treacherous man I ever heard of," and Whittier may well have found the suggestion for his great poem "Ichabod" in Lowell's query, "Shall not the Recording Angel write *Ichabod* after the name of this man in the great book of Doom?" [43]

Despite the valiant service he rendered, however, Lowell was quite right when he wrote Sydney Gay that he had come into the anti-slavery ranks after the chief burden and heat of the day was over. He might have added that he made a separate peace long before the battle was won. It was not that he took anything back; he simply ceased to be an agitator. He once told George William Curtis that there was nothing of the martyr in him and that if there had been, it would have been early exorcised "by the folio Foxe in my father's library." There may be something in this, but it does not cover the case. Lowell might admire fanaticism, but he could never possess it for long, even in behalf of a cause in which he believed. There was simply too much of him, and his interests were too wide, for him to be able to spend his time, year after year, hammering away at one particular evil. "The truth is," he wrote Sydney Gay, "that our position is so purely *destructive*, that one must look at everything from a point of *criticism* which is wearisome." He did not feel quite at home with the professional agitators who were his colleagues, and they do not seem to have entirely trusted him. Nor did he admire John Brown, and though, in the early days, he flirted with Garrisonian mistrust of political action as a means of opposing slavery, and with Garrisonian disunionism too, he never really committed himself to either.[44] Increasingly, as he grew older, he saw the "inextricable connection" of every social wrong with all others, like a great underground network of original sin, and in some ways he found himself more inclined to methods of indirect attack. When the *Atlantic* was on the drawing board, he wrote Norton that it would be "free without being fanatical and we hope to unite in it all available talent of all shades of opinion." His own *Atlantic* articles seem to me uncompromising enough, but Higginson complained bitterly that the magazine had only spoken out on emancipation once in three months and then on the wrong side.

Did Lowell *like* Negroes? I really do not know. His abolitionism was a matter of principle, not sentiment, and this was well, for if the rights of Negroes or any other group are to depend upon the emotional reactions of others to them, then are they of all men most miserable. As early as 1848 Lowell knew that there is no scientific basis for any beliefs about superior and inferior races,[45] and when he found Negroes sitting with the rest of the congregation, "promiscuously," as he oddly calls it, in a New York church, he thought this an improvement over the segregation which was practised in Boston. He praised President Quincy of Harvard for giving his seat in a public vehicle to a Negro woman, and he almost resigned from the Town and Country Club in his disgust over Emerson's refusal to accept Frederick Douglass as a member. After the war he advocated making Negroes landowners and giving them the vote; existing prejudices he thought would disappear with proximity; but he disappoints us when he adds, "We believe the white race, by their intellectual and traditional superiority, will retain sufficient ascendancy to prevent any serious mischief from the new order of things." But though he acknowledged the contributions of the Negroes to American music and was capable of speaking of them as a gentler, less selfish race than the whites, he had unpleasant encounters with them too, and he did not always handle them quite so skillfully as he handled the haughty porter on the Pullman he took home from Chicago in 1887: "I beg that you will be patient with one so ignorant as I. I shall try to be as respectful as possible." In the dining car he refused to drink the tea or eat the potatoes the waiter brought him. "Ain't they good?" "I dare say they were day before yesterday."

As to other races, the only comment on Orientals I have found in Lowell is his remark about Bret Harte's "Plain Language from Truthful James" ("The Heathen Chinee")—that, "with a deadly thrust of humor," it "gave the *coup de grace* to the barbarian cant on the Chinese question."[46]

One of the mysteries of American racism has always been the question why a people which regards "Negro blood" as a disgrace should be so eager to claim descent from Indians.

Lowell's comment on this is more savage than ironic, however, for he speaks of "an ancestry of filthy barbarians, who daubed themselves for ornament with a mixture of bear's-grease and soot, or colored clay," after which, apparently determined to insult as many people as possible, he proceeds to compare Indians to Scottish Highlanders, "between whom and our Indians there was a very close analogy," and both groups "have become romantic in proportion as they ceased to be dangerous." In his Anti-Slavery paper on "The Prejudice of Color," Lowell might be said to illustrate his title as well as discussing it when he complains that

the red men, having returned blow for blow,—having displayed, perhaps, more hideous qualities than any other savages,—become the theme of novels and romances, are made the subject of rhymes almost as atrocious as one of their own war songs, and furnish even our children's books with pernicious examples of utterly barbarous and pagan virtues.

On the other hand, he idealizes the natives of the West Indies, whom Columbus encountered, and he was on the Indian side in the Seminole War. His Class Poem shows far more sympathy toward Indians than it does toward Negroes, and if we postulate Lowell's dislike of sentimentalism as the explanation for what seems like his anti-Indian position in general, we may be thrown off by the very sentimental passage on the Indian lovers in Section XXII.

Lowell knew—or believed—that immigrants untrained in democratic processes must make the administration of democracy more difficult in America, and in his New England immigration meant largely Irish immigration. I would not say that he never spoke an unjust word against the Irish, but I can say that he never lent himself to any scheme of discrimination against them; once he even indicated his dissent from an expression of anti-Irish feeling on the part of so liberal a young man as William Dean Howells. Americans might begin by enduring immigrants from "all the four corners of the world," but Lowell felt quite sure that from here they must pass on to toleration, and at last to liking, and, much more importantly, to the understanding "that each added a certain virtue of his own to that precious amalgam of which we are in due time to fashion a great nation." When the Irish bought up worn-out farms in Massachusetts and made them "productive again by the same virtues of industry and thrift that once made them profitable to the English ancestors of the men who are deserting them," he admired them and gladly acknowledged their contribution to the commonwealth.

The really interesting matter is Lowell's attitude toward the Jews. Not even Hitler ever had them more on the brain. By this I do not at all mean that Lowell would in any sense have approved of Nazism, for there is not the slightest suggestion that he ever even considered the possibility of adopting repressive measures toward Jews or anybody else.[47] What he did do was to detect them everywhere. Gladstone was a Jew. Mark Twain was a Jew because he had a Jewish nose. Browning was a Jew—because he looked like it, because he once used a Hebrew line in a poem, then cancelled it, and because he associated freely with Jews. In 1890 Story wrote Lowell, "What do you think now of the Jews? or have you forgotten our talk about them? and do you still think that you and I are the only two persons you know who are *not* Jews?" "To say the truth," wrote Sir Leslie Stephen, "this was the only subject upon which I could conceive Lowell approaching within measurable distance of boring."

The odd thing is that Lowell professed not to dislike Jews but rather to admire them. Story to the contrary, he wondered whether the "Russell" in his name did not indicate a Jewish inheritance, and S. Weir Mitchell told Albert Mordell "that Lowell regretted that he was not a Jew and even wished that he had a Hebrew nose." [48] He called the Jews "perhaps the ablest, certainly the most tenacious" of all races—

the race to whom we owed our religion and the purest spiritual stimulus and consolation to be found in all literature—a race in which ability seems as natural and hereditary as the curve of their noses, and whose blood, furtively mingling with the bluest bloods in Europe, has quickened them with its own indomitable impulsion.

He knew too that many traits which Gentiles profess to dislike in Jews were fostered by Christian intolerance and persecution, and he sympathized with Shylock and believed Shakespeare intended him to do so.[49] And yet—and yet—he perpetuates so many Jewish stereotypes that I cannot believe him wholly admiring.[50]

VI

In Lowell's time the slavery issue crossed the peace-and-war issue, and if one were to take the first series of *The Biglow Papers* and stop there, he would find it difficult to avoid the conclusion that Lowell was one of the most uncompromising pacifists who ever lived, for he makes Hosea Biglow say,

> Ez fer war, I call it murder,—
>   There you hev it plain an' flat;
> I don't want to go no furder
>   Than my Testyment fer that.

It has hardly been said better even yet.

> Ef you take a sword an' dror it,
>   An' go stick a feller thru,

Guv'ment ain't to answer for it,
God'll send the bill to you.

How could the essential Puritan refusal to allow any man or institution to come between the individual soul and its God, or the Puritan determination to hold every man directly responsible to God, be better expressed?

Parson Wilbur adds that the devil was the first recruiting sergeant and is proud that none of his flock has gone to the war. He is not sure that it is God who gives victory in war; perhaps it may be the devil. "Our country right or wrong" is a "pestilent fallacy," suitable to shooters, not fishers, of men. Christians live in two worlds and "owe a double, not a divided, allegiance," but the "patriotism of the soul" sets us free from lower claims, and "our true country is that ideal realm which we represent to ourselves under the names of religion, duty, and the like."

As an expression of Lowell's anti-war views, *Biglow* I does not stand alone among Lowell's writings. Perhaps the closest he came to dogmatic formulation was in a couple of paragraphs headed "Nonresistance" in a Notebook of rough drafts in the Houghton Library:[51]

There are fixed laws in the spiritual as well as the material world. If we infringe material laws, the body becomes diseased, if spiritual, the soul suffers. But in obeying these laws we have God on our side. Therefore if it be absolutely Right not to resist evil, we hold up the very strongest shield against violence by submission, since then we obey a spiritual law, and a claim on the protection of God.

So if we are murdered in secret and forgive the murderer, our example is not lost. There is a power in nature which will not let a good deed be thrown away. It enters into the atmosphere and unconsciously influences others. The murderer himself shall one day proclaim it.

In their own way, some early poems come pretty close to this. "An Extract" declares that "force never yet gained one true victory," and that all war can offer is

> So many vultures forged with human flesh;
> So many widows made, so many orphans;
> So many cinders for so many homes;
> So many caps flung up as there are fools,

while the dead soldier's reward is to have his picture hung up in taverns.

> His features struggle through the barroom's smoke,
> Trimmed round the edges with some toper's score.

The "Hymn" beginning "Friends of Freedom! ye who stand" advocates passive, non-violent resistance, and the poem called "The Fatherland" declares that the true man's fatherland is "world-wide." So too:

> In the gain or loss or one race all the rest have equal claim.
> ("The Present Crisis")

> Man is more than Constitutions; better rot beneath the sod,
> Than be true to Church and State while we are doubly false to God!
> ("On the Capture of Fugitive Slaves near Washington")

> Give to Caesar what is Caesar's? yes, but tell me, if you can,
> Is this superscription Caesar's here upon our brother man?
> ("Anti-Apis")

In the second number of *The Pioneer*, he flayed Macaulay's *Lays of Ancient Rome* for what he considered its appeal to base and brutalizing martial passions:

If Mr. Macauley [*sic*] must write ballads founded on stirring incidents, he had been better employed, in our mind, in turning the tide of public opinion against the vilest crusade of modern times, the Chinese massacre, by beautifying with his polished and spirited verses, the self-devotion of Chinese women, who chose rather to die by their own hands than suffer pollution, or the act of that Tartar general who burnt himself alive at his post, a deed of barbarous heroism which neither Greece nor Rome can parallel.[52]

Reviewing Halleck's *Alnwick Castle* in 1845, he went after him for:

> The Moslem tramples on the Greek,
> And on the Cross and altar stone,
> And Christendom looks tamely on,
>
> .   .   .
>
> And not a sabre blow is given
> For Greece and fame, for faith and heaven,
> By Europe's craven chivalry.

"When 'faith and heaven' require to be defended by 'sabre blows' and bloodshed," says Lowell, "they must have sadly degenerated from what they were in Christ's time." On

> Lord Stafford mines for coal and salt,
> The Duke of Norfolk deals in malt,
> The Douglas in red herrings,

which Halleck had presented as examples of the death of romance, Lowell declares that

all these peers are much more creditably employed than any of their ruffian ancestors ever were. Moreover, there is more that is truly poetical in the operations connected with mining, the raising of malt, and the herring fishery, than in all the "chivalry" that ever went about breaking the heads of peaceable neighbors and the hearts of their wives and children. The man who thinks that the age of romance has gone by today, would have thought the same in Spenser's time. Poetry is as rife in the world as ever, but the secret of it lies in the heart and eye and ear of the poet, not in any combination of circumstances.

From the pacifist point of view, *Biglow* I represents Lowell's finest hour, yet his motives for opposing the Mexican War were far from being exclusively pacifist motives. For the Mexican War was a war for the extension of slavery, and not even militarists approve of wars undertaken to achieve results of which they disapprove. Perhaps this may explain the apparent ease with which Lowell shifted from a pacifist to a non-pacifist position between *Biglow* I and *Biglow* II, or between the Mexican War and the Civil War. At no point does he give any indication that this change caused him any mental anguish, nor does he comment upon the inconsistency between the two *Biglows*.

Moreover, though Lowell's early poetry is predominantly pacifistic in tone, it is not exclusively so. He had a tradition of opposition to unjust wars behind him. John Lowell the Rebel had heartily opposed the War of 1812 (though Lowell himself praised it in "The Power of Sound"). The poet speaks harshly of the Revolutionary War loyalists, and though he once expressed the opinion that sooner or later the separation from the mother country could have been achieved without war, he nowhere questions the justice of the Revolutionary cause. "Ye Yankees of the Bay State" and "A Rallying-Cry for New-England against the Annexation of Texas" are certainly not pacific in tone, and it is interesting that Lowell did not put his name to the latter because, though he thought the situation called for violence, he did not wish to advocate it himself. In 1859 he believed it to be "the manifest destiny of the English race to occupy this whole continent," and in a review of a history of New England,[53] he went out of his way to take up a completely amoral point of view on the Acadian expulsion:

If our forefathers were ever wise and farseeing, if they ever showed a capacity for large political views, it is proved by their early perception that the first question to be settled on this continent was whether its destiny should be shaped by English or Keltic, by Romish or Protestant ideas. By what means they attempted to realize their thought is quite another question. Great events are not settled by sentimentalists, nor history written in milk-and-water. Uninteresting in many ways the Puritans doubtless were, but not in the least *spoony*.

The year before, attacking Rufus Choate for an address in Boston, he had written: "There is no man who believes that the ship of State, any more than an ordinary vessel, can be navigated by the New Testament alone; but neither will be the worse for having it aboard." [54] But how and why, one wonders, since it is not a charm nor a talisman, if its teachings are not followed? What function can it possibly serve?

Lowell feared civil war as early as 1845—

Out from the land of bondage 'tis decreed our slaves shall go,
And signs to us are offered, as erst to Pharaoh;
If we are blind, their exodus, like Israel's of yore,
Through a Red Sea is doomed to be, whose surges are of gore—

and by 1857 he may surely be said to have accepted it—

But, oh! fair Freedom, if our choice must be
'Twixt war and craven recreance to thee,
Sooner, dear land, let each manchild of thine
Sleep death's red sleep within the enemy's line, . . .
Sooner than brook, what only slaves hold dear,
A suppliant peace that is not Peace, but Fear! [55]

In 1860 he told Thomas Hughes that he was not for peace at any price. Up to the time the war began, he was apparently not even for union at any price, since he insists that a dissolution of the Union would itself be preferable to Northern acquiescence in Southern demands.[56] All his emphasis, however, falls on the idea that Union firmness is the great hope; it seems strange that anybody should have considered the Southerners so utterly unreasonable as Lowell did and at the same time so underestimated their determination to resist.

Once the war had begun, there was no longer any question about where Lowell stood. Parson Wilbur, who had rejoiced that none of his parishioners fought in Mexico, now sends his own son to war with his blessing. Lowell's own personal stake took the form of three dearly loved, slaughtered nephews, and after that questioning the sacredness of the cause would have been impious. Now the end in view was so noble that a ten years' war would be a cheap price to achieve it. "There is something magnificent in having a country to love. It is almost like what one feels for a woman." And New England has vindicated her nobility above that of

> Plantagenets,
> Hapsburgs, and Guelfs, whose thin bloods crawl
> Down from some victor in a border-brawl! [57]

Not much consolation there, one would think, especially for those who live outside of New England, but Lowell no longer desires such peace as

> "lulls to sleep,
> But sword on thigh, and brow with purpose knit!" [58]

Peace will not keep house with cowardice, and "craven submission to manifest wrong" is a greater evil than war. Peace is not to be sacrificed to honor either, and he passes over the "little more present suffering, self-sacrifice, and earnestness of purpose" called for, as cavalierly as he acknowledges but excuses the administration's riding rough-shod over civil liberties.[59] There were even moments (fortunately not many) when he praised war itself. "Moralize as we will about the victories of peace and the superiority of the goose-quill over the sword, there is no achievement of human genius on which a country so prides itself as on success in war, no disgrace over which it broods so inconsolably as military disaster." And he sneers that "a man's education seems more complete who has smelt hostile powder from a less aesthetic distance than Goethe." But since the closest Lowell himself ever came to smelling it was when he remarked in 1864 that, "If I had enough to leave behind me, I would enlist this very day and get knocked in the head," he must, I fear, share Goethe's limitations in this regard. What he ignores, of course, is the fact that the vast majority of those who have got themselves knocked in the head in the Civil War or any other left nothing behind them.[60] All in all, there was not much left of

> Ez fer war, I call it murder,—
> There you hev it plain an' flat.

Instead we read that

> "Soft-heartedness, in times like these,
> Shows sof'ness in the upper story!" [61]

and that "the doing good to those that despitefully entreat us was not meant for the enemies of the commonwealth," which, whether Lowell realized it or not, is simply to admit that the state is amoral and that Christian virtues and ethical standards can apply only between individuals.[62]

The tribute to Lincoln in the Commemoration Ode is probably still the most famous that has ever been paid him; it is interesting to remember that it was an afterthought, not included in the first draft and not read at the Harvard exercises. In later years, Lowell was proud of having been one of the first in his circle to discern that Lincoln was one of Plutarch's men. He did not always discern it clearly, however. He had wanted Seward nominated in 1860, but he soon came to feel that Lincoln had both ability and integrity—"experience enough in public affairs to make him a statesman, and not enough to make him a politician." But he thought the First Inaugural and the President's conduct afterwards too conciliatory, and there is no recognition of the greatness he afterwards discerned in Lincoln in his article "Self-Possession vs. Prepossession" in the *Atlantic* for December 1861.[63] At one time he thought Lincoln determined to win the war without injuring the enemy—"an ounce of Frémont is worth a pound of long Abraham"—and as late as 1864 he wrote Norton that he was hearing "bad things" about Lincoln's management of the war. In retrospect he acknowledged his impatience with Lincoln but also acknowledged that he had been wrong. The President showed his wisdom, he thought, in moving slowly until he had a united country behind him.

But if, then, Lowell's pacifism had oozed out at the palms of his hands since Mexican War days, what about his abolitionism? It had fared somewhat better, though he was no longer nearly passionate enough to satisfy those who had supported the war only because it promised to abolish slavery. Lowell knew that slavery had *caused* the war, but, like Lincoln, he insisted that slavery was not the *issue*. "If the destruction of slavery is to be a consequence of the war, shall we regret it? If it be needful to the successful prosecution of the war, shall anyone oppose it?"

Yet he was also sure "that the people, instructed by the experience of the past three years, will never consent to any plan of adjustment that does not include emancipation," [64] and one of the reasons why he opposed McClellan against Lincoln in 1864 was that he believed this would mean a negotiated peace and the survival of slavery into the post-war country. Nevertheless, the purpose of the war was to put down the rebellion, vindicate the supremacy of law, and prove the capability of democracy. What was at stake was nothing less than "the august foundation on which the very possibility of government, above all of self-government, rests as in the hollow of God's own hand."

While the war was brewing, and while it raged, Lowell said many harsh things about the barbarous, ignorant Southerners, both in verse and in prose; I cannot recollect any kind thing said about the South in *The Biglow Papers* except one expression of sympathy for Southern mothers. But the war was not yet over when he began to change his tune. In an article published at the beginning of 1865 he was sure that multitudes in the South had been "guilty only of weakness." In 1868 he felt "strong sympathy with men who sacrificed everything even to a bad cause which they could see only the good side of." In 1869 he saw great qualities in Southerners, defended Hawthorne's memory against war-time charges of lack of patriotism, and even admitted that there might have been two sides to the war. At first sympathetic toward Andrew Johnson, he later grew less so, but he opposed impeachment proceedings, and never embraced Thaddeus Stevens, the results of whose Reconstruction policy disgusted him more and more as time went on.[65] When, in 1875, he read "Under the Old Elm" at Cambridge, in honor of the hundredth anniversary of Washington's taking command of the army there, he went out of his way to hold out the olive branch to Virginia.

VII

Disgusted and embittered by the corruptions of the Gilded Age, Lowell, during his later years, opposed Benjamin F. Butler in Massachusetts and James G. Blaine upon the national scene. His reference to America as "the Land of Broken Promises" shocked even Howells, who was generally considered so much more radical than he. But though there were a number of bitter poems,[66] he retained a certain faith in the ability of society to weather a crisis, and when he went west, he was reassured, in the midst of corruption, by the smiling face of the land itself. After the defeat of the international copyright bill in 1890, he wrote Kate Field, "I have had too long experience of the providential thickness of the human skull, as well as of the eventual success of all reasonable reforms, to be discouraged by the temporary defeat of any measure which I believe to be sound."

But Lowell did more than write bitter poems about the political situation. He interested himself actively in civil service, international copyright, tariff reform, and a decent administration of law; he had long ceased to be a party man. In 1887 he publicly declared that he had stood outside all parties for twenty-five years, and in 1890 he told E. M. Bacon that he had been a Mugwump ever since Lincoln's death. This was not a completely new development. Lowell had supported a coalition ticket of Democrats and Free-Soilers against the Whigs as far back as 1850, and though he thought Andrew Jackson a semi-barbarian, he called Jefferson "the first *American* man" and as good a thinker and writer as we have had. His admiration for Cleveland, freely expressed to the disgust of many rock-ribbed Republicans, survived even his loss of his ambassadorship, though he was hurt that others were retained when he was cashiered, and considered his letter of dismissal too curt to send to a dog. How widely all this was recognized appears in the fact that he was the only Hayes elector who in 1876 was believed in many quarters likely to vote for Tilden when it appeared that Tilden had fairly won the popular vote, but he decided against this because the people had elected him to vote for Hayes. "They did not choose me because they had confidence in my judgment, but because they thought they knew what that judgment would be. . . . It is a plain question of trust." Besides, Lowell did not trust Tilden and he did trust Hayes. Though he was losing his old faith in the Republicans, he had not become a Democrat, for he never got over the feeling that the Democratic Party, still tainted with rebellion, was no haven for gentlemen. He remained therefore an independent voter.

Early in 1876, at the request of a group of concerned young men in Cambridge, Lowell presided over a public meeting called to rally the forces of decency in politics, later becoming permanent chairman of the Cambridge committee and a delegate to the Republican convention (the experience turned him against the convention system), where he and those like-minded with him succeeded in preventing Blaine's nomination, though they did not achieve victory for their own favorite candidate, Benjamin Bristow. Lowell could have had the Republican nomination for Congress but refused to consider it, and E. L. Godkin says that Hayes asked his advice about a Cabinet position for Lowell, and that he advised against it, "because he would not accept, because he was not fit physically and otherwise for executive drudgery, and because even an offer to him would give the enterprise a slightly fancy or literary air, that would be injurious."[67] What Lowell did do, for the first time in his life, was to attend caucuses and perform other political drudgery at the grass-roots level. When he died Charles Eliot Norton wrote J. B. Harris that he had done more than any other man of his time to maintain a level of decency and good sense in political affairs.

Though he worked, for the most part, through the Republicans, he can hardly be said to have maintained a consistently Republican point of view. He did not believe in a protective tariff, which, from the Republican point of view, was, as he says, rather worse than not believing in God. The free silver heresy did not seduce him; neither did he accept the Single Tax, though he admired Henry George in some aspects; and he shrank from accepting state Socialism because he feared it would stamp out the variety and color of life, undercut personal initiative, and wither the roots of character.[68] Yet he understood the problems posed by urbanization, industrialization, and the disappearance of the frontier, recognized "a common interest which vastly transcends the claims of individual freedom and action," and acknowledged the need of governmental regulation to protect that common interest.[69] As far back as 1848, he had refused to be shocked by the French government's promising its people food and work, and he takes the bull boldly by the horns when he declares that "the humanity of our day is willing (as our ancestors were not) that the state should support its inefficient members." He knew that it was poverty, not capital, which bore the heaviest burdens of the state, and he could not believe that trade-unions, which were "now debating instead of conspiring," represented an ever-present danger. State Socialism was one thing, but "the practical application of Christianity to life" through "cooperation and community of interests, sympathy, the giving of the hands not so large a share as the brains, but a larger share than hitherto in the wealth they must combine to produce" was quite another, and the benevolences which wealth had so far achieved were "remedies . . . partial and palliative merely." None of this means that Lowell had solved all the problems of our social order, but it does mean that he comes pretty close to at least the non-Marxian phases of our contemporary thinking about them.

At his best, moreover, he achieved a toleration which we today would do well to emulate. It finds its best expression, of all places, in his essay on witchcraft:

> If any lesson may be drawn from the tragical and too often disgustful history of witchcraft, it is not one of exultation at our superior enlightenment or shame at the shortcomings of the human intellect. It is rather one of charity and self-distrust. When we see what inhuman absurdities men in other respects wise and good have clung to as the corner-stone of their faith in immortality and a divine ordering of the world, may we not suspect that those who now maintain political or other doctrines which seem to us barbarous and unenlightened may be, for all that, in the main as virtuous and clear-sighted as ourselves?

If a wiser word was ever spoken, I know not where to look for it.

CHAPTER SEVEN

ULTIMATE HORIZON

Of course, in whatever the man himself has made a part of the record we are entitled to find what intimations we can of his genuine self, of the real man, veiled under the draperies of convention and circumstance, who was visible for so many years, yet perhaps never truly seen, obscurely known to himself, conjectured even by his intimates, and a mere name to all beside.

JRL, 1886

I

Lowell was strongly predisposed in favor of religion by his idealistic, anti-materialistic temperament.[1] In opposition to the law, which "calls only the earth and what is immovably attached to it *real* property," it was his feeling that only a "very small part of the world we truly live in is represented by what speaks to us through the senses," and that "those only are the real possessions which abide with a man after he has been stripped of those others falsely so called." He once spoke of himself as "a sceptic, with a superstitious imagination," and though this may have been true in some aspects (he believed that fables embody truths, for example, and he hated to give up even the sea serpent), reverent imagination would have been more accurate. That which good men have regarded as sacred had an aura about it for him, whether he could believe in it or not. He would not have the death sacrifice in an Elizabethan drama compared to Christ's, and

192

"sweats blood and water" in a story by Henry James struck him as irreverent.[2]

Brownell says that Lowell never cites the Bible, but this is not true. Howells quotes Lowell himself as having said that the truth was in the New Testament but that "they had covered it up with their hagiology." The son of a father who refused to take sides in the Trinitarian-Unitarian controversy, Lowell was not long on theological formulation, but he makes his religious *feelings* unmistakably clear, and even doctrine is less completely neglected than some would have us believe.

Like the Puritans, Lowell cherished "faith in God, faith in man, faith in work." He saw the Puritan faith as the foundation of New England's greatness. For him, God, the source of all good, manifested Himself in all things; without this consciousness, life on this earth was exile. "Every man's duty is to represent some quality of God"; as for himself, Lowell had no doubt that his work had been assigned to him by God.

When his first child was born, he expressed his sense of gratitude to God; in every crisis and every loss, he expresses the idea that there is no hope except in prayer and trust. After Maria's death, prayer may actually have saved him from suicide. "We have the promise of God's Word and God's nature on our side," he writes Motley, and he assures Mabel that her dead mother watches over her and that he himself never goes to sleep without praying for her. After he was gone, F. J. Child wrote,

There is a thing which I regret, and that is J. R. L. did not die in his full mind. Could I have sat by his bed or his chair, his lamp slowly declining, and could we have talked of the other life, in which we both believed, could I have read him cherished places from the Bible, there would have been much happiness to remember from the last days.

I doubt, however, that Lowell possessed what a theologian

would call a Christology. His emphasis, as all readers of "The Search" and "The Vision of Sir Launfal" must know, was on what we later called the Social Gospel; with him, Christ's throne was "with the outcast and the weak." He saw the Christian life as a continual aggression against evil and believed that in its fullness it was possible only to a few. He was not even sure that the New Testament offered good preparation for American citizenship, but he did think it possible (at least when he wrote his antislavery papers) "that Jesus Christ may be right and the glorious framers if our Constitution wrong." In one of his writing books he wrote: "Christ in coming down through the ages hath left the prints of his bleeding feet everywhere with here and there the ashes of a martyr."

In "The Vision of Sir Launfal," Christ is

> Himself the Gate whereby men can
> Enter the temple of God in man.

But I think Lowell speaks of incarnation and atonement only in his essay on Dante:

A man does not receive the statements that "two and two make four," and that "the pure in heart shall see God" on the same terms. The one can be proved to him with four grains of corn; he can never arrive at a belief in the other till he realize it in the intimate persuasion of his whole being. This is typified in the mystery of the incarnation. The divine reason must forever manifest itself anew in the lives of men, and that as individuals. This atonement with God, this identification of the man with the truth, so that right action shall not result from the lower reason of utility, but from the higher of a will so purified of self as to sympathize by instinct with the eternal laws, is not something that can be done once for all, that can become historic and traditional, a dead flower pressed between the leaves of the family Bible, but must be renewed in every generation, and in the soul of every man, that it may be valid.

That is why Lowell regarded the revival, which attempts to engineer the job of redemption, once and for all. under high pressure, as merely mechanical. Yet, for all his emphasis upon what I have called the Social Gospel, he was quite clear that our final reliance must rest upon the hope of remolding individual character.

He had reached the high altar [he writes, again of Dante] where the miracle of transubstantiation is wrought, itself also a type of the great conversion that may be accomplished in our own nature (the lower thing assuming the qualities of the higher), not by any process of reason, but by the very fire of divine love.

I have noted only one reference to the Virgin Birth:

> A maiden and undefiled
> Like her who bore the world's redeeming child.[3]

In *The Biglow Papers*,[4] the Second Advent is treated the reverse of seriously, but in "A Christmas Carol for Geordie's Children," which is dated 186? at the Houghton Library, we read:

> 'Tis eighteen hundred years and more
> Since those sweet oracles were dumb;
> We wait for Him like them of yore;
> Alas, He seems so slow to come!

This *sounds* like an expression of faith in the Second Coming, but this is hard to accept. Perhaps it is to be regarded as a kind of poetic license.

As for Providence, Lowell knew that the doctrine of rewards and punishments must be interpreted in the large, and that, in this world, something must be allowed for chance. "God's livery in this world is but a plain one, and the wages are not very inviting. The devil pays his scullions better." Yet in the long run he did believe that good comes out of evil and that we are living in a safe universe.

I take great comfort in God. I think he is considerably amused with us sometimes, but that he likes us, on the whole, and would not let us get at the match-box so carelessly as he does, unless he knew that the frame of the Universe was fire-proof. How many times have I not seen the fire-engines of Church and State clanging and lumbering along to put out—a false alarm! And when the heavens are cloudy, what a glare can be cast by a burning shanty!

Lowell's most elaborate meditation upon spiritual matters is in "The Cathedral," and there is no substitute for reading and studying this work as a whole. Some of its high points must, however, be noted here. The sense of alienation which the Protestant Lowell felt at Chartres made it impossible to avoid raising the question whether religion itself might not now be outmoded:

> Was all this grandeur but anachronism,
> A shell divorced of its informing life,
> Where the priest housed him like a hermit-crab,
> An alien to the faith of elder days
> That gathered round it this fair shape of stone?
> Is old Religion but a spectre now,
> Haunting the solitude of darkened minds,
> Mocked out of memory by the sceptic day?
> Is there no corner safe from peeping Doubt,
> Since Gutenberg made thought cosmopolite
> And stretched electric threads from mind to mind?

But whatever he may believe or disbelieve, Lowell cannot throw off the idea that there is a sacred quality in life itself:

> I turned and saw a beldame on her knees;
> With eyes astray, she told mechanic beads
> Before some shrine of saintly womanhood,
> Bribed intercessor with the far-off Judge:

Such my first thought, by kindlier soon rebuked,
Pleading for whatsoever touches life
With upward impulse: be He nowhere else,
God is in all that liberates and lifts,
In all that humbles, sweetens, and consoles:
Blessëd the natures shored on every side
With landmarks of hereditary thought!
Thrice happy they who wander not life long,
Beyond near succor of the household faith,
The guarded fold that shelters, not confines!

If science cannot be outlawed, neither can God:

Man cannot be God's outlaw if he would,
Nor so abscond him in the caves of sense
But Nature still shall search some crevice out
With messages of splendor from that Source
Which, dive he, soar he, baffles still and lures.
This life were brutish did we not sometimes
Have intimation clear of wider scope,
Hints of occasion infinite, to keep
The soul alert with noble discontent
And onward yearnings of unstilled desire;
Fruitless, except we now and then divined
A mystery of Purpose, gleaming through
The secular confusions of the world,
Whose will we darkly accomplish, doing ours.
No man can think nor in himself perceive,
Sometimes at waking, in the street sometimes,
Or on the hillside, always unforewarned,
A grace of being, finer than himself,
That beckons and is gone,—a larger life
Upon his own impinging, with swift glimpse
Of spacious circles luminous with mind,
To which the ethereal substance of his own
Seems but gross cloud to make that visible,
Touched to a sudden glory round the edge.
Who that hath known these visitations fleet

Would strive to make them trite and ritual?
I, that still pray at morning and at eve,
Loving those roots that feed us from the past,
And prizing more than Plato things I learned
At that best academe, a mother's knee,
Thrice in my life perhaps have truly prayed,
Thrice, stirred below my conscious self, have felt
That perfect disenthralment which is God;
Nor know I which to hold worst enemy,
Him who on speculation's windy waste
Would turn me loose, stript of the raiment warm
By Faith contrived against our nakedness,
Or him who, cruel-kind, would fain obscure,
With painted saints and paraphrase of God,
The soul's east-window of divine surprise.

Religious symbols have changed since the Middle Ages, but the
Cross is still a

> bold type of shame to homage turned,
> Of an unfinished life that sways the world,

and if modern religious experience, as compared, say, to that of
the faith of the men who built the cathedrals, is, and must,
through our time, remain incomplete, what is this but to say that
modern religion partakes of the nature of modern man himself
and the spirit of the age in which he lives. Since its roots lie deep
in the nature of man himself—

I think man's soul dwells nearer to the east,
Nearer the morning's fountains than the sun;
Herself the source whence all tradition sprang,
Herself at once both labyrinth and clue.
The miracle fades out of history,
But faith and wonder and the primal earth
Are born into the world with every child—

religion itself can never be destroyed; neither need we fear God's withdrawal from the world:

> My soul shall not be taken in their snare,
> To change her inward surety for their doubt
> Muffled from sight in formal robes of proof:
> While she can only feel herself through Thee,
> I fear not Thy withdrawal; more I fear,
> Seeing, to know Thee not, hoodwinked with dreams
> Of signs and wonders, while, unnoticed, Thou,
> Walking Thy garden still, commun'st with men,
> Missed in the commonplace of miracle.

A kind of mystical awareness thus becomes the final basis for Lowell's faith. As he says, he wiped out the distinction between natural and supernatural because he was himself as supernatural as any ghost that had ever manifested. Harry Hayden Clark is quite right when he describes Lowell's "theistic speculation" as taking the form of "fragmentary and often contradictory ideas" and his faith as having "subsisted chiefly on shadowy, evanescent intimations of a supernal existence." He adds: "He puts far more store by religious sensibility than by systematic theology." And Lowell himself says, "I suppose I am an intuitionist, and there I mean to stick." But it was not only in the religious field that he operated thus. As we have already seen, intuition played a considerable role in his criticism.

Professor Clark seems to feel that this is an unsatisfactory basis for religious faith. This is a matter which every man must decide for himself. But there can be no question that Lowell's way was the mystic's way. "To the non-beholders," says Rufus Jones, "he can only cry in the wilderness: 'I have seen and here are my tokens.' "

In the light of these considerations, it may be easier to understand, even in these days of neo-orthodoxy, why Lowell, with his vague theology, still became a great inspirational force to many people. As late as 1902, Herbert W. Horwell reported that "the younger ministry in the free churches [of England] is better acquainted with Lowell's poetry than with that of any other writer." [5] Minot J. Savage wrote:

> O Lowell! I first gave to thee
> My boyhood's love and loyalty,
> My youth took fire at thy words,
> And thou my manhood's spirit stirred
> To lofty faith and noble trust.

To W. T. Stead, the great Christian journalist of *The Review of Reviews*, who went down with the *Titanic*, Lowell was "the greatest of contemporary Americans," "one of the prophets of the nineteenth century," and "the most potent preacher of the living Christ." "In some of the critical moments of my life I found in Lowell such help as I found in none other outside Carlyle's *Cromwell* and Holy Writ." Lowell inspired Stead's *If Christ Came to Chicago*, where he is quoted on the title page. He was admired by Washington Gadden and by Lyman Abbott. The philosopher Rufus M. Jones, the leading American Quaker since Woolman and Whittier, undeterred by Lowell's antagonism toward Friends, called him his favorite poet and gave his only son his name. *The Biglow Papers*, said Jones, "first woke me up to see and feel the gleam of beauty on the common fields and flowers, the woods and sky of New England," and when Jones became editor of *The Friends Review*, Lowell's "Godminster Chimes" was the first thing he printed in it.[6] But I do not know that any testimony along this line has impressed me more than that of Bret Harte, who is not usually considered an authority in such matters. If Lowell was, like Bramah, "the Doubter and the Doubt," says Harte, he was also "the hymn the Brahmin sings." And he proceeds to comment very suggestively on "The

Courtin'," which everybody else who writes about Lowell's religion has passed over:

In the first word the keynote of the Puritan life is struck:—

God makes sech nights, all white and still.

The familiar personal Deity is there—no Pantheistic abstraction, conventional muse, nor wanton classic Goddess, but the New Englander's Very God. Again and again through the verses of that matchless pastoral the religious chord is struck; weak human passion and grim poetry walk hand-in-hand to its grave measure; to look at the pretty Huldy in her cosy kitchen was "kin' o' kingdom come"; when, on Sunday, in the choir, Zekel "made Old Hundred ring," she knowed the Lord was nigher; with his eyes on the cover of her meetin' bonnet she blushes scarlet "right in prayer," and the loving but discreet pastoral closes with the assurance that

They was cried
In meetin' come nex Sunday.[7]

II

Lowell seems to have had a special interest in that side of religion which connects with thoughts of a hereafter. The very orthodox Elmer J. Bailey thought him confident of God but not of immortality, but Bailey did not sufficiently allow for the difference between poetry and preaching, nor yet for the poet's inclination to present various states of emotion and varying points of view. Lowell recognized the decline of faith in immortality which has occurred in modern times. "That crawling prose of death too well I know," he wrote, and heaven knows he had enough experience with it in his family. The touching poem "After the Burial" does not reject immortality, but it does assert that no spiritual source of comfort can cure the ache in a human heart. He

> Would give all my incomes from dreamland
> For a touch of her hand on my cheek.

Sometimes it seemed to him, as it must have seemed to the Greeks, that even if we could be sure of immortality, it would be less desirable than the life we had lived here.

> Truly this life is precious to the root,
> And good the feel of grass beneath the foot;
> To lie in buttercups and clover-bloom,
>   Tenants in common with the bees,
> And watch the white clouds drift through gulfs of trees,
> Is better than long waiting in the tomb.

Who would wish to change all this for "casual hope of being elsewhere blest"?

Nevertheless he believed. Even in the ode on Agassiz, from which these words are taken, he refers to Agassiz's own orthodoxy:

> But God to him was very God,
> And not a visionary wraith
> Skulking in murky corners of the mind.

If Agassiz survived death at all, it must have been in the Christian sense of personal immortality, and "not with His essence mystically combined." In his review of Thoreau's *Week*, Lowell expressed the opinion that the Hindu philosophy in these matters might be more satisfying to men if they were oysters!

He knew that "death knits as well as parts," and he felt

> our souls grow fine
> With keen vibrations from the touch divine
> Of noble natures gone.[8]

His considered word on the subject of survival is "Auf Wieder-sehen," as in the poem of that title. "I hate farewells," he wrote Thomas Hughes, when leaving London—"they always seem to ignore another world by the stress they lay upon the chance of never meeting again in this. We shall meet somewhere, for we love one another." He did not care

where the notion of immortality came from. If it sprang out of a controlling necessity of our nature, some instinct of self-protection and preservation, like the color of some of Darwin's butterflies, at any rate it is there and as real as that, and I mean to hold it fast. Suppose we don't *know*, how much *do* we know after all? There are times when one doubts his own identity, even his own material identity, even the solidity of the very earth on which he walks.

After Maria had died, he cherished her promise to be near him. And many years later he wrote of Fanny, "But she is surely with God, for never was there a soul readier for him, or that would have been more welcome."

Belief in a hereafter often involves the thought of punishment as well as reward. In "Sunthin' in the Pastoral Line" we read:

> I thought o' the Rebellion, then o' Hell,
> Which some folks tell ye now is jest a metterfor
> (A the'ry, p'raps, it wun't *feel* none the better for.)

In "Si Descendero in Infernum, Ades," Lowell affirms fellow feeling with the damned, but is also unwilling to set bounds to the love of God. He praised the devil for his diligence, as Latimer did, as "the faithfullest of bishops, going up and down con-tinually in his diocese, and distraining for rent when his parish-ioners were on their death-beds, and that not for *tithes* merely, but for the whole of his debtor's eternal substance." In view of Satan's distressed circumstances, Lowell playfully judged the loyalty which he still commanded "on the whole, creditable to poor human nature." He was the only "stage-property of poetry" that the Pilgrims brought with them to the new world, but "even he could not stand the climate." Lowell knew, however, that if he had departed, he had left many behind him to do his work for him.

Other things being equal, persons with a strong interest in immortality would seem more predisposed than others to be attracted to spiritualism and occult phenomena, but Lowell scornfully rejected spiritualism as "the weakest-kneed of all whimsies that have come upon the parish from the days of the augurs down to our own" [9] In 1858 when he wished to flay the politician Caleb Cushing for a letter he had written, he wrote that "the epistles of Jacob Behmen [Boehme] himself are not farther removed from any contamination with the delights of sense," [10] certainly a remark which would bring up the eyebrows of many modern students of mysticism.

Lowell was, in fact, as scornful toward spiritualism as Hawthorne was, and it is interesting that these two should probably have been the most "sensitive" of all the leading New England writers; Lowell, indeed, might not unfairly be described as mediumistic. No wonder he was offended when Mrs. Longfellow "expressed her fears that I was deranged because I believed in ghosts." He added, "I have a crack in my brain, but it is just where the light comes in." [11]

When I speak of him thus, I am not thinking of such things as the rather fuzzy mysticism of "A Mystical Ballad," nor the suggestion of pre-existence in "The Token"—

> As now sometimes we seem to find,
> In a dark crevice of the mind,
> Some relic, which, long pondered o'er,
> Hints faintly at a life before—

nor yet the idea that those on the other side of life and death may be as curious about us here as we are about them, which he might have taken from Dante. Nor am I forgetting the nice capacity for careful discrimination which never deserted him. (We reminded ourselves at the outset that nothing about Lowell was simple, and it might be well to recall the reminder, now that we draw near to the end of our inquiry.) The essay on witchcraft opens with a brilliant discussion of the difference between genuine superstition and the fancies of those who only play with inherited folk beliefs for the sake of the fillip they can give to the imagination:

Credulity, as a mental and moral phenomenon, manifests itself in widely different ways, according as it chances to be the daughter of fancy or terror. The one lies warm about the heart as Folk-lore, fills moonlit dells with dancing fairies, sets out a meal for the Brownie, hears the tinkle of airy bridle-bells as Tamlane rides away with the Queen of Dreams, changes Pluto and Proserpine into Oberon and Titania, and makes friends with unseen powers as Good Folk; the other is a bird of night, whose shadow sends a chill among the roots of the hair; it sucks with the vampire, forges with the ghoul, is choked by the nighthag, pines away under the witch's charm, and commits uncleanness with the embodied Principle of Evil, giving up the fair realm of innocent belief to a murky throng from the slums and stews of the debauched brain.

He believed that nightmare could "explain the testimony of witnesses in trials for witchcraft, that they had been hag-ridden by the accused," but he was puzzled "to explain the appearance of the *first* ghost, especially among men who thought death to be the end-all here below." Against Grimm's profession of ignorance as to "when broomsticks, spits, and similar utensils were first assumed to be the canonical instruments of . . . nocturnal equitation," Lowell suspected it to be "as old as the first child that ever bestrode his father's staff and fancied it into a courser shod with wind, like those of Pindar." And he is even more penetrating when he declares that "even now the territory which Reason holds firmly as Lord Warden of the marches during daylight, is subject to sudden raids of Imagination by night, a statement which recalls Sir Osbert Sitwell's reply to the question whether he believed in ghosts—that he so believed only at night.

We do not know a great deal about Lowell's dream life, but we do know that it must have been rich. He makes the speaker in "Sunthin' in the Pastoral Line" say,

> I'm gret on dreams, an' often when I wake,
> I've lived so much it makes my mem'ry ache,
> An' can't skurce take a cat-nap in my cheer
> 'thout havin' 'em, some good, some bad, all queer.

From boyhood he was visited, usually in the evening, by a figure in a medieval costume, and he told Howells he had seen many ghosts and Doppelgängers besides. He seems to have seen his own Doppelgänger and to have felt himself "dispersed through space in some inconceivable fashion, and mixed with the milky way." He believed that human beings are encircled by a spirit world, and he did not dislike this, for he thought the spirits inspired insight and purpose. As a youngster he spent a night in the graveyard with C. W. Scates, trying to raise spirits; as a man he was beyond such hocus-pocus, but he still believed at times that "there is something in the flesh that is superior to the flesh, something that can in finer moments abolish matter and pain." [12]

The most remarkable passage bearing on such matters is in a letter of September 20, 1842, to G. B. Loring:

I had a revelation last Friday evening. I was at Mary's, and happening to say something of the presence of spirits (of whom, I said, I was often dimly aware), Mr. Putnam entered into an argument with me on spiritual matters. As I was speaking the whole system rose up before me like a vague Destiny looming from the abyss. I never before so clearly felt the spirit of God in me and around me. The

whole room seemed to me full of God. The air seemed to waver to
and fro with the presence of Something I knew not what. I spoke
with the calmness and clearness of a prophet.
I cannot yet tell you what this revelation was. I have not yet
studied it enough. But I shall perfect it one day, and then you shall
hear it and acknowledge its grandeur. It embraces all other systems.

There is no further light on what this revelation was, but I doubt
that it was a unique experience, for he writes elsewhere:

I find myself very curiously compounded of two utterly distinct
characters. One half of me is clear mystic and enthusiast, and the
other humorist. If I had lived as solitary as a hermit of the Thebais,
I doubt not that I should have had as authentic interviews with the
Evil One as they, and without any disrespect to the saint, it would
have taken very little to have made a Saint Francis of me. Indeed,
during that part of my life when I lived most alone, I was never
a single night unvisited by visions, and once I thought I had a personal revelation from God Himself. I can believe perfectly in the
sincerity of those who are commonly called religious impostors,
for at one time, a meteor could not fall, nor lightning flash, that I
did not in some way connect it with my own interior life and
destiny. On the other hand, had I mixed more with the world than
I have, I should probably have become a Pantagruelist.

Did such experiences cease as he grew older, or did he merely
learn not to talk about them? And if the former view be taken,
must they, then, be placed under the Wordsworthian heading
of

> Those shadowy recollections
> Which, be they what they may,
> Are yet the fountain light of all our day,
> Are yet a master light of all our seeing,

those recollections of a better world and a purer state of being
which must at last "fade into the light of common day"? I am

not sure this follows. For though these visions certainly represent Lowell's most spectacular and elaborate mysticim, there may
be more religious significance to the sense of spiritual impinge-
ments which he described in "How I Consulted the Oracle of the
Goldfishes," which draws a parallel between the goldfish globe
and the world outside of it on the óne hand and our world and
whatever lies beyond it on the other, and even more in certain
passages of "The Cathedral."

> What know we of the world immense
> Beyond the narrow ring of sense?
> What should we know, who lounge about
> The house we dwell in, nor find out,
> Masked by a wall, the secret cell
> Where the soul's priests in hiding dwell?

As we have already seen, in "The Cathedral" it is mystical
awareness that saves religion for Lowell even after all traditional
sanctions have faded away.

III

Friendly as he is toward Christianity, Lowell can hardly be
called a great admirer of the church. In the early days, this was
because he was angered by the association of the church with
established evils—especially slavery—and the use of the Bible to
defend them. "Such strange things have been found in the Bible
that we are not without hope of the discovery of Christianity
there, one of these days." In 1840 he declared that "Christ has
declared war against the Christianity of the world," and in 1845
he wrote Edward M. Davis that "Christ cast out devils, but the
Church nowadays casts about diligently for ways and means by
which to expel whatever ángels there may chance to be in it." [13]

This is not the whole story however. Even without the

slavery issue, Lowell would not have made a good churchman. Though he knew he was an indefatigable preacher himself, he disliked both sermons and hymns, thought creeds "malarious," and detested all religious exclusivism as evil.

God sends his teachers unto every age,
To every clime, and every race of men,
With revelations fitted to their growth
And shape of mind, nor gives the realm of Truth
Into the selfish rule of one sole race.[14]

Once permit religious establishment,[15] and you find the church usurping the place of God. "People worship preacher," "preacher worships salary," and the Sabbath is devoted to the "manufacture of wooden-nutmegs." At one period of his youth, Lowell seems to have paraded the piazza ostentatiously during family prayers ("James is not serious, as yet," said his father, "but he has a good heart, and is a foe to every mortal wrong"), and he denounced the infidelity of the church in his Harvard Class Poem even before he had become an abolitionist. In 1842 he overtly repudiated churchianity in a hymn written for a Congregational church in Watertown:

Let us not think thy presence falls
Only within these narrow walls,
Nor that this handiwork of clods
Can prison up the God of gods. . . .

The world too many homes doth own,
Shall God the Father have but one?
Shall we his loving presence seek,
But one poor day of all the week? . . .

Thy presence here we then shall seek,
As but an emblem of the week;

> Secure that thou wilt bless us when
> We strive to bless our fellow men.
>
> Then shall this house indeed be thine,
> A visible and outward sign
> Of that unseen, encircling love,
> Which doth in all our spirits move.

These are stern words, and he might have been a little less obvious about it later, but his basic viewpoint never changed. In "Turner's Old Téméraire" he called the church "the fairest of all man-made things."

Lowell was brought up in the Congregational Church; in later years, if he had any preference, it would seem to have been for the Episcopal Church. The church his first wife attended in Watertown was Unitarian from the 1820's, and Scudder, Howells, and W. J. Stillman all call the second wife Swedenborgian. Yet she and Lowell were married by Episcopal rites, with Lowell's brother Robert performing the ceremony; she apparently attended an Episcopal church after her marriage, and he went with her when he attended church at all. It is interesting, however, that Swedenborgianism is the only marginal Christian religious movement of which Lowell can always be trusted to speak respectfully. He was extremely contemptuous toward Mormonism, and neither the prominence of Quakers among abolitionists nor his own happy contacts with them in Philadelphia could disabuse him of the idea that George Fox was a crazy fanatic, though a fanatic of imagination, who made come-outism a cause in itself, regardless of the particular issue at stake, nor that contemporary Quakerism was ruled by a dead authority.

During his early life, Lowell shared the traditional Puritan dislike of the Roman Catholic Church;[16] once he even suggests that foreigners can become good Americans only if they are Protestants! In 1851, in Rome, he tended to think of Romanism as dead in Italy, with the Pope a relic. At Christmastime he went to the church ceremonies "merely that I may see for myself that they are not worth seeing," and quite naturally found what he expected. He was more responsive at Chartres in 1855, as my references to "The Cathedral" have already shown, but as late as 1868, the Pope is still "that pagan full of pride," and when Cardinal Newman died, he thought of him as "a beautiful old man" who had lived "a futile life if ever there was one, trying to make a past unreality supply the place of a present that was becoming past, and forgetting that God is always 'I am,' never 'I was.' "

Nevertheless there are indications that, as he grew older, Lowell became in some aspects more sympathetic toward the Catholic Church, and though I doubt he ever went quite as far in this direction as Longfellow, it would have been surprising if something like this had not happened to a scholar who was as familiar as Lowell became with the Catholic civilization of Europe. In the *Fifth Annual Report of the Dante Society* (1886), he outlined the Catholic scheme of redemption, as set forth in the *Comedy*, and commented: "Here are general rules which any Christian may accept and find comfort in." He was sensitive enough to be disagreeably impressed by the irreverent behavior of English tourists in Roman churches, when they went there to hear the music and not to worship, and he loved the nuns who nursed his second wife when she was sick in Spain. For whatever it may be worth, it may be well to record here that he wished Hawthorne had not deprived himself of the "psychologically admirable" effect he might have secured by carrying out his original notion of having Dimmesdale confess his sin to a priest. When Raymond Blathwayt interviewed him, near the end of his life, he discerned Puritan influence in American Catholicism and even said a good word for Catholic schools and for Cardinal Manning.[17]

Lowell's closest ancestral relationship, theologically speaking, was of course not with Catholicism but with Calvinism, and in spite of what many have regarded as his theological indifferentism, it seems clear that he never did quite succeed in sweating this inheritance out of his bones.

The inheritance shows clearly enough in the "New Year's Eve" fragment of 1844, which speaks of "the great hopes we have had for men" as

> Foes in disguise, because they based belief
> On man's endeavor, not on God's decree,—

but it would not be well to make too much of this, for he had plenty of time to change his mind afterward. Later, when he read Lyman Beecher's autobiography, it caused him to wonder "as in a land of earthquakes, how the work of life can go on at all with that gloomy faith hanging between men and heaven." But he adds, "the truth is, that creeds, though intellectually unbending, are always pliant to the moral needs of men." [18] When he was editing the *Atlantic* he offended Emerson by refusing to print one passage of "May Day"—

> One, in Judaean manger,
> And one by Avon stream,
> One over against the mouths of Nile,
> And one in the Academe—

and in 1875 he told James Freeman Clarke, apparently about some question that had been raised at Harvard as to Charles Eliot Norton's religious views, that he himself was "orthodox enough to think a great part of the Board of Overseers heterodox."

Underwood says Lowell once told him that the five points of Calvinism were about as reasonable as other formulations, but this is certainly no more than he said elsewhere of the Catholic formulation in the *Comedy*. Lowell told Mrs. Herrick that he sympathized with some Calvinistic doctrines, but apparently did not particularize. His strongest statement was made to Harriet Beecher Stowe in 1859: "I confess a strong sympathy with many parts of Calvinistic theology, and, for one thing, believe in hell with all my might, and in the goodness of God for all that." [19] On this point, Howells, having first made the universal error of having Lowell "bred a Unitarian," says that, though he had "more and more liberated himself from all creeds, he humorously affected an abiding belief in hell, and similarly contended for the eternal punishment of the wicked." This report may be tempered somewhat by Howells's own skepticism and gentleness. Lowell did not believe that he was living in a world in which a man can go on forever sinning with impunity. It does not seem, however, that his notion of hell could have been physical, since he specifically told Sir Leslie Stephen that he could not agree with Jonathan Edwards on this point: "If he had only conceived of damnation as a spiritual state, the very horror of which consists . . . in its being delightful to who is in it, I could go along with him altogether."

IV

It was science that got in the way of faith in the minds of many nineteenth-century men and women—how did Lowell fare here? [20] One of his 1836 letters mentions chemistry and mineralogy, and he was nearing the end of his life when he wrote Mabel, apropos of her son's interest in entomology, that it had been his own earliest passion, though in his case it had led to nothing. In 1845 Maria wrote her mother-in-law from Philadelphia that she and James had been reading Babbage's *Vestiges of*

Creation: "It overthrows all former theories and opens a most wonderful and interesting view of the formation of the planets bringing all science to support it." Twice Lowell himself speaks of having visited a dissecting room.

In 1919, when the centenary of Lowell's birth was celebrated at Harvard, Bliss Perry declared that the poet "had little or no interest in science or philosophy," while President Eliot, though admitting his delighted observation of "trees, flowers, birds, and landscape," denied him "even an elementary training in any exact science, and without knowledge of the great part played by the imagination in scientific research, or perception of the oneness or identity of modern methods of advancing knowledge in all fields of inquiry." Since then both Harry Hayden Clark and William White have made it clear both that he read more science than he has generally been given credit for and that he made more use of what he learned about it in his writings.[21] In a sense, however, Perry and Eliot are still right. Lowell was a "bookman" and a humanist. Essentially, science interested him to the extent and in the degree to which it affected poetry, imagination, and religion.

Of course this does not mean that he was a Fundamentalist in his attitude toward science. The author of "The Cathedral" was quite clear that

> Nothing that keeps thought out is safe from thought.
> For there's no virgin-fort but self-respect,
> And Truth defensive hath lost hold on God.
> Shall we treat Him as if He were a child
> That knew not His own purpose? nor dare trust
> The Rock of Ages to their chemic tests,
> Lest some day the all-sustaining base divine
> Should fail from under us, dissolved in gas?

He spelled it out in prose too. "Science has scuttled the old ship of Faith," he wrote Norton, and he told his daughter that "nobody ever quarreled with Science who did not come off second best." [22]

Lowell respected Huxley and Darwin, and his friendship with Agassiz inspired one of his most ambitious poems, but Agassiz was not a Darwinian, and it may be significant that Lowell confessed understanding and liking him better "as I grew older (perhaps less provincial)." He wrote a memorial poem too for the scientist Jeffries Wyman in which he declares that "to touch, if not to grasp" the "endless clue" of nature is one of the blessings of life. There is even an early sonnet which begins "I grieve not that ripe knowledge takes away."

Friendship aside, however, none of this came out of the depths for Lowell. Eliot to the contrary notwithstanding, he does sometimes catch a glimpse of "oneness or identity." In his essay on Disraeli he remarks that "many examples, were it necessary, might be brought to prove that the great mathematical or scientific mind is not so different in kind from the poetical as is generally taken for granted." But there was no question as to where his own heart lay. "The man who gives his life for a principle has done more for his kind than he who discovers a new metal or names a new gas, for the great motors of the race are moral, not intellectual, and their force lies ready to the use of the poorest and weakest of us all." In "The Function of the Poet," the evolutionary hypothesis is just that, and science is bleak and bare without imagination. In "The Progress of the World" he accepts evolution but characteristically stresses the human and religious aspects which he finds in it or reads into it. He may not have agreed with Thoreau about many things, but the two were agreed that technology was no unmixed blessing. In 1859 he reviewed Actaea's *A First Lesson in Natural History*,[23] but though the facts contained in it had been vouched for by Agassiz, he was obviously more interested in "the feminine grace and charm with which they are told." Science here was "living poetry," not the "vile compound of treacle and brimstone" which was "sometimes forced down youthful throats by the Mrs. Squeerses of polite learning."

Like Disraeli, Lowell was "on the side of the angels"; like Oliver Wendell Holmes, he believed that "facts of chemistry are one thing . . . and facts of consciousness" another, and like him too, he could not but regard the evolutionists' "mush" of protoplasm as "a poor substitute for the Rock of Ages." This is the explanation for those utterances of Lowell's which *seem* Fundamentalistic. "I am a conservative . . . and keep on the safe side—with God as against Evolution." "Let whoever wishes to, believe that the idea of Hamlet or Lear was developed from a clod; I will not." "I can't help being fond of particular scientific men . . . but I would trudge over to Smithfield . . . to make a bonfire of the rest of 'em all the same. Why wake the Seven Sleepers of Ephesus before their time—especially when their dreams are so pleasant? Not that *I* call 'em dreams, but visions rather." And, the most extreme statement of all, to Mrs. W. E. Darwin: "I hate it [science] as a savage does writing, because he fears it will hurt him somehow."

Actually, however, Lowell accepted science so long as it remained upon its own ground, though this did not concern him very much because that was not the ground where he lived. But he was not impressed by "all the science that ever undertook to tell me what it doesn't know." He speaks of the teachings of Huxley & Co. as "the new nursery-tales of science," [24] and when George Henry Lewes thought he found Positivism in the Commemoration Ode, he was horrified. "The old ship of Faith" might have been "scuttled," but he could see nothing "dishonest" or "undignified in drifting about on the hencoop" he had contrived to secure in the confusion."

VI

When Lowell died, *The Christian Union* achieved a far more perspicacious evaluation of his strength and weakness than piety and journalistic acumen can always be trusted to arrive at:

His working moods were often fitful, and his work is uneven, but there is more impulse in it, more color and fire, more spontaneity, more rich human feeling, than in that of any of the men with whom he was most intimately associated. So fertile was his mind, so strong his personality, so rich the tides of thought and feeling that registered their ebb and flow in his talk and work, that, in spite of all he has done, he seemed never to realize his possibilities; there was always in him a thought deeper than he expressed, a life profounder than he disclosed. This is true only of men of real greatness; such men are always richer and ampler than their work.

Writing later, out of more expert professional knowledge, in *The Cambridge History of American Literature*, Ashley H. Thorndike was in essential agreement. Admitting the "somewhat miscellaneous appeal" of Lowell's work, he did not claim that his subject had possessed the "literary power" which achieves "the great conquests of the imagination," but he also found Lowell's failure

due in large measure to the variety of responses which his rich personality made to the changing movements of American life. Other writers were surer of their message or of their art, but perhaps the career of no other affords a more varied and interesting commentary on the course of American letters, or responds as constantly to the occasions and needs of the nation's experience.

Lowell would not have asked for anything better than that, though we can never know whether he was thinking of himself when he declared, long before either Thorndike or *The Christian Union*, that "it is only a great mind or a strong character that knows how to respect its own provincialism and can dare to be in fashion with itself." He had this kind of strength. Insofar as his insufficiencies and contradictions were due to willfulness on his part, they indicated a weakness in his character, but they had also a higher significance. He trusted his own insights, accepted his temperament, and stood upon his own feet. What he saw, what he expressed, was not all there was to see or to express, but there was nothing second-hand in it. Everything had been passed through the alembic of his own personality and verified, for him, in his own experience. Whatever his individual limitations may have been, this is important, because it is only on some such basis that literature can be created or character achieved.

NOTES

The following abbreviations are employed in both the Notes and the Bibliography.

It should be noted that all books not otherwise assigned are published by Houghton Mifflin Company.

ABC	American Book Company	HM	Harper's Magazine
AL	American Literature	HUP	Harvard University Press
AM	The Atlantic Monthly	HW	Harper's Weekly
AMP	The Atlantic Monthly Press	JRL	James Russell Lowell
AS	American Speech	L	James Russell Lowell
BNYPL	Bulletin of the New York Public Library	LB	Little, Brown & Company
BPLQ	Boston Public Library Quarterly	LG	Longmans, Green and Co.
Ce	Century Magazine	Li	J. B. Lippincott Company
CER	Catholic Educational Review	M	The Macmillan Company
CLQ	Colby Library Quarterly	MHS	Massachusetts Historical Society
CR	Contemporary Review	MLN	Modern Language Notes
CW	Classical Weekly	MLQ	Modern Language Quarterly
D	Doubleday & Co. (and their predecessors)	NAR	North American Review
ESQ	Emerson Society Quarterly	NEM	New England Magazine
FR	Fortnightly Review	NEQ	New England Quarterly
H	Harper and Brothers	NQ	Notes and Queries
HC	Harvard Crimson	OED	Oxford English Dictionary
HL	Houghton Library, Harvard University	OUP	Oxford University Press
HLQ	Huntington Library Quarterly		

P	G. P. Putnam's Sons	S	Charles Scribner's Sons
PBSA	*Publications of the Bibliographical Society of America*	*SB*	*Studies in Bibliography*
		SM	*Scribner's Magazine*
		SP	*Studies in Philology*
PMHS	*Publications of the Massachusetts Historical Society*	*TSLL*	*Texas Studies in Language and Literature*
		UCP	The University of Chicago Press
PMLA	*Publications of the Modern Language Association*	Van	Vanderbilt University Press
PQ	*Philological Quarterly*	*YR*	*The Yale Review*
RES	*Review of English Studies*	YUP	Yale University Press

CHAPTER ONE: THE LOWELL PROBLEM

1 A typical example is Seth Low, "L as an Educator," *Educational Review*, II (1891), 417–21.

2 Boston *Evening Transcript,* Feb. 19, 1919.

3 Quoted by Russell Kirk, *A Program for Conservatives* (Regnery, 1954), p. 32.

4 Published by Albert Mason, New York.

5 *The Chief American Poets* (1905), p. 684.

6 "Reading Lowell today is likely to awaken a stronger sense of unrealized potential than is the case with any other of the 'schoolroom poets.' No other one of them brings us so close to Whitman or, in thought, to Henry Adams, or to Lowell's English contemporaries Tennyson and Arnold, yet leaves us in the end so far away from them."—*American Poets from the Puritans to the Present* (1968).

7 *HC,* Feb. 21, 1919.

8 For a lively account of the whole Lowell family, see Ferris Greenslet, *The Lowells and their Seven Worlds*, especially the interesting comparison between Lowells and Adamses in the Epilogue. Ellery Sedgwick's review article, "Lowells, Inc.," *Saturday Review of Literature*, XXIX, Sept. 21, 1946, pp. 5-6, 37–38, is excellent on family characteristics.

9 "JRL," VI (1891), 477–98.

10 *Book and Heart* (H, 1877), p. 48.

11   See "Memoir of the Rev. Charles Lowell, D.D.," *PMHS*, 1860–61, pp. 427–40.

12   According to Barrett Wendell, there was also a connection with the family of Sir Walter Raleigh, but I have found no other reference to this.

13   In the Scudder box—bMS Am800.30.

14   Scudder, *JRL*, I, 13.

15   According to Higginson, Lowell was rusticated because he appeared in chapel under the influence of wine, but this is doubtful and unsupported by college or other records. See M. A. DeWolfe Howe, *Barrett Wendell and his Letters* (AMP, 1924), p. 28; Howard, *Victorian Knight-Errant*, pp. 367–68; and especially Duberman, *JRL*, pp. 394–95, n. 11. Frederic M. Holland, "Reading Dante with L," *NEM*, N.s. XIII (1895–96), 575–76, remembered L giving most of the blame for what happened to him to Professor Edward T. Channing, whose formalized methods of teaching English composition may well have been antipathetic to him.

CHAPTER TWO: BASIC EQUIPMENT

1   "Early Recollections of L," HL, bMS Am 1162.9.

2   "He looked as he should have looked. He spoke as he should have spoken. Distinction marked him as her own, and he responded without effort to her election."—*Eight Decades* (1937), p. 14.

3   M. A. DeWolfe Howe, *John Jay Chapman and His Letters* (1937).

4   William Shepard, ed., *Pen Pictures of Modern Authors* (P, 1882), pp. 137–38.

5   Howells, *Literary Friends and Aquaintance*.

6   See Scudder, *JRL*, I, 404–406, and, for more detailed accounts, William J. Stillman, *The Autobiography of a Journalist* (1901) and two papers—"The Subjective of It" and "The Philosophers' Camp"—in *The Old Rome and the New* (1898).

7   *Harvardiana*, IV (1838), 18–25.

8   There are some amusing doggerel verses on cheese in Martin Duberman, "Twenty-Seven Poems by JRL," *AL*, XXXV (1963–64), 322–55.

9 Whiskey punch is mentioned in letters to Nathan Hale, Jr., in 1840. For ale and hock, see also *TSLL*, III (1962), 569, 570, 575.

10 See Howard, *Victorian Knight-Errant*, p. 183. In a leter to Nathan Hale, Jr., June 22, 1840, Lowell described a "blow" he had attended the night before at which at least one guest was drunk. "*I was as sober as a judge, for having been sick the day before, everything that I drank came up in a short time, and on its way to my head came out at my mouth.*" On July 25 he wrote the same correspondent that, after having drunk a bottle of "devilish good wine," he met Mrs. Hooper on the ferry "with a piece of tobacco in my mouth. Rather strange sensation produced by the awkwardness of my situation and the winegiven independence."—*TSLL*, III (1962), 574, 577. These are the most dissipated references that I have found in Lowell.

11 *Woman's Journal*, Sept. 12, 1891. Higginson also records (*Old Cambridge*) that Lowell "kept the rhymed records of the Hasty Pudding Club, but in later life requested, quite to the disapproval of the immediate members, to be permitted to cut them out of the record book, which he did."

12 *JRL and his Friends* (1899), p. 42: "Now, let me say that from his birth to his death I never saw him [Lowell] in the least under any influence of liquor that could be detected in any way. I never, till within five years, heard any suggestion of the gossip which I have referred to above."

13 Duberman, *JRL*, p. 398, n. 15.

14 See L's article on Fredrika Bremer, *NAR*, LVIII (1844), 480–508.

15 See Holmes's reply in John T. Morse, Jr., *Life and Letters of Oliver Wendell Holmes* (1896), II, 295 ff.

16 *NAR*, CV (1867), 592–626.

17 In the Boston *Evening Transcript*, Feb. 19, 1919, E. W. Metcalf spoke of Lowell as "puffing his meerschaum and carrying his heavy oaken stick to and from college. He also smoked, as did his students, during the Dante sessions he conducted in his study at Elmwood—"my reeky old den," he calls it. "When editor of the *Atlantic Monthly*," continues Metcalf, "he extended his walk to [the] Riverside [Press], where the magazine was printed, and going through the office, regaled the printers with a bit of cascarilla bark

in the bowl of his pipe, the odor from which was caviare to the general." To this last point I have found no other reference.

18 For a detailed analysis of the *Pioneer* debt, see Sculley Bradley's introduction to his edition of that periodical, pp. xxiv-xxvi, and cf. Leon Howard, "The Case of the Sanded Signature," *Manuscripts*, XIII (1961), 13–17.

19 *The American Spirit in Literature* ("Chronicles of America") (YUP, 1918).

20 In *The Function of the Poet*. . . .

21 See also "Sonnets," XI, XII. The conservative is bitterly assailed in "The Sower."

22 Cf. "To the Past."

23 Lowell's humor seems to me forced all through the essay "A Plea for Freedom from Speech and Figures of Speech-Makers," reprinted in *The Function of the Poet*. . . . For an authoritative study of "L's Puns," see Kathryn Anderson McEuen, *AS*, XXII (1947), 24–33. She finds and reports that *The Biglow Papers* are not rich in puns. The short poems "yield but few ingenious puns and not many of any kind." There are few good puns in letters written before 1846, "and they tend to taper off after 1863." In letters written between 1871 and 1876 there are hardly any. Lowell's punning is determined primarily by his mood. He did not pun when he was in a serious frame of mind.

24 "Mr. Worseley's Nightmare," *Nation*, II (1866), 426–28. Was Lowell's animosity increased by the fact that the book was dedicated to Lee?

25 There are whole nonsense letters of Lowell's, like this undated one to Sydney Gay, written when he was ill (Houghton Library, bMS Am 1246 [75]:

It isn't iritis, my eye wholly right is; nor pneumonitis, though fearful my plight is; it isn't a quinsy, though bad enough *in se*; it isn't scrofula, but something awfuller; it isn't podagra, but it's a staggerer; it isn't lumbago, though I say to it, pray go; it isn't the cholera, but beats it all hollerer;

> It's a thing that much wus is,—
> I swears and I cusses,
> And thinks about husses
> (Death's black omnibuses)

> I can't think of noffin
> Except of my coffin,
> For what can I else with this horrible *tussis?*

He can break into nonsense too in a serious letter, as in this to J. G. Palfrey, dated only "Elmwood, 28th July," which furnishes an excellent illustration of Lowell's volatile quality and his capacity for yielding to the impulse of the moment:

> My dear Sir,
> I have been meaning to bring my answer in person, but one thing and another stood in the way. The book is *Memoirs of a Frontier Missionary* being the life of Rev. Jacob Bayley. But unfortunately it relates (if a fly who insists on occupying the end of my nose will let me tell you) to the middle of the 18th Century. It is very enter (I wish his father and prince, Beelzebub had him!) taining. Would you like to see it? On the whole I will send it at a venture.
> With great regard, and my nose nearly knocked off, faithfully yours
> J. R. Lowell

A good example of a somewhat less irresponsibly playful style in correspondence may be found in this to Howells:

> Elmwood
> Friday
> My dear Howells,
> Who writes me casts his bread on the waters. The carrier handed me your note on the road, I put it in my pocket and straightway forgot all about it. We are told in a book (which I still look on as quite up to the level of any that have come out in my time) to do whatever we do with all our might. That's the way I forget my letters and I hope I shall find my reward in the next world, for I certainly don't in this. On the contrary, happening to thrust my hands into my pockets (I don't know why —there is seldom anything in them) I found your note, and it stuck into me like an unexpected pin in the girdle of Saccharissa. If you didn't want our company, you might our room! Therefore to be categorical, *I* am coming, as I said I would; Mrs. Lowell has unhappily an inflamed eye and is very sorry (for

she prefers *My Summer in a Garden*, I fear, to some more solid
works done under her immediate supervision); and Miss Dunlap
is in Portland. So the whole of our family can sit in one chair
like St. Thomas Aquinas's angels.

With kind regards to Mrs. Howells,

Affectionately yours always

J. R. Lowell.

See also the "lisping" verses to Thomas Hughes's daughter May, in
Mack and Armytage, *Thomas Hughes.* . . , pp. 186–87, and the
nonsense verses described in Duberman's "A Brahmin's Laughter,"
Manuscripts, XV (1963), 23–26. These trace the Lowell family back
to the dawn of time, and, as Duberman says, show that Lowell was
capable of laughing at them—and himself.

26 *Ce*, n.s. XXXVII (1899–1900), 49–50.
27 *NAR*, CVIII (1869), 324.

CHAPTER THREE: STORING THE WELL

1 Cf. "To George William Curtis."
2 "Birthday Verses Written in a Child's Album."
3 "An Indian Summer Reverie."
4 Scudder, *JRL*, II, 98.
5 See, for example, "The Bobolink," "Al Fresco," and "The
Nightingale in the Study." The same point of view seems involved
in "The Shepherd of King Admetus." In *Conversations* he even says
that the leaf of a tree has more of "the love of God . . . than a leaf
of Taylor or Barrow."
6 *AM*, XI (1863), 515.
7 Hyatt H. Waggoner, *American Poets*, pp. 64–65, cites
"Rhoecus" as showing L's understanding of a pure and undivided
approach to nature, illuminating "at once the background in romantic theory of Buber's contemporary philosophy and the contemporary relevance of romantic metaphysics." He adds that L "wavered
between restating Bryant and anticipating Robinson."
8 Howe, *New Letters*, pp. 107–11.
9 "A Legend of Brittany," XXXII.
10 "Our Own," Progression C; see Smith, *Uncollected Poems*,
p. 90.

11   *AM*, XI (1863), 515.

12   *AM*, XII (1860), 761.

13   If "The Pennsylvania Academy of Fine Arts," *Broadway Journal*, I (1845), 121–22, which Cooke ascribes to L, was really written by him, it is unlike any of his other productions. A sarcastic blast at the Academy, it singles out Sully and West for specific attack. West's "Death on a Pale Horse," Allston's "Dead Man Restored to Life," and Opie's Gil Blas picture are all severely handled, and the "exposure" in a picture of "Time Flogging Cupid" inspires hysterics.

14   Vernon, The *Poems of Maria Lowell*. . . .

15   "Music in Lowell's Prose and Verse," *Musical Quarterly*, X (1924), 546–72.

16   Smith, *Uncollected Poems*, pp. 110–26.

17   For interesting references to organ and piano, see also "Getting Up," in *L's Early Prose Writings*, pp. 44–45.

18   There is an interesting reference to L's early theater-going in one of his *Anti-Slavery Papers*—"Turncoats."

19   "An Ember Picture."

20   "JRL and Science," *Today's Japan*, V, August, 1960, pp. 45–53.

21   See Martin B. Ruud, "JRL: An American University Man," *The Quarterly Journal of the University of North Dakota*, IX (1918–19), 251–59.

22   *HC*, Feb. 21, 1919. L's reaction to the new, technical Germanic type of scholarship in the field of literary study is a bit wavering. Though he could not but perceive its value, its scientific, dryasdust, anti-humanistic aspects (as he conceived them) repelled him. He was oddly insensitive to the value of annotating English texts and declared that "he who loves the comic side of human nature will find the serious notes of a *variorum* edition of Shakespeare as funny reading as the funny ones are serious."

23   Russel B. Nye, "L and American Speech," *PQ*, XVIII (1939), 249–56.

24   Besides the long introduction to *The Biglow Papers*, Second Series, see, for L's philological knowledge, his *AM* reviews of the following books: Richard Grant White's edition of Shakespeare, III (1859), 111–21, 241–60; John Bartlett's *Dictionary of Americanisms*, IV (1859), 638–44; Hesleigh Wedgwood's *Dictionary of English*

Etymology, VI (1860), 248–54; Max Müller's *Lectures on the Science of Languages*, IX (1862), 140–42; the dictionaries of Worcester and Webster, V (1860), 631–37. See also the later review of Webster in *NAR*, C (1865), 299–302. For L on incompetent editorial scholarship, see his "Library of Old Authors" in *My Study Windows*.

25   See Jayne Crane Harder, "JRL: Linguistic Patriot," *AS*, XXIX (1954), 181–86.

26   According to *OED*, the macaronic is "a burlesque form of verse in which vernacular words are introduced into a Latin context with Latin terminations and in Latin constructions." See Frederick D. Smith, "Mr. Wilbur's Postumous [*sic*] Macaronics," *University of North Dakota Quarterly Journal*, X (1920), 436–44, which translates the "Kettelopotomachia" into English, with Commentary, and Edgar Hill Duncan, "L's Battle of the Kettle and Pot," *AL*, XV (1943–44), 127–38. George P. Clark, "JRL's Study of the Classics before Entering Harvard," *Jahrbuch für Amerikastudien*, VIII (1963), 206–209, gives the most careful study of L's early education and shows reason to consider that he was well prepared in Latin and (to a lesser extent) in Greek when he entered Harvard.

27   See W. T. Bandy, "JRL, Sainte-Beuve, and The *Atlantic Monthly*," *Comparative Literature*, XI (1959), 229–32.

28   The author of "Conversations with Mr. L" says L declared in Paris in 1883 that it was still difficult for him to speak French, but the article itself contains material which refutes this view.

29   See also Henry A. Pochmann, *German Culture in America* . . . (*1600–1900*) (University of Wisconsin Press, 1961.

30   Ethel F. Fisk, ed., *The Letters of John Fiske* (M, 1940), p. 103.

31   Frank P. Stearns, *Cambridge Sketches* (Li, 1905), p. 101.

32   *The Memoirs of Julian Hawthorne* (M, 1938), pp. 186–87.

33   See also Frederic M. Holland, "Reading Dante with L," *NEM*, N. s. XIII (1895–96), 63–69.

34   John P. Pritchard, "Aristotle's *Poetics* and Certain American Literary Critics: III, JRL and Aristotle's *Poetics*," *CW*, XXVII (1933–34), 89–93. See, by the same author, "L's Debt to Horace's *Ars Poetica*," *AL*, III (1931–32), 259–76; *Return to the Fountains* (Duke, 1942); and "A Glance at L's Classical Reading," *AL*, XXI (1949–50), 442–55; also Edmund G. Berry, "L and the Classics," *CW*, XXXVIII (1944), 11–12.

35   Reprinted in *The Function of the Poet*. . . . L's review of Lord Derby's translation of the *Iliad, NAR,* CI (1865), 303–310, shows his familiarity with both Homer and his English translators.

36   *NAR,* CXII (1871), 460–63.

37   At his address in 1886 at the 250th anniversary of the founding of Harvard College, L still championed a classical education, though obviously now somewhat on the defensive. "Only those languages can properly be called dead in which nothing living has been written." Classical literature "is as contemporary with us to-day as with the ears it first enraptured, for it appeals not to the man of then or now, but to the entire round of human nature itself." But by the time he gave his presidential address before the Modern Language Association three years later, Lowell was much less certain that the modern languages might not take over the place formerly accorded unquestioningly to Greek and Latin. "I hold this evening a brief for the Modern Languages, and am bound to put their case in as fair a light as I conscientiously can. Your kindness has put me in a position where I am forced to reconsider my opinions and to discover, if I can, how far prejudice and tradition have had a hand in forming them." "Is it less instructive to study the growth of modern ideas than of ancient?" For all that, L was pleased when his grandson took kindly to his Homer. "I had rather he should choose Greek than any modern tongue, and I say this as a hint that I am making allowance for the personal equation. The wise gods have put difficulty between man and everything that is worth having. But where the mind is of softer fibre, and less eager of emprise, may it not be prudent to open and make easy every avenue that leads to literature, even though it may not directly lead to those summits that tax the mind and muscle only to reward the climber at last with the repose of a more ethereal air?" Surely this conclusion is condescending toward those who choose the modern languages.

38   French influences upon L are studied in detail by Charles Oran Stewart, *L and France* (Van, 1951); see also C. M. Lombard, "L and French Romanticism," *Revue de Litterature Comparée,* XXXVIII (1968), 582–88.

39   See also the letter printed in *BPLQ,* VI (1954), 190–191.

40   George Wurfl, "L's Debt to Goethe: A Study of Literary Influence," *Penn State College Studies,* Vol. I, No. 2 (1936), is an exhaustive study, arguing that L's critical method was importantly

indebted to Goethe: "he adopted a number of Goethe's principles of criticism without even making changes, took over ideas, adjusted them to his uses, and deduced some of his theoretical definitions from specific practical applications."

41   *Part of a Man's Life* (1905), facing p. 300.

42   See the second paragraph of the section on Webster in *The Old English Dramatists*.

43   Nelson F. Adkins, "A Borrowing of L from George Chapman," *AL*, V (1933), 172–75, suggests *Bussy D'Ambois* as the source of a famous passage in "Sir Launfal."

44   "A Persian poet says, 'When the owl boasts, he boasts of catching mice on the edge of a hole.' Shakespeare would have understood this! Milton would have made him talk like an eagle."

45   On October 17, 1866, L wrote William C. Church, "I suppose I must have mentioned to some indiscreet person the fact that so long ago as 1853 I had planned to write a story of moral life (so to speak) in New England, had sketched the characters, and even written the first chapter—but something happened during that year which broke forever the continuity of my life and left all my literary schemes at loose ends. I am just now trying to knit some of them together again but I altogether doubt my ability to write a good story, least of all one calculated to be popular, which is what *you* want." The manuscript is preserved in HL. "Chapter First. The Place in which" is all background and description, rich in New England history and tradition, but with no hint of story. The style is much like that of L's prose in general, which is to say that it is a little finely-wrought for fiction.

The Baptist Meetinghouse stood just north of the tavern. It was a Grecian temple with an Egyptian doorway and gothic windows, over which, on the South side, green blinds could be closed in the summer. These had been omitted on the North Side through economy or an instinctive recognition of that artistic principle which has left Cologne Cathedral plainer toward that quarter of the heavens. A nest of boxes piled one on top of the other in a diminishing series, crowned by a kind of extinguisher, made the spire. At the apex, a vane in the shape of a comet seemed to rush against the wind, leaving a somewhat formal train of gilded fire behind it.

L once planned a tragedy about Anne Hutchinson, and he actually wrote part of a play about the conquest of Mexico, based on Prescott, and designed for Edwin Forrest. Walter Blair rightly gives him credit for having created "a changing, a developing, character" in Birdofredum Sawin.

46   In denying imagination, in its highest sense, to Wordsworth, L is in agreement with Irving Babbitt, "The Primitivism of Wordsworth," in *On Being Creative and Other Essays* (1932). Babbitt found so many opinions against him on this point that he professed himself appalled by his own temerity! This is interesting in view of the kinship some have discerned between L and the "new humanists."

47   See his letter to Edmund Quincy in Howe, *New Letters*, pp. 146-47, and cf. my account of the Byron-Stowe matter in *Harriet Beecher Stowe: The Known and the Unknown* (OUP, 1965), pp. 83-88.

48   See the sonnet "To the Spirit of Keats" in his collected poems and "Sonnet—To Keats" in Smith. See also the note on p. 467 of Clark and Foerster, *JRL: Representative Selections,* for the influence of Keats on JRL's own writing, including the echoes of "Isabella" in "A Legend of Brittany."

49   L's authorship of the review of *Enoch Arden, NAR,* XCIX (1864), 626, has been seriously questioned; see another review, C (1865), 305-307. See also, for his review of *The Princess, Massachusetts Quarterly,* I (1847-48), 256-59.

50   Reprinted in *The Round Table.*

51   Charles J. Rooney, Jr., "A New Letter by L," *AL,* XXXVI (1964-65), 214-15.

52   "Some Letters of Walter Savage Landor," in *Latest Literary Essays;* "The Works of Walter Savage Landor," reprinted in *The Round Table.* The essay on Carlyle is in *My Study Windows.*

53   See Edward F. Payne, *Dickens Days in Boston* (1927).

54   *NAR,* LXV (1847), 201-24, reprinted in *The Round Table.*

55   The best passage on this point is a lecture reported in *HC,* May 4, 1894, in which L at some length contrasts Don Quixote with a character who in the paper is called both Pecksniff and Pickwick. The former, I think, is intended. Parson Wilbur's letter prefixed to *Biglow Papers,* Second Series, V, may be indebted to Mr. Pickwick's interpretation of the stone engraved "BILL STUMPS HIS MARK."

56   The only real exception I have found is in a letter to W. A. White, Jan. 7, 1842, where Emerson is criticized for having attacked the abolitionists in a lecture. Since he himself lacks "energy or enthusiasm of character to fight for truth amid the practical and undeniable dust and heat of the market," he "has reasoned himself into the faith that those who do are fanatics."

57   JRL to W. H. Furness, July 13, 1879, in *Proceedings of the Colonial Society of Massachusetts*, VIII (1906), 135.

58   L did admit, however, after Emerson's death, that he must give him up as a metrist. He was "absolutely insensitive to the harmony of verse. . . . I never shall forget the good-humoredly puzzled smile with which he once confessed to me his inability to apprehend the value of accent in verse." In addition to the paper on "Emerson the Lecturer" in *My Study Windows*, see L's review of *Conduct of Life*, *AM*, VII (1861), 254-55. Killis Campbell, "Three Notes on L," *MLN*, XXXVIII (1923), 121-22, suggests the influence of Emerson upon the following poems by L: "To Perdita, Singing," "Ode" (1847), "The Landlord," "Bibliolatres," and "The Fountain of Youth."

59   Samuel Longfellow, *Final Memorials of Henry Wadsworth Longfellow* (Ticknor, 1887), p. 311.

60   Both reprinted in *The Function of the Poet*. . . .

61   L admired Longfellow's second wife, Fanny Appleton, and always remembered gratefully that she had been one of the first to praise his work. See his poem, "On My New Year's Candlestick," in the Appendix to my *Mrs. Longfellow* . . . (LG, 1956), pp. 247-48, and the many references to L in the index to that work.

62   *NAR*, CIV (1867), 194-97.

63   All reviews are reprinted in *The Function of the Poet*. . . .

64   "Mrs. Passion J. Howe has brought out a play in New York. The critics seem to have been too gallant or goodnatured to damn it, but they have at least sent it to a kind of Limbo, neither hell nor heaven." He summarizes the plot and then burlesques it by writing a soliloquy in blank verse for a New England character about to hang himself after committing a crime similar to that dealt with in the play.

65   *AM*, III (1859), 651-52.

66   Reprinted in *The Round Table*.

67   Austin Warren, "L on Thoreau," *SP*, XXVII (1930), 442-

61, is important. E. J. Nichols, "Identification of Characters in L's *A Fable for Critics*," *AL*, IV (1932–33), 191–94, debates the relative claims of Thoreau and William Ellery Channing, nephew of the preacher, as the original of ll. 618–27.

68   "The Origin of L's 'Miss Fooler,'" *AL*, XXXVII (1965–66), 473–75.

69   C. E. Stowe, *Life of Harriet Beecher Stowe* (1889), pp. 326–36.

70   Walter Blair, *Horse Sense in American Humor* (UCP, 1942), p. 99, cites *Margaret* as a source for *The Biglow Papers*, though without particularizing or naming the author.

71   E. H. House recalled L's saying that he had no great liking for Poe's stories. Though he would have been glad to be able to print a "Gold Bug" or a "Rue Morgue" in *AM* every month, he did not consider such tales as representing "a high order of composition. It is the last line of fiction I should wish to see followed by anyone under my guardianship." Poe's review of L's 1844 *Poems* has been reprinted in James A. Harrison, ed., *The Complete Works of Edgar Allan Poe*, "Virginia Edition" (Crowell, 1902), XI, 243–49, L's 1845 general essay on Poe in *The Function of the Poet*. Beside the fact that "A Mystical Ballad" (Smith, *Uncollected Poems*) seems very Poe-like, I have found little or nothing to support Leon Howard's opinion (*Literature and the American Tradition*, D, 1960, p. 163) that Poe influenced L. On the personal relations between the two men, see Max L. Griffin, "L and the South," *Tulane Studies in English*, II (1950), 75–102, especially pp. 84–87, and I. B. Cauthen, Jr., "L on Poe: An Unpublished Comment, 1879," *AL*, XXIV (1952–53). See also my *Edgar Allan Poe: The Man Behind the Legend* (OUP, 1963).

72   L told E. H. House that the *Atlantic* was open to Whitman. "He has a clear right to be heard; there can be no question of that." "As to my liking, it doesn't matter in this instance. Considering how he stands, and the cry that is raised against him, I shall probably print whatever he sends, whether I like it or not. But I should very much prefer to like it." Flaying "The New Tariff-Bill," *AM*, VI (1860), 124, he found its style suggestive "of some of the poems of Mr. Whitman." Horace L. Traubel, "L-Whitman: A Contrast," *Poet-Lore*, IV (1892), 22–31, is a labored and tiresome, but also very cautious, attempt to exalt Whitman at L's expense.

73   See William T. Stafford, "L 'Edits' James: Some Revisions in *French Poets and Novelists*," *NEQ*, XXXII (1959), 92–98, and, more importantly, Miriam Allott, "JRL: A Link between Tennyson and Henry James," *RES*, N.S. VI (1955), 399–401, for L as a source for "The Romance of Certain Old Clothes" and a possible influence upon *The Sense of the Past*.

74   Ernest Samuels, *Henry Adams: The Middle Years* (HUP, 1958).

75   *NAR*, CXII (1871), 234–35.

CHAPTER FOUR: THE CREATIVE LIFE

1   The essentially poetic quality of L's mind shows clearly in the style of his prose. Jeremy Taylor is "a kind of Spenser in a cassock." Carlyle is forever "calling down fire from Heaven whenever he cannot readily lay his hand on the matchbox." Wordsworth's mind "had not that reach and elemental movement of Milton's which, like the trade wind, gathered to itself thoughts and images like stately fleets from every quarter; some deep with silks and spicery, some brooding over the silent thunders of their battailous armaments, but all swept forward in their destined track, over the long billows of his verse, every inch of canvas strained by the unifying breath of their common epic origin." Except for *Areopagitica*, "Milton's tracts are wearisome reading, and going through them is like a long sea-voyage whose monotony is more than compensated for the moment by a stripe of phosphorescence heaping before you in a drift of star-sown snow, coiling away behind in winking discs of silver, as if the conscious element were giving out all the moonlight it had garnered in its loyal depths since first it gazed upon its pallid regent." It is interesting that this last sentence should be followed by "Which, being interpreted," and an explication in the usual manner of prose.

2   These troubles were not wholly confined to poetry. L would not write a critical essay without rereading the subject's whole oeuvre, but he put the actual writing off as long as possible. In 1855 he began delivering a course of Lowell lectures with only the manuscript of one in hand. For his excellent advice about writing, see George Bainton, ed., *The Art of Authorship* . . . (Appleton, 1890), pp. 29–30.

3 See Howard, *Victorian Knight-Errant*, pp. 329–30, and the illustrations following, especially on pp. 334, 338–39, 354–55.

4 See also John C. Broderick's demonstration, "L's 'Sunthin' in the Pastoral Line,'" *AL*, XXXI (1959–60), 163–72, that this piece is a "made" poem. "Moreover, that part of the poem which has seemed the most spontaneous—the descriptive introduction—emerges as the most contrived."

5 F. DeWolfe Miller, "An Artist Sits for L," *BPLQ*, II (1950), 378–79.

6 For a detailed study, see G. Thomas Tanselle, "The Craftsmanship of L: Revisions in *The Cathedral*," *BNYPL*, LXX (1966), 60–63. See also Arthur W. M. Voss, "L's 'A Legend of Brittany,'" *MLN*, LXI (1946), 343–45, which shows that in revising this poem for the 1849 edition, L omitted much moralizing which had been criticized by Poe and Felton. This "indicates that for once, at least, he was capable of exercising a self-criticism hardly to be expected of a young poet so filled with the urge to preach to mankind."

7 A comprehensive critical examination of L's poetic theory and practice is not called for here, where our interest is in painting a character portrait. The most elaborate attempt to formulate L's critical credo was Norman Foerster's, in his *American Criticism* (1928), reprinted in Clark and Foerster, *JRL: Representative Selections*. This has often been attacked as too schematic, but all its elements are present in L's own writings; see "The Function of the Poet" and "The Imagination," both reprinted in *The Function of the Poet . . .* , and especially the manuscript of his first Lowell lecture, preserved in HL—bMS Am765 (899). (This MS, not in L's hand, is marked "being in large part a rewriting of the first Lecture of the Lowell Institute course.") See also Alexis F. Lange, "JRL as a Critic," *University [of California] Chronicle*, VIII (1906), 352–64; E. S. Parsons, "L's Conception of Poetry," *Colorado College Publication*, General Series, No. 37, Language Series, II (1908), 67–84; Harry Hayden Clark, "L's Criticism of Romantic Literature," *PMLA*, XLI (1926), 209–28; J. P. Pritchard, "Aristotle's *Poetics* and Certain American Literary Critics, III: JRL and Aristotle's *Poetics*," *CW*, XXVII (1933–34), 89–93. Austin Warren, "L on Thoreau," *SP*, XXVII (1930), 442–62, finds L a humanist, allied in spirit to Arnold, Santayana, and Babbitt, citing in his support not only the paper on Thoreau but also those on Lessing, Carlyle, Percival, and

Rousseau. "All of these studies imply the same critical background: humanism *versus* romanticism." Richard D. Altick asks, "Was L an Historical Critic?" *AL*, XIV (1942–43), 250–59, and answers in the affirmative. More interesting still are two older articles by J. M. Robertson, "L as a Critic," *NAR*, CCIX (1919), 246–62, and "Criticism and Science," pp. 690–96. Robertson begins by considering Reilly's charges against L, many of which he sustains (he is excellent on L's inconsistencies and contradictions), but if L is not a critic, he wonders who is. At its best, his criticism "is the response of a very fine receptive faculty to a great many forms of literary appeal. . . . Few critics put so much material . . . in their readers' way; and surely no English critic has explored quite so much ground with such vivacity and variety of craftsmanlike observation." He was one of the pathbreakers for a more scientific criticism than his own, and there was no generic gap between his product and that of his successors. Percy H. Boynton, "L in his Times," *New Republic*, XVIII (1919), 113–14, remarks interestingly that L "did little thinking that was original, but much that was independent."

8   Review of *No Love Lost, NAR*, CVIII (1869), 326.

9   The low doggerel of most so-called religious poetry distressed L deeply. "When we think what religion is and what poetry is, and what their marriage ought to be, a great part of what is published as religious poetry seems to us a scandalous mockery." *NAR*, C (1865), 303–304.

10   Review of Fitz-Greene Halleck's *Alnwick Castle, Broadway Journal*, I (1845), 281–83.

11   See *The Function of the Poet*. . . .

12   L gave Peter Bell credit for perceiving that the primrose was a primrose, not a theophany, and I am sure he would also have accounted it to Peter's credit that he knew it was not a hyacinth nor a tulip.

13   "He reads most wisely who thinks everything into a book that it is capable of holding, and it is the stamp and token of a great book so to incorporate itself with our own being, so to quicken our insight and stimulate our thought, as to make us feel as if we helped to create it while we read. Whatever we can find in a book that aids us in the conduct of life, or to a truer interpretation of it, or to a franker reconcilement with it, we may with a good conscience believe is not there by accident, but that the author meant

that we should find it there."—"Don Quixote," *Literary and Political Essays*.

14   In his "Rhymed Lecture" on "The Power of Sound," L wrote:

> And what is Art? 'tis Nature reproduced
> In forms ideal, from the actual loosed;—
> Nature sublimed in life's more gracious hours
> By high Imagination's plastic powers. . . .

In an *NAR* review of 1866 (CII, 633–34), he wrote: "Whenever a novelist speaks of the pretty boots, or the white hands, or the 'golden-beaded purple silk purses' of his heroes and heroines, or describes the silver and fruit on their dinner-tables, or the abundance of their breakfasts, that moment he shows either that his characters are not accustomed to such things, and therefore are disproportionately regardful of them, or else that he himself, in so carefully observing them, is wasting his force on non-essential particulars." J. P. Pritchard is right when he points out (*Return to the Fountains*, p. 103) that L's insistence on the superiority of poetry to history is thoroughly Aristotelian. But it is also thoroughly idealistic, and it must be admitted that when it came to autobiography, L showed a somewhat divided mind. On the one hand, he thought that reserved autobiography was useless: "But what do we want of a hospitality that makes strangers of us, or of confidences that keep us at arm's-length?" But when one of his authors does write of himself without reserve, he is hardly pleased. "We think there is getting to be altogether too much unreserve in the world. We doubt if any man have the right to take mankind by the button and tell all about himself, unless, like Dante, he can symbolize his experience. Even Goethe we only half thank, especially when he kisses and tells, and prefer Shakespeare's indifference to the intimacy of the German."—*AM*, IV (1859), 770–73. In a review of Julia Ward Howe's *A Trip to Cuba*—*AM*, IV (1860), 510—he says: "Here and there it seems to us a little too personal, and the public is made the confidant of matters in which it has properly no concern." Yet he knew that the only travelers worth reading were those who told what they saw, not what they went to see—see *AM*, V (1860), 629.

15   In *NAR*, CXII (1871), 236–37, he gave *Suburban Sketches* a "rave" review: "Yes, truly, these are poems, if the supreme gift of

the poet be to rim the trivial things of our ordinary and prosaic experience with an ideal light. Here is something of the gracious ease of Chaucer, which cost him so much pains. . . . Let us make the most of Mr. Howells, for in the midst of our vulgar self-conceits and crudenesses, and noisy contempt of those conventions which are the safeguards of letters, and the best legacy of culture, we have got a gentleman and artist worthy to be ranked with Hawthorne in sensitiveness of observation, with Longfellow in perfection of style." Howard M. Munford, "The Disciple Proves Independent: Howells and L," *PMLA*, LXXIV (1959), 484–87, points out that Howells gives *The Biglow Papers* part of the credit for helping him realize the importance of the commonplace, but I cannot agree when he cites L on *The Lady of the Aroostook* as an example of L's desire to have Howells avoid the colloquial even in dialogue: "No Bostonian ever said, 'Was his wife along?' . . . Change it in a new edition—of which there will be lots." L objected to "Was his wife along" not because it was colloquial but only because it was not a New England colloquialism. And surely "of which there will be lots" should have been sufficient to warn Mr. Munford that L had no objection to colloquialism as such.

16 In bMS Am 765 (899)—HL—lines are drawn through this passage, possibly indicating that L thought he had gone too far. But he expresses essentially the same point of view, though less emphatically, elsewhere.

17 "A Legend of Brittany."

18 "whom if I had not the higher privilege of revering as a parent, I should still have honored as a man and loved as a friend, this volume containing many opinions from which he will wholly, yet with the large charity of a Christian heart, dissent, is inscribed, by his youngest child."

19 "My former volume of Essays has been so kindly received that I am emboldened to make another and more miscellaneous collection." He was shutting them up between covers so that they should haunt him no more and free his mind for new enterprises. "I should have preferred a simpler title, but publishers nowadays are inexorable on this point, and I was too much occupied for happiness of choice." The dedication was to Francis James Child, reminding him that he had liked the essay on Chaucer, "about whom you know so much more than I."

20   Ferris Greenslet's suggestion (*JRL*, p. 272) that L's letters "contain perhaps the very best" of him expresses, I think, a not indefensible point of view.

21   Once when L had written Child that nothing was ever quite so good as it should be "except a rose now and then," Child replied:

> "Nothing is good as it should be—
> 'Cept now and then a rose"—
> And now and then your poetry—
> And now and then your prose.

22   "Bellerophon," in *A Year's Life*.

23   Max Müller, *Auld Lang Syne*, pp. 180–81.

24   Lilian Whiting, *Boston Days* (LB, 1902), p. 83.

25   The failures of craftsmanship involved in certain structural deficiencies in both writers connect here. In *Conversations* the statement is made: "If some of the topics introduced seem foreign to the subject, I can only say, that they are not so to my mind, and that an author's object in writing criticisms is not only to bring to light the beauties of the works he is considering, but also to express his own opinions upon those and other matters." This is not a fault in *Conversations*, the scheme of the work being what it is, but he would be a bold man who should say that L never did the same thing elsewhere. Van Wyck Brooks (*The Flowering of New England*, Dutton, 1936) found "general ideas" in only two of L's essays, and Reilly declares that "his essays lack a unity which comes from the presence of a dominant idea, a thesis to be supported, or a point of view steadily maintained." But L was not interested in "general ideas" in the Van Wyck Brooks sense, and Reilly's illustrations leave the impression that he was not greatly concerned about the validity or the idea or thesis maintained. Comparing L's comments on Gray with Matthew Arnold's, he remarks, "Whether or not one agree with Arnold's conclusion one comes to realize that there is a difference between that penetration which stops short and that other which seeks to pierce to the heart of things." Seeking is no doubt an excellent thing. But is it as good as finding?

CHAPTER FIVE: LOWELL THE LOVER

1   Farewell! those forms that in thy noontide shade
Rest near their little plots of oaten glade,
Those steadfast eyes that beating breasts inspire
To throw the "sultry ray" of young Desire;
Those lips whose tides of fragrance come and go
Accordant to the cheek's unquiet glow;
Those shadowy breasts in love's soft light arrayed,
And rising by the moon of passion swayed.

2   Gurdon, *Suffolk Tales and Other Stories* (LG, 1887), p. 135.

3   Anderson, *A Few Memories* (H, 1896), p. 84. L's dislike of grossness extended to other forms of coarseness. Howells, who records one "Damn," also declares that he used this rarely and never anything stronger. There is a letter to Cranch in which he says he does not give a "d" and then mischievously explains that "d" stands for penny. But Howells also furnishes material to help prove that L's fastidiousness was not absurd. He could relish—and even tell—a story "unmeet for ladies," provided the emphasis was on "the human nature of it" and not on the filth. A letter to Child, Jan. 17, 1884, includes a guarded report on a coarse version of "Little Billee" which he had heard Thackeray sing privately.

4   In *Conversations*, John says that "Christianity differs not more widely from Plato than from the Puritans." Cf. "Plutarch's Morals," in *The Function of the Poet.* . . .

5   "He is, of all our poets, the most truly sensuous, using the word as Milton probably meant it when he said that poetry should be 'simple, sensuous, and passionate' "—"Spenser."

6   They did not, but the pigments deteriorated, and the picture no longer exists. Two Venus pictures reproduced in Joshua Taylor, *William Page* (UCP, 1957), probably give some idea of what it was like. Page was a "spiritual" painter, but he was not squeamish about nakedness.

7   See, for example, "Caesarian operation," in "Nationality in Literature," *The Round Table*, p. 13, and the first two pages of "Mr. Calhoun's Report," in *Anti-Slavery Papers*.

8   "With a Copy of Aucassin and Nicolette."

9   See Duberman, *JRL*, p. 121. Perhaps L's understanding of the pain which unattractive girls must feel shows his kindness of heart even more than his toleration of frailty. See in "The Unlovely" (*A Year's Life*) the lament of a girl in whom nothing charms that charms in others, "because I am not fair." One cannot but recall H. L. Mencken's amusing notion that it would be accounted unto a man for righteousness that he had winked at a homely girl!

10   Gordon Milne, *George William Curtis and the Genteel Tradition* (Indiana University Press, 1955), p. 143.

11   HL—bMS Am765 (902).

12   "She will make a cuckold of him at any rate for she will become a *Hoar* as soon as she is married." So writes L to G. B. Loring, Aug. 9, 1838, after which he apologizes for his "pun or *rather* smutty joke." So far as my researches have gone, this is the bawdiest passage he ever wrote. I may remark in passing that "Rosaline" in the 1848 *Poems*, which deals with a lover haunted by the low-born bride he has murdered, is about as Gothic as anything in Poe. I am surprised that the Freudian critics seem so far to have overlooked it.

13   "Marian," *Graham's Magazine*, XX, 305–306. One item in HL—bMS Am765 (895)—contains poems written or copied for "Miss Jackson," but they are not love poems.

14   Duberman, pp. 396–97, n. 9.

15   L's exalted estimate of Maria was not peculiar to him. Edmund Quincy called her "truly an angelic creature." When C. F. Briggs came into her presence he wanted to say, "Sancta Maria, ora pro nobis!" "Younger in years than he," writes Norton, "she was more mature in feeling, more disciplined in character, and to her L owed all that a man may owe to the woman he loves." Mrs. Longfellow, however, was disappointed in her appearance at her wedding: "She did not look so charmingly as was expected, her dress being exceedingly simple but not well arranged." We are also told that Maria teased the younger members of her family mercilessly, which does not seem quite angelic. But the only vigorously dissenting view, that of a woman who knew L during his engagement, does not much impress me. According to her, Maria "was then only considered a pretty girl, pleasing and gentle in her manners, but without the least claim to beauty, while one of her sisters was generally conceded greater praise in that direction. In these Philistine days Mrs. Lowell

would probably be described as sentimental and lackadaisical."

16 In the light of later events, one passage from a letter of L's to Mabel, written from Dresden, Oct. 19, 1855, when he was characteristically complaining about the absence of letters, is amusing:

> And what is the matter with Miss Dunlap that she is grown so stately? Pray show her this message—"Mr. J. R. Lowell presents his compliments to Miss F. H. Dunlap and begs that (if pen and ink and paper are to be got in America) she will write him a *quarterly* or *semiannual* report of the progress and general condition of her pupil, by doing which she will confer an additional obligation on Mr. Lowell."

17 Wagenknecht, *Mrs. Longfellow*, pp. 210–11. When Jane Norton died in 1877 without ever having married anybody, L wrote Mabel that she had always been like a sister to him and had left a gap in his life that nothing could fill. "I never knew anyone more entirely lovely." But it is interesting that he also wrote her sister Grace: "I was always conscious that she was a woman with whom I might have fallen in love, though she never occurred to me as one who might have fallen in love with me."

18 There is a fairly detailed account of Frances Dunlap Lowell's illness in Duberman, but the fullest record of its ebb and flow is in L's unpublished letters to Mabel in HL.

19 HL has many charming letters from L to Charles Eliot Norton's daughter, Elizabeth Gaskell Norton (Lily), in which the writer gallantly avails himself of an old man's privileges.

20 HL has a number of poems to Mrs. Smalley, all lover-like in tone, though in a rather literary, neo-Elizabethan way. These were "sent with a pair of Moorish slippers to P.G.S.":

> Happy that go where she is going,
> If you are honored by her feet,
> So influence them without her knowing
> That all her paths and mine may meet.

There are others—"On an inkstand lent me by P.G.S." and "To P.G.S. on her birthday, 8th April, 1881." I might add that there are also a number of late published poems about the sorrows of love which might suggest personal experience, but if they had any experiential basis, it would seem that they, or their preliminary drafts, must have been kept unpublished in L's folders for many years. See "Estrangement," "Absence," "The Broken Tryst," and "Foreboding," all in *Heartsease and Rue.*

21   There is a hand-printed letter from her to her GODPAPA, produced at the age of six, in HL—bMS Am1659 (282). (Is this her earliest surviving letter?) There is also a copy of his reply, apparently in her father's hand—bMS Am765 (935). See "Verses Intended to Go with a Posset-Dish to my Dear Little God-daughter, 1882," in L's *Last Poems.*

22   The greatest grief which the Civil War brought L was the death of his three nephews, on which see Greenslet, *The Lowells and their Seven Worlds.* Greenslet's speculations (pp. 299–300) on the possibility of General Charles Russell L, Jr.'s, having become Governor of Massachusetts and/or President of the United States if he had lived, are not absurd.

23   Even in this connection L did not lose his capacity for facing facts. When W. J. Stillman, father of an incurably sick and suffering child, remarked that he was afraid the boy would die, L shocked him by replying, "I should be afraid he would not die."

24   *Three Houses* (Thomas Todd Company, 1955).

CHAPTER SIX: THE WORLD AND THE PARISH

1   Mary Thacher Higginson, *Letters and Journals of Thomas Wentworth Higginson, 1846–1906* (1921), p. 8.

2   *The Autobiography of Nathaniel Southgate Shaler* (1909) has the most extreme statement. Shaler found L "the most perfect and most natural poser I have ever known"; "at times it made me fairly ache to look at him."

3   Moncure D. Conway, *Autobiography, Memories, and Experiences* (1904), I, 158.

4   Odell Shepard, ed., *The Journals of Bronson Alcott* (LB, 1938), p. 218.

5   Colonel Henry Lee declared that the Lowells, Higginsons, and Jacksons were "social and kindly people." Their difficulty was that "they got some Cabot women that shut them up."—Greenslet, *The Lowells and their Seven Worlds,* p. 112.

6   It is hard to believe that L has not given something of himself to the "common" but sensitive and intelligent countryman of "Sunthin' in the Pastoral Line"—

> Ther's times when I'm unsoshle ez a stone,
> An' sort o' suffercate to be alone,—
> I'm crowded jes' to think thet folks are nigh,
> An' can't bear nothin' closer than the sky. . . .

There is no dramatic element in "Under the Willows":

> Hating the crowd, where we gregarious men
> Lead lonely lives, I love society,
> Nor seldom find the best with simple souls
> Unswerved by culture from their native bent,
> Thy [nature's] ground we meet on being primal man
> And nearer the deep bases of our lives.

Another poem, "Without and Within," expresses an impatience with formal society close to that of Howells in *Stops of Various Quills.*

7   Which was a two-volume work of 653 pages, *Memoirs of Lieut.-General Scott, LL.D., Written by Himself.* The review is in *NAR*, C (1865), 242–44. "A great part of the book reminds one of a collection of certificates to the efficacy of a quack medicine."

8   On this point L was quite in agreement with the Transcendentalists, who tended to underrate the advantages of travel because they thought all the essential needs and elements of human experience everywhere available. Cf. "Gold-Egg: A Dream Fantasy":

> Each day the world is born anew
>   For him who takes it rightly;
> Not fresher that which Adam knew,
> Not sweeter that whose moonlit dew
>   Entranced Arcadia nightly.

See also "Under the Willows" and "An Invitation." But a deeper note is sounded in "Si Descendero in Infernum, Ades," which constitutes a moving Christian confession:

> Looking within myself, I note how thin
>   A plank of station, chance, or prosperous fate,

Doth fence me from the clutching waves of sin;
In my own heart I find the worst man's mate,
And see not dimly the smooth-hingèd gate
    That opens to those abysses
Where ye grope darkly. . . .

9   Nothing could be more delightful than L's playful letters to the Gilders. Specimens are given in Rosamond Gilder, ed., *Letters of Richard Watson Gilder* (1916).

10   It is an interesting little sidelight on L's temperament that he hated to incur obligations, even in such little matters as allowing somebody to run a personal errand for him. He had no objection, however, to running one for somebody else, which was most amusingly illustrated when, at a party for Agnes Repplier, as a young writer on her first visit to Boston, she came downstairs without her glasses, and L, having learned of her plight, gallantly climbed the stairs to fetch them for her, greatly to the consternation of their proper Bostonian hostess. See George Stewart Stokes, *Agnes Repplier, Lady of Letters* (University of Pennsylvania Press, 1949), pp. 88–90.

11   He did get Gilder to print Landor's letters in Mary Boyle's collection, with an introduction by L himself, because he knew Miss Boyle needed the money. Sarah Warner Brooks, "L as a Helpful and Kindly Critic," Cambridge *Tribune*, Feb. 20, 1892, p. 3, gives an example of his care in revising a poem she had sent him. See also Clara M. Parker, "A Bold Visit to JRL," *Christian Union*, XLV (1892), 1146–47, for L's kindness to a young lady who had resented his criticism of Mrs. Browning. His letters to Christopher Pearce Cranch in the Boston Public Library, written in a delightfully humorous style, make a very attractive record of his efforts to aid that writer.

12   Charles Akers, "Personal Glimpses of our New England Poets," *NEM*, n.s. LXXVII (1897), 446–56.

13   Whitman and Thoreau have been spoken of elsewhere in these pages. There were also Cornelius Mathews, Francis Bowen, and Julian Hawthorne; see Duberman, *JRL*, pp. 401–402, n. 37; pp. 412–13, n. 12; pp. 487–89, n. 56. On Hawthorne, see also Carl J. Weber, "L's 'Dead Rat in the Wall,'" *NEQ*, IX (1936), 468–72, and "More about L's 'Dead Rat,'" 686–88, and the fullest account in

George Knox, "The Hawthorne–L Affair," *NEQ,* XXIX (1956), 493–502. See also L's letters to Duyckinck, *BNYPL,* IV (1900), 339–41, 344–45: "I left my trick of 'getting mad' with people—at school and I thought everybody else did." "I knew that he had done me a great injustice about a matter very trifling in itself. I knew that he had assailed me in print, and I retaliated as I would not do now. The traditions of literary animosity would justify all I did and more, but my heart has never justified it, and I have been sorry for it more times than I can think of since." In the light of the record of L's work on the *Fable* preserved in his published letters, it is difficult, however, to see how the two sentences which follow this passage can be accepted: "But when I wrote the Fable for Critics I had no thought of publishing it. The greater part of it was written in a week for my own amusement." Julian Hawthorne, if we accept L's view of the matter, printed the record of a private conversation, thus seriously embarrassing his host. L himself was at fault, however, when he printed a private letter of Thomas Hughes in E. E. Brown, ed., *True Manliness,* from the Writings of Thomas Hughes, with an introduction by JRL (Boston, D. Lothrop and Co., 1880). L had asked Hughes for material to write an autobiographical note. Hughes refused but sent "an autobiographical letter," which L found "so interesting" that he quoted most of it. He did not send a copy of the book to Hughes, who never saw it until after L's death, when he seems inexplicably to have believed that L was not responsible for what had occurred; see Mack and Armytage, *The Life of Thomas Hughes, Appendix,* pp. 289–91.

14 Lowell's own criticism of Poe was motivated by his resentment of Poe's treatment of Longfellow, quite as much as by personal considerations.

15 "A Passing Word on Mr. L," Manchester *Guardian,* August 19, 1891.

16 *AM,* LXXIX (1897), 127–30.

17 L was also very capricious on one occasion with Howells; see the latter's *Literary Friends and Acquaintance,* Part VII, Section III. Max Müller (*Auld Lang Syne,* p. 179) says that L sometimes lost his temper and used very emphatic language, but the illustration he gives does not support this charge, for he merely records his telling a young lady, "But, Madam, I do not accept your major premise!"

18   Charles Francis Adams, *Autobiography* (1916).

19   *AM,* XI (1863), 517—review of Story's *Roba di Roma.*

20   *PMHS,* XI (1871), 365–68.

21   In February 1887 L went to Chicago to speak on "American Politics" at a Washington's Birthday meeting in the Music Hall, where he disappointed his audience by giving instead a literary address on the Shakespearean—or, as he saw it, non-Shakespearean—authorship of *King Richard III.* The usual explanation is that he was in political disagreement with the Union League Club, which was sponsoring the meeting, and did not see his way clear to expressing his honest views at a meeting held under their auspices. See Scudder, *JRL,* I, 351–52; also "A Page of Ancient History," *Dial,* LV (1913), 5–9. However, a letter to Lily Norton, written the day before he left home, shows that he had already made up his mind to give the address on *Richard III* at that time and makes no mention of the motive usually alleged: "Give my love to Papa and tell him that after writing a political address, I found it so lifeless that I have fallen back on the Richard III thing I read him which I gave in Edinburgh. Twill be new to them, but I [am] wretched about it, I can't help it."

22   In her *Times and Tendencies* (1931).

23   When L traveled in the Middle West in 1855, he found it "the East over again—only dirtier and worse-mannered" in taverns and railways and "the East grown more openhanded" in homes. His letter to Norton from Madison, Wisconsin (April 6, 1855) in HL is full of anecdotes of Western manners that are worthy of Mark Twain. Harry Hayden Clark comments on his understanding of the importance of the frontier and notes that he "opposed protection of [Eastern] wealth by means of tariff and trusts as an unfair kind of class legislation." See *JRL: Representative Selections,* p. lxxxviii and pp. xcii–iii, n. 288.

24   In "An Indian Summer Reverie."

25   The italics are mine. In a review of *Life and Letters of Wilder Dwight, NAR,* CVIII (1869), 328, L wrote: "Governor Andrew once said, that there was not a family that had been in Massachusetts two hundred years that did not hold a commission in her volunteers [during the Civil War], and not one had disgraced itself. Colonel Dwight was a good example of this. Of the best blood

in New England (and there is none better), he showed the best qualities of the stock from which he sprang."

26 L to C. G. Leland, 1867, quoted by Elizabeth Robins Pennell, *Charles Godfrey Leland: A Biography* (1906), I, 294.

27 *Broadway Journal*, I (1845), 281–83.

28 I hope he did not mean to indicate Victoria in

> And, for that scarlet woman
> Who sits in places high,
> There cometh vengeance swift to quench
> The lewdness in her eye.

Or if he did, I hope she never found it out. She regarded him highly during his ambassadorship. But he was referring to England's "crowned ghoules who devour this unhappy people" as late as 1883; see *The Scholar-Friends*, p. 55.

29 *NAR*, CI (1865), 303.

30 A good example of his early sensitiveness is his furious attack upon Mary Howitt for her criticism of American translators of Fredrika Bremer. Her statement—a "literary curiosity" coming from a Quaker—was "the most coarse, ill-natured, unjust, and unwomanly production that we have ever read." After which he spends about ten pages belaboring Mrs. Howitt's own shortcomings as translator and writer.—*NAR*, LVIII (1844), 480–508.

31 The letter is in MHS.

32 It is only fair to add that even during the war L's anti-English utterances were often written more in sorrow than in anger. In "Mason and Slidell: A Yankee Idyll," which is No. II in the second *Biglow* series, Concord Bridge is violently anti-British, but Bunker Hill Monument is conciliatory. So is Parson Wilbur's letter which precedes the poem, and there can be no question that Wilbur here speaks for L; he has ceased to be a figure of fun.

33 *NAR*, XCVIII (1864), 619.

34 L's sensible, thoughtful, considerate letter of Dec. 21, 1874, to J. H. Clifford (MHS) gives the fullest statement of his reasons for refusing.

35 The Spanish appointment had been under consideration as early as 1869. When it went instead to Daniel Sickles, L wrote Mabel that he had come "within an ace of it—or, if I may be allowed a

little natural bitterness under the circumstances—within an ass of it."

36   See Ferris Greenslet's exciting account of this case—"Love and Death in Dedham"—in *The Lowells and their Seven Worlds,* Book III, Ch. 2.

37   There is, however, an excellent summary and analysis of his political principles in Warren G. Jenkins, "L's Criteria of Political Values," *NEQ,* VII (1934), 115–41. See also Dorothy Leeds Werner, *The Idea of Union in American Verse (1776–1876)* (Philadelphia, n.p., 1932)—Ph.D. thesis, University of Pennsylvania.

38   "A Sample of Consistency," *AM,* II (1858), 754; see also "The Election in November" (1860) in his *Political Essays.* One passage in a letter of L's printed by Scudder (I, 342–43) must strike the contemporary reader with far greater horror than L can have intended: "I cannot help believing that in some respects we represent more truly the old Roman Power and sentiment than any other people. Our art, our literature, are, as theirs, in some sort exotics; but our genius for politics, for law, and, above all, for colonization, our instinct for aggrandizement and for trade, are all Roman. I believe we are laying the basis of a more enduring power and prosperity, and that we shall not pass away till we have stamped ourselves upon the whole western hemisphere so deeply, so nobly, that if, in the far-away future, some Gibbon shall muse among our ruins, the history of our Decline and Fall shall be more mournful and more epic than that of the huge Empire amid the dust of whose once world-shaking heart these feelings so often come upon me."

39   *AM,* I (1857), 756.

40   L was proud to believe that his grandfather John Lowell had introduced the clause in the state constitution which was afterwards considered to have made slavery illegal in Massachusetts. The accuracy of this claim has been doubted, but the point here is L's belief in it and what that shows about him.

41   To G. B. Loring, Nov. 15, 1838. Norton prints the letter in part, *Letters,* I, 41–43. See also letter to John W. Field, Dec. 13, 1885, Norton, III, 141–42.

42   *JRL: Representative Selections,* p. xvi.

43   In 1930, Claude M. Fuess, "Some Forgotten Political Essays by L," *PMHS,* LXII, 3–13, remarks, with reference to L's attacks on Choate and Cushing, that "in literary and political warfare, L adopted methods not unlike those employed by Mr. Mencken. He did not

try to meet Choate's arguments; he endeavored to overwhelm him by ridicule, banter, sarcasm, irony, rhetorical exaggeration, and burlesque—in fact, all the devices of the experienced controversialist." But this statement seems as extreme as anything L himself ever wrote and suggests that, like many of us around 1930, Fuess had Mencken on the brain.

Considerable interest attaches to a little-known series of articles by L on "Anti-Slavery in the United States," in the London *Daily News,* Feb. 2, March 18, April 17, May 17, 1846. This was the liberal newspaper founded, and very briefly edited, by Charles Dickens. My quotations are from the manuscript of these articles, apparently a first draft, in the Houghton Library. "The whole force of public opinion in America presents its front against the Abolition Movement, but this other and mightier element of man's progress works with them." L admits that the people of the free states compromised with slavery when the Constitution was framed. "But the history of guilt in nations and individuals is the same; the prosperous sin of yesterday begins on the morrow to exact daily payments of shame and sorrow and must be undone again sooner or later at a vast sacrifice of that very profit for whose enjoyment it was committed." "Never in the world's history has truth come into fair and open conflict with Falsehood, but her cause has been triumphant. That which contains within itself a spark of the divine is indestructible, unconquerable." Slavery became more aggressive with the admission of Missouri as a slave state, and this was made possible by the treachery of northern members.

44   Cf. the end of the first *Biglow Paper*:

> Ef I'd *my* way I hed ruther
>   We should go to work an' part,
> They take one way, we take t'other,
>   Guess it wouldn't break my heart;
> Man hed ough' to put asunder
>   Them thet God has noways jined;
> An' I shouldn't gretly wonder
>   Ef there's thousands o' my mind.

But when the disunion issue was presented at the New England Anti-Slavery Convention, in Boston, May 28, 1844, both L and Maria voted against disunion. Maria herself accused abolitionists of stridency and intolerance. "They are like people who live with the deaf, or hear water-falls, and whose voices become high and harsh."

45   "A Sample of Consistency," *AM*, II (1858), 759. See also Duberman, *JRL*, pp. 78–79.

46   *NAR*, CXII (1871), 235.

47   In the *AM* article, "Conversations with Mr. L," he is said to have been asked what he thought the Jews would do with the rest of us when they had secured control of everything, to which he replied, "That is the question which will eventually drive me mad." L may have said this, though if he did, I should think he must have been employing humorous exaggeration, and it is well to remember that we have nothing so absurd as this over his signature or in an unquestionable context.

48   Which, actually, when it occurs, is Hittite, not Hebrew.

49   See the essay on Marlowe, in *Works*, VIII, 218–19; *also Anti-Slavery Papers*, I, 20, and this passage quoted from the manuscript of his Lowell lecture on metrical romances, where he says of the knights: "They looked upon the rich Jew with thirty two sound teeth in his head as a providential contrivance, and practised upon him a comprehensive kind of dental surgery—at once for profit and amusement, and then put into some chapel a painted window with a Jewish prophet on it for piety, as if they were the Jewish profits they cared about."

50   The divided mind I fancy I see in him is shown in his reference (in "The Progress of the World") to the Jewish gift "for commerce and (strange paradox) for the higher divinations of the soul." There is a blatant appeal to religious hatred and prejudice in the Class Poem:

> Such doctrines new! they've been repeated oft
> Since first the Jews at their Redeemer scoffed,
> Stained their vile hands with the Messiah's gore,
> And filled the bitter cup to running o'er!

I will give two other examples of what I mean from unpublished verses in the Houghton Library:

> Abram was happy when he met
>   Rebecca at the well;
> With patriarchal, mild regret

He saw the white arms curve to set
The pitcher on the braided jet
That o'er smooth shoulders fell.

Then, as he felt the garments sweep
    Muskodored by his side,
He sat, good Jew, and reckoned deep
How many camels, oxen, sheep,
The lucky son in law would reap
    Who made the fair his bride.

(L did not often remember Bible stories as inaccurately as that!)
The other poem, "No, 'tis not for their religion," is a rough pencil
draft (18 lines) of some uncompleted verses about Jews. L pays
tribute to their "brains without an ounce of fat," but again perpetuates clichés, and the admiration seems grudging.

    51 bMS Am765 (961). See George Hendrick, "JRL in Gandhi's
Indian Opinion," *ESQ*, No. 10 (1958), pp. 31–32, which reprints an
article by Mansukhlal Hiralal Nazar (Jan. 27, 1906), which shows a
recognition of kinship in L on the part of persons involved in
Gandhi's *Satayagraha* movement.

    52 As late as 1859, L wrote a correspondent in China: "So you
are to have another war over there. I think it a shabby piece of
business. Can you thrash a nation into friendly relations? And if a
man doesn't like your society, can you change his views by giving
him a black eye? The Chinese are not a nation of savages, and with
two hundred and forty millions of people they can hold out a great
while in killed, wounded, and missing. I think John Bull and Johnny
Crapaud will have their hands full before they are done with it.
What has a Bull to do in a China-shop?"

    53 *AM*, IV (1859), 645.

    54 *AM*, II (1858), 379.

    55 "On the Capture of Fugitive Slaves near Washington"; "The
Power of Sound," in Smith, *Uncollected Poems*.

    56 See "Mr. Buchanan's Administration," *AM*, I (1857), 757;
"The Question of the Hour," VII (1961), 117–21.

    57 "Ode Recited at the Harvard Commemoration."

    58 "The Washers of the Shroud."

    59 See *NAR*, XCVIII (1864), 258: "Mr. Lincoln probably
thought it more convenient . . . to have a country left without a

constitution, than a constitution without a country." "We have no sympathy to spare for the pretended anxieties of men who, only two years gone, were willing that Jefferson Davis should break all the commandments together, and would now impeach Mr. Lincoln for a scratch on the surface of the tables where they are engraved."

60 L had the White Queen's habit of experiencing his sorrows in anticipation. Long ago he had looked forward to the death of his wife and children; now he anticipated the loss of his nephews. "If they should die in battle well on into the enemy's lines, it would be all that one could ask, but it would be dreadful to have them picked off by those murdering cowards." As late as 1869, L's review of *Life and Letters of Wilder Dwight* (*NAR*, CVIII, 327–28) approaches hysteria: ". . . to die for one's country as this youth did, with a clear understanding of what it was he gave his life for, and to do it before one had otherwise made that mark in the world which he might fairly expect to make, 'to cease and make no noise,' may be fairly reckoned among the highest kinds of success; for it was nothing less than that most splendid of human achievements, the sacrificing of the seen and calculable to the unseen and incalculable, the recognition of the idea as infinitely more real than the actual."

61 *Biglow Papers*, Second Series, VII.

62 If it be asked whether L returned to this old anti-war point of view after the Civil War, I do not think we can honestly say he did. Nothing could have been more gauche than his address to the deputation from the Workmen's Peace Association which came to pay their respects to him as ambassador before he left England, for he not only harked back to English-American relations during the Civil War but even discussed the possibility of war between the two countries in the future! He hoped no need for arbitration would ever arise, and he did not believe it would, yet he believed also "that there are occasions when war is less disastrous than peace; that there are times when one must resort to what goes before all law, and what, indeed, forms the foundation of it—the law of the strongest; and that, as a general rule, the strongest deserve to get the best of the struggle. They say, satirically, that God is on the side of the strong battalions, but I think they are sometimes in the right, and my experience goes to prove that." This is Nietzscheism or social Darwinism of the kind that Lowell elsewhere gives the impression of having loathed. He favored Prussia at the time of the Franco-

Prussian War, and though he afterwards found the arrogance of the Germans "*ganz colossal,*" he still blamed the French for not facing up to the "wormholing of their own moral fibre." In 1878 he wrote Thomas Hughes he hoped England would not have to fight Russia, but that if she did, it would be a war between civilization and barbarism.

63   Volume VIII, pp. 761–69.

64   *NAR,* XCVIII (1864), 269.

65   One of L's most caustic, allusive, and least endearing papers was a bitterly sarcastic screed on Andrew Johnson's father, occasioned by the President's trip to Raleigh, N.C., in 1867, to assist in dedicating a memorial to him. He left it to be published by LeRoy P. Graf and Ralph W. Haskins, " 'This Clangor of Belated Mourning': JRL on Andrew Johnson's Father," *South Atlantic Quarterly,* LXII (1963), 423–34. Jay Hubbell's comments in *The South in American Literature* (Duke, 1954) contains a much more intelligent evaluation than Beatty's of L's utterances on the South from a Southern point of view, but see further Max Griffin's excellent article, "L and the South," *Tulane Studies in English,* II (1950), 75–102, which is especially valuable in its account of L's relationships with individual Southerners. Though Griffin's purpose was to allay Southern prejudices against L, fostered by Poe, Simms, and others, he does not overstate the case nor force the evidence at any point. L's post-war friendliness toward the South appears also in his comments on Lucian Minor; see "A Virginian in New England Thirty-Five Years Ago," *AM,* XXVI (1870), 162–79. In a paper on "The Seward-Johnson Reaction" (1866) in *Political Essays,* he seems to me to come dangerously close to granting Southern contentions: "The war can in no respect be called a civil war, though that was what the South, in its rash ignorance, threatened the North with. It was as much a war between two different nations, and the geographical line was a distinctly drawn between them, as in the late war between North and South Germany."

66   See, in the collected poems, "An Ode for the Fourth of July 1876," "Agassiz," "To George William Curtis," "Tempora tantur," "On a Bust of General Grant," and "Bankside," which concludes with the statement that public office has become "a tramps' boosingken." Smith's *Uncollected Poems* adds "The World's Fair, 1876," "A Coincidence," and the savage "Epitaph" on Jim Fisk—

World, Flesh, and Devil gave him all they could,
Wealth, harlots, wine and disbelief in good . . . .
Living, Gould's friendship, dead, the tears of Tweed!

67 Rollo Ogden, *Life and Letters of Edwin Lawrence Godkin* (M, 1907), I, 290–91. Grant is said to have wanted L for Secretary of State if he won a third term, and Whittier in 1883 wanted him to return from England and oppose Butler for the governorship of Massachusetts. In 1888, L was wryly amused by Higginson's curious idea of doing him honor by sending him to the General Court and the lower house at that. "I couldn't help laughing. Why, it was all I could do to prevent their sending me to Congress, would I, nould I, in '76."

68 L called Howells "the sweetest socialist that ever was" and added that "there is a good bit of that leaven in me, but it struggled vainly with the dough of commonsense." Having finished *A Hazard of New Fortunes*, he felt as he had used to feel in the old days, "when the slave would not let me sleep. I don't see my way out of the labyrinth except with the clue of coöperation, but I am not sure even of that with over-population looming in the near distance. I wouldn't live in any of the Socialist or Communist worlds into the plans of which I have looked, for I should be bored to death by the everlasting Dutch landscape. Nothing but the guillotine will ever make men equal on compulsion, and even then they will leap up again in some other world to begin again on the old terms."

69 Clark and Foerster, *JRL: Representative Selections*, pp. lxxxvi–xciii, is very important on this aspect of L's thinking.

CHAPTER SEVEN: ULTIMATE HORIZON

1 Commentary on L's religion includes Minot J. Savage, "The Religion of L's Poems," *Arena*, IX (1893–94), 705–22; William A. Quayle, *Modern Poets and Christian Teaching: L* (Eaton and Mains, 1906); Augustus H. Strong, *American Poets and Their Theology* (Griffith and Rowland Press, 1916); Lewis H. Chrisman, "L and his Interpretation of Life," *Methodist Review*, CII (1919), 366–78; Elmer J. Bailey, *Religious Thought in the Greater American Poets* (Pilgrim Press, 1922); H. T. Henry, "Religious Intimations in the Writings of JRL," *CER*, XXI (1923), 398–408; Leo Martin Shea,

L's Religious Outlook; G. P. Voight, "L," in *The Religious and Ethical Element in the Major American Poets, Bulletin of the University of South Carolina, The Graduate School,* June 1, 1925, pp. 100–123.

2   Reviewing Froude's History of England, *NAR,* CIII (1866), 606–607, L finds the author's "apparent fairness in judging moral questions . . . the result of a certain religious apathy, rather than of judicial impartiality of temper. . . . Left apparently by the result of the politico-religious revival at Oxford without any very resolved convictions, he is a master of casuistry, and often weighs a question with such a show of conscientious nicety, that nothing but the dust left in one side of the balances decides the turning of the scale. His method of treatment leads us sometimes to ask ourselves whether there is such a thing as positive right and wrong, and whether morals (as the name signifies) are really anything more than what is for the time customary."

3   "Ode to France."

4   First Series, IV; Second Series, VII, IX.

5   "L's Influence in England," *NEM,* N.S. XXVII (1902), 321–25.

6   See David Hinshaw, *Rufus Jones, Master Quaker* (P, 1951); Elizabeth Gray Vining, *Friend of Life* (Li, 1958).

7   Bret Harte, "A Few Words about Mr. L," *New Review,* V (1891), 193–201.

8   "Memoriae Positum."

9   *AM,* III (1859), 777–79. See, further, the gay and disrespectful enumeration of occult literature in "The Unhappy Lot of Mr. Knott" and the discussion in the "Preliminary Note" to "Kettelopotomachia," *Biglow Papers,* Second Series, VIII.

10   *AM,* X (1858), 751.

11   See, further, Wagenknecht, *Mrs. Longfellow,* pp. 97–98.

12   In his Lowell lecture on the Ballads, Lowell says: "I remember hearing Hawthorne say once that it was painful to him to live in an old house, for the shadows of former occupants that haunted it. But I think this is contrary to the general feeling, and I have observed that the instinct of most persons leads them to endeavor to establish some link between themselves and the past of the old dwelling they may have come to live in, even by so desperate an expedient as fancying that a ghost walks there. Of course it is not their ghost

—that would not be so pleasant—but merely a kind of minister resident of the departer days." See "A Glance Behind the Curtain"; also L's letter to S. Weir Mitchell, *Letters*, III, 230–32, with Norton's note.

13   See, further, "The Pious Editor's Creed," *Biglow Papers*, First Series, VI; "The Church and Clergy" and "The Church and Clergy Again," in *Anti-Slavery Papers*. On this point a comparison with Whittier is in order; see my *John Greenleaf Whittier: A Portrait in Paradox* (OUP, 1967), Appendix B.

14   "Rhoecus." See also "Godminster Chimes" and "Bibliolatres."

15   See "Calling Things By Their Right Names," in *Anti-Slavery Papers*, a completely successful short story, which deserves to be better known.

16   See H. T. Henry's article cited in n. 1 to this chapter; also his "Lowell's Moral Intuitions," *CER*, XXII (1924), 6–17. More recently, Leo Martin Shea, who has made a much fuller study of L's religious aspects from the Catholic point of view, has remarked, "we know of many Catholic priests who consistently read L with consolation and never a shock."

17   *Review of Reviews*, IV (1891), 309.

18   *NAR*, XCVIII (1864), 623.

19   Charles Edward Stowe, *Life of Harriet Beecher Stowe*, pp. 335–36; see also his comments on *The Minister's Wooing*, pp. 327–32.

20   L says nothing specific about the new Biblical scholarship, which was disturbing nearly as many people at the time as natural science, though there is one passage in which he classifies those who opposed *Essays and Reviews* with those who persecuted witches.

21   Clark's discussion is in his introduction to *JRL: Representative Selections*. For White, see, besides the article cited elsewhere, "Two Versions of L's 'Function of the Poet,'" *PQ*, XX (1941), 587–96.

22   The poem "Credidimus Jovem Regnare" offended some Christians, but L afterwards stated that he originally meant to call it "A Humorist's Growl" and that it "was not argumentative, but only the expression of a mood." In any case, it hardly seems complimentary to the new orthodoxy of science.

23   *AM*, IV (1859), 773–74.

24   When the children ask L to tell what becomes "Uncle

Cobus's Story," *Our Young Folks*, III (1867), 411–18, he fears his kind of story is now out of fashion. Should he begin, "Once upon a time there was a gas whose name was Hydrogen and he lived in an India-rubber bag" or "One of the most curious circumstances in relation to the coleopterous insects is . . ."? He does not like the kind of children's literature in which when the pie is opened, the birds begin to preach. Later in the story he tells the children that "everyone of us has two pair of eyes, one withinside, and the other without." It is interesting to remember, however, that by supporting Gurney against Peabody as president of Harvard in 1868, L placed himself on the side of those who sought to secularize the college.

SELECTED BIBLIOGRAPHY

A general reference to the manuscript material used in the preparation of this volume is made in the Preface, and there are some specific citations in the Notes. This section contains a fairly comprehensive but not complete list of the printed sources drawn upon. Articles cited in the Notes are generally not relisted here. For a list of the abbreviations employed see the beginning of the Notes.

It may be repeated here that all books not assigned to other publishers are published by Houghton Mifflin Company.

The most extensive bibliography is G. W. Cooke, *A Bibliography of JRL* (1906), but this needs to be supplemented, and in some cases corrected, by later studies. Among the sources which should be consulted for books and articles about L are Harry Hayden Clark and Norman Foerster, eds., *JRL: Representative Selections* (ABC, 1947), which also contains an outstanding biographical and critical introduction; the *Bibliography* volume of Robert E. Spiller et al., eds., *Literary History of the United States* (M, 1948), with its *Bibliography Supplement*, edited by Richard M. Ludwig (1959); Martin Duberman, *JRL* (1966); and, for periodicals, Lewis Leary, *Articles on American Literature, 1900–1950* (Duke, 1954), which is supplemented in every issue of *American Literature*.

I have used the "Edition de Luxe" of *The Complete Writings of JRL*, 16 vols. (1904), which is the large paper form of the "Elmwood Edition," and the one-volume "Cambridge Edition" of the *Complete Poetical Works* (1897), edited by Horace E. Scudder. For additional poetry, see JRL, *A Year's Life* (Boston, C. C. Little and J. Brown, 1841); *The Power of Sound: A Rhymed Lecture* (Privately printed, 1896); *Undergraduate Verses: Rhymed Minutes of the Hasty Pudding Club* (Hartford, The Thistle Press, 1956); and especially Thelma M. Smith, ed., *Uncollected Poems of JRL* (University of Pennsylvania Press, 1950).

Additional important prose appears in *Conversations on Some of the Old Poets,* Second Edition (Cambridge, John Owen, 1846); *Lectures on English Poets* (Cleveland, the Rowfant Club, 1897); *Impressions of Spain,* ed. Joseph B. Gilder (1899); *The Anti-Slavery Papers of JRL,* 2 vols. (1902); *Early Prose Writings* (John Lane, The Bodley Head, 1902); *The Round Table* (Richard G. Badger, 1913); *The Function of the Poet and Oher Essays,* ed. Albert Mordell (1920). There is a memoir of Shelley by JRL in *The Poetical Works of Percy Bysshe Shelley,* ed. Mrs. Shelley (LB, 1857). Sculley Bradley edited a reprint of *The Pioneer, A Literary Magazine* (Scholars' Facsimiles and Reprints, 1947). Some L material not elsewhere available appears in *American Ideas for English Readers,* with an introduction by Harry Stone (Boston, J. G. Cupples Co., 1892) and in *L: Essays, Poems and Letters,* ed. William Smith Clark II (Odyssey Press, 1948). George Peirce Clark's article, "L's Part in the Harvard Exhibition of 1837," *AL,* XXII (1950–51), 497–500, contains L's "Ancient Epics as Proofs of Genius," which was written during his senior year at Harvard; this has also been reprinted in *ESQ,* No. 22 (1961), 63–64.

See also the following miscellaneous items: Anon., "A Supposedly New Poem by JRL," *NQ,* CLXXXVIII (1945), 34; Martin Duberman, "Twenty-Seven Poems by JRL," *AL,* XXXV (1963–64), 322–55; Ethel Golann, "A L Autobiography," *NEQ,* VII (1934), 356–64; William Knight, ed., *Wordsworthiana: A Selection from Papers Read to the Wordsworth Society* (M, 1889), which contains L's presidential address of 1884; F. DeWolfe Miller, "Twenty-Seven Additions to the Canon of L's Criticism," *SB,* IV (1951-52), 205–210; Evelyn Smalley, "Verses Written in a Copy of Shakespeare by JRL," *Ce,* N.S. XXXVI (1899–1900), 49–50; Arthur Voss, "An Uncollected Letter of L's Parson Wilbur," *NEQ,* XXVII (1953), 396–99.

The most extensive collection of L's letters is still Charles Eliot Norton's *Letters of JRL,* 2 vols. (H, 1894); this was republished, with some additions, in three volumes, in the "Elmwood" and "de Luxe" editions. In 1932 M. A. DeWolfe Howe supplemented it importantly with *New Letters of JRL* (H). *The Scholar-Friends,* ed. Howe and G. W. Cottrell, Jr. (HUP, 1952) contains L's correspondence with Francis J. Child. Another important collection is Gertrude Reese Hudson, ed., *Browning and his American Friends:*

Letters between the Brownings, the Storys, and JRL (Bowes and Bowes, 1965). There are also many letters in Scudder's biography. For other letters see W. H. G. Armytage, "Some New Letters of JRL," *NQ*, CXCV (1950), 207–208; W. T. Bandy, "JRL, Sainte-Beuve, and The *Atlantic Monthly*," *Comparative Literature*, XI (1959), 229–32; Richard Cary, "L to Cabot," *CLQ*, VI (1962–64), 208–15; Mary A. Clarke, "Three Letters from JRL," *Ce*, N.S. XXIX (1895–96), 545–46; George T. Goodspeed, "A Unique L Item," *American Collector*, III (1926–27), 241–43; Philip Graham, ed., "Some L Letters," *TSLL*, III (1961–62), 557–82; Paul P. Kies, "L and the Two Doras," *Research Studies of the State College of Washington*, XVI (1948), 179–84; Robert A. Rees, "JRL in Spain and England: New Letters," *ESQ*, No. 47 (1967), 7–13; James L. Woodress, Jr., "Comfort Me, O My Publisher: Some Unpublished Letters from JRL to James T. Fields," *HLQ*, XV (1951–52), 73–86, and "The L–Howells Friendship: Some Unpublished Letters," *NEQ*, XXVI (1953), 523–28.

The authorized biography was Horace E. Scudder, *JRL: A Biography*, 2 vols. (1901). The definitive modern biography is Martin Duberman, *JRL* (1966). Other book publications are Richmond C. Beatty, *JRL* (Van, 1942); Henry S. Borneman, *JRL in Philadelphia* (City History Society of Philadelphia, 1931); E. E. Brown, *Life of JRL* (D. Lothrop Company, 1887); George William Curtis, *JRL, An Address* (H, 1893); Ferris Greenslet, *JRL, His Life and Work* (1905) and *The Lowells and their Seven Worlds* (1946); Edward Everett Hale, *JRL and His Friends* (1899); Edward Everett Hale, Jr., JRL (Small, Maynard, 1899); Leon Howard, *Victorian Knight-Errant: A Study of the Early Literary Career of JRL* (California, 1952); William Henry Hudson, *L and his Poetry* (Harrap, 1911); Lawrence H. Klibbe, *JRL's Residence in Spain, 1877–1880* (Newark, Washington Irving Publishing Co., 1964)—cf. his article, *Hispania*, XLI (1958), 190–93; Claire McGlinchee, *JRL* (Twayne, 1967); Joseph J. Reilly, *JRL as a Critic* (P, 1915); Leo Martin Shea, *L's Religious Outlook* (Catholic University of America, 1926); Charles Oran Stewart, *L and France* (Van, 1951); Francis H. Underwood, *JRL, A Biographical Sketch* (Osgood, 1882) and *The Poet and the Man: Recollections and Appreciations of JRL* (Lee and Shepard, 1893).

See, further, Hope Jillson Vernon, ed., *The Poems of Maria*

Lowell, with Unpublished Letters and a Biography (Brown University, 1936) and a number of commemoratives: *Addresses Delivered at the L Commemoration Held in Arkitektenhaus, Berlin, February 19, 1897* (Berlin, Mayer & Müller, n.d.); *American Academy of Arts and Letters, Commemoration of the Centenary of the Birth of JRL* (S, 1919); *Celebration of the One Hundredth Anniversary of the Birth of JRL by the Cambridge Historical Society, February 22, 1919;* "A Welcome to L," *Literary World,* XVI (1885), 217–26; "L Birthday Number" of *The Critic,* XI (1889), 85–96; and the symposium in *The Review of Reviews,* IV (1891–92), 287–310.

Though I have read nearly all of Lowell's uncollected articles, they are not listed in this Bibliography. Those from which I quote, or to which I am particularly indebted, are mentioned in the Notes.

The following volumes deal with L in part: Gay Wilson Allen, *American Prosody* (ABC, 1935); George Arms, *The Fields Were Green* (Stanford University Press, 1953); James C. Austin, *Fields of The Atlantic Monthly* (Huntington Library, 1953); Van Wyck Brooks, *America's Coming of Age* (Huebsch, 1915) and *The Flowering of New England* (Dutton, 1936); W. C. Brownell, *American Prose Masters* (S, 1909); George E. DeMille, *Literary Criticism in America* (Dial, 1931); E. W. Emerson, *The Early Years of the Saturday Club, 1855–1870* (1918); George Hamlin Fitch, *Great Spiritual Writers of America* (San Francisco, Paul Elder & Company, 1916); Norman Foerster, *Nature in American Literature* (M, 1923) and *American Criticism* (1928), which latter is reprinted in the introduction to Clark and Foerster, *JRL: Representative Selections;* H. R. Haweis, *American Humorists* (Chatto & Windus, 1883); Thomas Wentworth Higginson, *Old Cambridge* (M, 1900); E. B. Holden, ed., *Memorials of Two Friends . . .* (Privately printed, 1902); W. D. Howells, *Literary Friends and Acquaintance* (H, 1900); Henry James, *Essays in London and Elsewhere* (H, 1893) and "JRL" in C. D. Warner, ed., *Library of the World's Best Literature* (Peale & Hill, 1897), XVI, 9229–37, both of which have been reprinted in Leon Edel, ed., *The American Essays of Henry James* (Vintage Books, 1956); Alfred Kreymborg, *Our Singing Strength* (Coward-McCann, 1919); William C. Lawton, *The New England Poets* (M, 1898); Robert C. LeClair, *Three American Travellers in England . . .* (University of Pennsylvania, 1945); Alexander Mackie,

Nature Knowledge in Modern Poetry (LG, 1906); John Macy, ed., *American Writers on American Literature* (Liveright, 1931); E. S. Nadal, *A Virginian Village and Other Papers* . . . (M, 1917); Bliss Perry, *The Praise of Folly and Other Papers* (1923); William Lyon Phelps, *Howells, James, Bryant, and Other Essays* (M, 1924); Gustav Pollak, *International Perspective in Criticism* (Dodd, Mead, 1914); John P. Pritchard, *Criticism in America* (University of Oklahoma Press, 1956); Frank Preston Stearns, *Cambridge Sketches* (Li, 1905); E. C. Stedman, *Poets of America* (1885); George Stewart, *Essays from Reviews* (Quebec, Dawson & Co., 1892); Francis Thompson, *The Real Robert Louis Stevenson and Other Critical Essays*, ed. Terence L. Connolly (University Publishers, 1959); Leon H. Vincent, *American Literary Masters* (1906); Beckles Willson, *America's Ambassadors to England, 1785-1928* (John Murray, 1928); Stanley T. Williams, *The Spanish Background of American Literature*, 2 vols. (YUP, 1955); George Edward Woodberry, *Makers of Literature* (M, 1900), reprinted in *Studies of a Litterateur* (Harcourt, 1921).

The following books contain significant references to L: George William Curtis, ed., *The Correspondence of John Lothrop Motley*, 2 vols. (H, 1889); Charles W. Eliot, *A Late Harvest* (AMP, 1924); John Galsworthy, *Addresses in America* (S, 1919); Zoltan Haraszti, ed., *Letters by T. W. Parsons* (Boston Public Library, n.d.); Virginia Harlow, ed., *Thomas Sergeant Perry: A Biography* (Duke, (1950); M. A. DeWolfe Howe, ed., *Memories of a Hostess* . . . (AMP, 1922); Mildred Howells, ed., *Life in Letters of William Dean Howells*, 2 vols. (D, 1928); Edward C. Mack and W. H. G. Armytage, *Thomas Hughes: The Life of the Author of* Tom Brown's Schooldays (Ernest Benn, 1952); Frederic William Maitland, *The Life and Letters of Leslie Stephen* (Duckworth, 1906); Frederick L. Mulhauser, ed., *The Correspondence of Arthur Hugh Clough* (OUP, 1957); F. Max Müller, *Auld Lang Syne* (S, 1898); Sara Norton and M. A. DeWolfe Howe, eds., *Letters of Charles Eliot Norton* . . . , 2 vols. (1913); Rollo Ogden, *Life and Letters of Edwin Lawrence Godkin*, 2 vols. (M, 1907); George W. Smalley, *London Letters and Some Others*, 2 vols. (H, 1891) and *Anglo-American Memories* (Duckworth, 1911); R. H. Stoddard, *Recollections Personal and Literary* (A. S. Barnes, 1903); William Roscoe

Thayer, ed., *Letters of John Holmes to JRL and Others* (1917); Ward Thoron, ed., *The Letters of Mrs. Henry Adams, 1865–1883* (LB, 1936).

These articles contain personal reminiscences of L: C. F. Briggs, "JRL," in Elbert Hubbard, ed., *Little Journeys to the Homes of American Authors* (P, 1896); Frederic W. Farrar, "An English Estimate of L," *Forum*, XII (1891–92), 141–52; Elizabeth Porter Gould, "Recollections of JRL," *Christian Register*, June 10, 1897; Lady Camilla Gurdon, "A Few Personal Reminiscences of Mr. L," *Suffolk Tales and Other Stories . . .* (LG, 1897); Mrs. S. Bledsoe Herrick, "JRL," *Southern Review*, XVIII (1875), 385–423; E. H. House, "A First Interview with L," *HW*, XXXVI (1892), 850; M.A. DeWolfe Howe, "Victorian Poets: A Side Light," *AM*, CLII (1933), 224–27; A. Lawrence Lowell, "Memoir of JRL, LL.D.," *PMHS*, Second Series, XI (1897); E. S. Nadal, "Some Impressions of Mr. L," *Critic*, N.S. XIX (1893), 105–107, and "London Recollections of L," *HM*, CXXXII (1915–16), 366–72; Minot J. Savage, "A Morning with L," *Arena*, XV (1895), 1–12; Eugenia Skelding, "A Poet's Yorkshire Haunts," *AM*, LXXVI (1895), 181–86; George W. Smalley, "Mr. L in England," *HM*, XCII (1896–96), 788–801; William Roscoe Thayer, "JRL as a Teacher: Recollections of His Last Pupil," *SM*, LXVIII (1920), 473–80; Barrett Wendell, "Mr. L as a Teacher," *Stelligeri and Other Essays Concerning America* (S, 1893).

The following articles deal with specialized topics as indicated: Anon, "JRL and Modern Literary Criticism," *International Review*, IV (1877), 264–81, and "Professor L as a Critic," *Lippincott's Magazine*, VII (1871), 641–50; John Q. Anderson, "L's 'The Washers of the Shroud' and the Celtic Legend of the Washer of the Ford," *AL*, XXXV (1963–64), 361–63; Hamilton Vaughan Ball, "Harvard's Commemoration Day, July 21, 1865," *NEQ*, XV (1942), 256–79, and "JRL's Ode, Recited at the Commemoration of the Living and Dead Soldiers of Harvard University, July 21, 1865," *PBSA*, XXXVII (1943), 169–202; R. C. Beatty, "L's Commonplace Books," *NEQ*, XVIII (1945), 391–401—cf. correction by William A. Jackson, XIX (1946), 113–14; Edward G. Bernard, "New Light on L as Editor," *NEQ*, X (1937), 337–41; Arthur Eugene Beston, Jr., "Concord Summons the Poets," *NEQ*, VI (1933), 602–13; Sculley Bradley, "L, Emerson, and *The Pioneer*," *AL*, XIX (1947–48), 231–44; Henry S.

Burrage, "JRL's Two Visits to Portland in 1857," *Maine Historical Memorials* (1922); Edward M. Chapman, "*The Biglow Papers* Fifty Years After" *YR*, n.s. VI (1916–17), 120–34; H. H. Clark, "L's Criticism of Romantic Literature," *PMLA*, XLI (1926), 209–28; Heyward Ehrlich, "Charles Frederick Briggs and L's *Fable for Critics*," *MLQ*, XXVIII (1967), 329–41; Nils Erik Enkvist, "*The Biglow Papers* in Nineteenth Century England," *NEQ*, XXVI (1953), 219–36; Lincoln R. Gibbs, "A Brahmin's Version of Democracy," *Antioch Review*, I (1941), 50–62; Ferris Lockwood, "JRL's Interest in Dante," *Italica*, XXXVI (1959), 77–100; Edwin D. Mead, "L's *Pioneer*," *NEM*, n.s. V (1891), 235–48; Edwin Mims, "L as a Citizen," *SAQ*, I (1902), 27–40; Clifford S. Parker, "Professor L: A Study of the Poet as Teacher," *The Colonnade*, XIII, May 1917, pp. 3–23; Richard C. Pettigrew, "L's Criticism of Milton," *AL*, III (1931–32), 451–64; Louise Pound, "L's 'Breton Legend,' " *AL*, XII (1940–41), 348–50; G. C. Scoggin, "JRL and 'Il Pesceballo,' " *Nation*, CV (1917), 436–37; Justin H. Smith, "*The Biglow Papers* as an Argument against the Mexican War," *PMHS*, XLV (1912); Arthur W. M. Voss, "The Evolution of L's 'The Courtin,' " *AL*, XV (1943–44), 42–50, "L, Hood and the Pun," *MLN*, LXIII (1948), 346–47, and "Backgrounds of L's Satire in *The Biglow Papers*," *NEQ*, XXIII (1950), 47–64; James L. Woodress, Jr., "A Note on Bibliography: The Review of Howells' *Venetian Life*," *SB*, IV (1951–52), 205–210.

This final paragraph is made up of articles comprising general critical comment: Anon, "Lowelliana," *Critic*, XVI (1891), 291–92, and "L: Poet and Friendly Critic," *CLQ*, I (1943), 19–23; William B. Cairns, "JRL: A Centenary View," *Nation*, CVIII (1919), 274–77; John W. Chadwick, "JRL," *Unitarian Review*, XXXVI (1891), 436–55; C. Hartley Grattan, "L," *American Mercury*, II (1924), 63–69; Sidney Low, "L in his Poetry," *FR*, LVI (1891), 310–24; C. E. Norton, "JRL," *HM*, LXXXVI (1892–93), 846–57; R. Ellis Roberts, "JRL: A British Estimate," *Living Age*, CCCI (1919), 231–35; Horace E. Scudder, "JRL," *Proceedings of the American Academy of Arts and Sciences*, n.s. XXI (1894), 423–32; H. D. Traill, "Mr. JRL," *FR*, XLIV (1885), 79–89; Arthur W. M. Voss, "JRL," *Univ. of Kansas City Review*, XV (1948), 224–53.

INDEX

American ambassador, 167–8; his convictions and activities as a reformer, and his consideration of ethical problems involved, 168–91. CHAPTER VII: his religious faith and practice, 192–218; mystical awareness, 196–9, 201–8; religious influence, 199–201; interest in hereafter, 201–4; attitude toward the church, 208–10; toward Catholicism, 211; toward Calvinism, 211–13; toward science, 213–16; his strength and weakness and the basic significance of his work, 216

Writings:

"Absence," 242
"After the Burial," 107, 201–2
"Agassiz," 106–7, 202
Among My Books, 17, 89
"Anti-Apis," 180
"Anti-Slavery in the United States," 249
Anti-Slavery Papers, 226
"Bankside," 153
"Beggar, The," 57
"Bellerophon," 57, 121, 231
"Bibliolatres," 256
Biglow Papers, The, 33, 44, 67, 70–71, 90, 106, 107, 116, 132, 147, 149, 150, 178–9, 182, 184–5, 187, 195, 200, 223, 226, 227, 230, 234, 237, 243, 255, 256
"Birthday Verses Written in a Child's Album," 54
"Bobolink, The," 225
"Broken Tryst, The," 142
"Calling Things by their Right Names," 256
"Cambridge Thirty Years Ago," 160

Cathedral, The, 17, 57–8, 59, 60–61, 106, 108, 196–9, 208, 211, 214, 234
"Charles Dickens," 155
"Chippewa Legend, A," 107
"Christmas Carol for Geordie's Children, A," 195
"Church and Clergy, The," 256
"Church and Clergy Again, The," 256
"Class Poem," 172
"Coincidence, A," 253
"Columbus," 111
Conversations on Some of the Old Poets, 16, 30, 85, 89, 112, 113, 117, 120, 130, 132, 135, 225, 239
"The Courtin'," 106, 200–201
"Credidimus Jovem Regnare," 256
"Cuckoo, The," 38
"Dante," 194–5
"Darkened Mind, The," 11
Democracy and Other Addresses, 18
"Donnazetti," 65
"Election in November, The," 248
"Ember Picture, An," 66–7
"Emerson the Lecturer," 231
"Endymion," 62
"Epigram on Certain Conservatives, An," 169
"Epitaph," 253–4
"Estrangement," 242
"Extract, An," 180
Fable for Critics, A, 4, 16, 37, 44, 65, 95, 100–101, 102, 122–3, 131, 161, 232, 245
"Fatherland, The," 180
Fireside Travels, 17
"First Snow-Fall, The," 107
"Fitz-Adam's Story," 50, 107

Poet and critic; philologist, teacher and editor; diplomat and political satirist; abolitionist, brilliant conversationalist, husband
and father—James Russell Lowell was both
professionally and personally a "many-sided
man." His good friend William Dean Howells once wrote of him, "Lowell was of the
richest nature I have known"; and when he
died in 1891, he was generally regarded as
America's leading man of letters.

Through the years Lowell's position in
American letters has become less certain—
even the distinction of his criticism has been
attacked—and his poetry has shown less
survival value than Longfellow's or Whittier's. The extraordinary variety of his interests has also added to the difficulty of
seeing him whole and plain. Yet during his
entire life Lowell remained an earnest
seeker, and his views and speculations about
his multitude of concerns have a remarkable
relevance to much of our contemporary
world.

Mr. Wagenknecht employs in depth the
methods of Sainte-Beuve and Gamaliel
Bradford, presenting the man and the writer
through a vast range of materials in manuscript and in print. Using this approach, he
is able to show that this "man of a thousand
impressions" did indeed have his inconsistencies and superficialities, but that he
operated within an overall well-defined
range, whose confines were marked off by
his own temperament. "All these Lowells
are unmistakeably the same Lowell," Mr.